A Lawyer among the Theologians

A Lawyer
among the Theologians

by

Norman Anderson

William B. Eerdmans Publishing Company
Grand Rapids, Michigan

Copyright © 1973 by J.N.D. Anderson
First Published 1973 by Hodder and Stoughton
London

First American edition February 1974
All Rights Reserved

Printed in the United States of America

Library of Congress Cataloging in Publication Data

Anderson, James Norman Dalrymple.
A lawyer among the theologians.

Includes bibliographical references.
1. Theology—Addresses, essays, lectures. 2. Jesus
Christ—Resurrection. I. Title.
BR85.A623 1974   230   73-21894
ISBN 0-8028-1565-0

Foreword

It was a great honour to be invited in 1972 to give the inaugural lectures of the "Bishop John McLean Lectureship in the University of Saskatchewan and the University of Emmanuel College, Saskatoon", and I am most grateful to the President of the University of Saskatchewan, the Principal of Emmanuel College and the Dean of the Law School for their welcome and kindness.

It was my preparation for these lectures which provided the genesis of this book. In the event I lectured on "The Jesus of History and the Christ of Faith" (chapter 2) and "The Difference in being a Christian Today" (chapter 6), and used some of the material from two other chapters. In its final form the book has, however, developed considerably beyond the scope of my lectures, and includes chapters on subjects in which I have long been interested (and about which I have lectured and written from time to time), but on which I have been able to read somewhat more widely in the course of preparing this book for publication.

Quite a number of friends have been generous enough to read some (or all) of these chapters in typescript, and I want to express my sincere gratitude to each of them for his criticisms, comments and advice. I shall not name them, since it is possible that some of them would prefer to remain *incognito*. Anyway, I alone am responsible for what I have written.

The reason why I have chosen *A Lawyer among the Theologians* as a title, and the sense in which I use these words, will be clear, I hope, to any who read the introductory chapter. But the thought behind them will also be a recurrent theme throughout the book.

NORMAN ANDERSON
Institute of Advanced Legal Studies
25 Russell Square, London WC1

ACKNOWLEDGMENTS are due to the following for permission to quote their copyright material: The Society for Promoting Christian Knowledge who publish Rudolf Bultmann's *Kerygma and Myth: a Theological Debate* (edited by H. W. Bartsch and translated by R. H. Fuller), 1953, paperback of Volumes I & II combined with enlarged bibliography and index, 1972; T. & T. Clark who publish Karl Barth's *Church Dogmatics* III 2 (English translation), 1966; SCM Press Ltd who publish W. Künneth's *The Theology of the Resurrection* (translated by J. W. Leitch), 1965; Fontana Paperbacks who publish John Robinson's *The Difference in Being a Christian Today*, 1972; Garnstone Press who publish Michael Ramsey's *The Resurrection of Christ*, 1945.

Contents

CHAPTER ONE

A Lawyer among the Theologians

I

At first sight, perhaps, the title of this book may appear
somewhat presumptuous or provocative. But it is certainly
not intended as the former. On the contrary, one reason
why I have chosen it is to make it perfectly clear that I
make no pretentions to being a theologian and am very
conscious that I am venturing to stray into an academic
discipline other than my own. Nor is it really intended to be
provocative, however much it may conjure up echoes of
"Daniel in the lions' den" or "A cat among the pigeons".
Unhappily, I share very few of the characteristics of Daniel;
and no member of my profession would admit for a moment
to any similarity between a lawyer and a cat. I doubt, moreover, if the metaphor of lions is particularly appropriate to
theologians, however easy they might find it to rend in
pieces this diminutive Daniel; and I certainly do not regard
them as characterised by the innocence and guilelessness of
pigeons. Nor is there the remotest possibility that what I
have written will have any such effect on them as the
approach of a cat might be expected to have on the denizens
of a pigeon cote. They are much more likely to treat me
with the detachment and disdain which was exhibited (in
that case quite contrary to nature) by King Darius's lions.

I must begin by making it clear that I have no quarrel
whatever with theologians or biblical scholars as such. On
the contrary, I often wish that I had myself chosen that
discipline and field of studies, and I have profited greatly
from the writings of many of the scholars to whom I shall
refer. My quarrel—if that is the right word—is only with
some of them; and I shall confine myself, for the most part,

9

to letting one theologian answer another, and to indicating which opinion seems to me to accord most closely with the available evidence. I must also state categorically that I write without any personal rancour. The sweeping and, to my mind, unfounded assertions of some writers whom I have never met do, I must confess, irritate me considerably; but I usually find that when I get to know a scholar personally I can esteem him greatly, however much I may disagree with some of his views. Indeed, I count as personal friends some of those whose opinions I shall criticise in the following pages.

But is a lawyer in any way qualified to discuss such questions? To this I would give a double answer. First, I do not suggest for a moment that everything in this book has been written in the manner, and with the special insights, of a professional lawyer. It would be nearer the mark to say that my comments are those of an academic who is interested in theology and biblical studies but who himself comes from another academic discipline, which may enable him to look at the subject from a somewhat different angle from that of the specialist as such. Secondly, this other discipline happens, in my case, to be the law; and this must inevitably colour my approach and make me view this subject not merely from a different angle but, for better or for worse, in the light of the way in which a lawyer is accustomed to assess evidence.

I am reminded, in this context, of the comments made by writers such as C. S. Lewis, Dorothy Sayers and Sherwin-White on various conclusions reached by New Testament scholars. Lewis was particularly outspoken in the remarks he made, on one occasion, to the students of Westcott House, Cambridge, about some of those who spend their lives steeped in the minutiae of New Testament criticism.[1] Approaching the subject from the angle of his own discipline, and in his inimitable style, he gave several examples of the sort of criticism which he found singularly unconvincing. The Fourth Gospel had been compared, he said, to "a

[1] Cf. *Christian Reflections*, ed. W. Hooper (Geoffrey Bles, London, 1967), pp. 152 ff.

spiritual romance", "a poem not a history", to be judged by the same canons as Nathan's parable, the book of Jonah, *Paradise Lost*, "or, more exactly, *Pilgrim's Progress*". This prompted him to ridicule the comparison with *Pilgrim's Progress* ("a story which professes to be a dream and flaunts its allegorical nature by every single proper name it uses"), and even with Milton or Jonah;[2] to invite a closer examination of the dialogues and pictures found in the Fourth Gospel; and to conclude:

> I have been reading poems, romances, vision-literature, legends, myths all my life. I know what they are like. I know that not one of them is like this. Of this text there are only two possible views. Either this is reportage— though it may no doubt contain errors—pretty close up to the facts; nearly as close as Boswell. Or else, some unknown writer in the second century, without known predecessors or successors, suddenly anticipated the whole technique of modern, novelistic, realistic narrative. If it is untrue, it must be narrative of that kind. The reader who doesn't see this has simply not learned to read.

Similarly, he criticised Bultmann's dictum that "The personality of Jesus has no importance for the kerygma either of Paul or of John ... Indeed, the tradition of the earliest Church did not even unconsciously preserve a picture of his personality. Every attempt to reconstruct one remains a play of subjective imagination." But there are only three characters in literature, Lewis asserted, whom we know to be historical and yet feel we know as "real people": Plato's Socrates, the Jesus of the Gospels, and Boswell's Johnson.

> Our acquaintance with them shows itself in a dozen ways. When we look into the Apocryphal gospels, we find ourselves constantly saying of this or that *logion*, 'No. It's a

---

[2] Cf. an article by Walter Lock in *A New Commentary on Holy Scripture*, ed. Charles Gore, Henry Leighton Goudge, Alfred Guillaume (SPCK, 1928), p. 241. But T. F. Glasser has pointed out that Lock misrepresents the views of J. Drummond in this article (*Theology*, June 1968, pp. 266 f.).

fine saying, but not His. That wasn't how He talked.'—
just as we do with all pseudo-Johnsoniana. . . . What
is gained by trying to evade or dissipate this shattering
immediacy of personal contact by talk about 'that significance which the early church found that it was impelled
to attribute to the Master'?

The question that hits us in the face, he said, is not what
they were impelled to do, but what so impelled them.

His next major criticism was a more personal one, but one
with which many authors can sympathise. The critics, he
said, spend much time attempting to reconstruct the genesis
of the books they study: "what vanished documents each
author used, when and where he wrote, with what purposes,
under what influences—the whole *Sitz im Leben* of the
text"; and it all seems singularly convincing. But in the
reviews of his own books, and those of authors whom he
had known intimately, attempts of this sort had almost always
proved to be wide of the mark—and he gave a series of
striking examples of how reviewers had made eminently
plausible suggestions which had invariably, he thought,
been completely mistaken. Yet New Testament critics make
the most dogmatic assertions about writers of whose circumstances they can have had far less knowledge. Happily for
them, whatever reconstructions they devise "can never be
crudely proved wrong. St. Mark is dead. When they meet St.
Peter, there will be more pressing matters to discuss."

One further criticism he made is eminently germane to our
purpose: namely, the way in which many critics assume
that any statement attributed to Our Lord in the Gospels
which, if he really made it, would constitute a prediction
of the future, is taken to have been put in after the occurrence which it seemed to predict. This, he said, would be
very sensible if we started by knowing that inspired prediction can never occur. Similarly, he continued,

the rejection as unhistorical of all passages which narrate
miracles is sensible if we start by knowing that the miraculous in general never occurs. Now I do not here want to

discuss whether the miraculous is possible. I only want to point out that this is a purely philosophical question. Scholars, as scholars, speak on it with no more authority than anyone else. The canon 'If miraculous, unhistorical' is one they bring to their study of the texts, not one they have learned from it.

What he pled for was, in effect, a wider agnosticism. "I do not want to reduce the sceptical element in your minds. I am suggesting that it need not be reserved exclusively for the New Testament and the Creeds. Try doubting something else."

This is precisely the sort of point that a lawyer would wish to make: that many theologians and biblical scholars impose their preconceived ideas on the evidence rather than assess the evidence as it stands and see where it leads them. But is a lawyer's approach at all suited to the New Testament? A friend who was kind enough to read most of this book in draft remarked that he would himself consider *parts* of the Gospels and Acts as

> great poetry, not sober narration. They are much more like *Hamlet* than they are like today's *Times*. You wouldn't expect a lawyer to have a distinctive contribution to the interpretation of *Hamlet*, except perhaps in curious little details. Above all, you wouldn't think it necessary to argue for Hamlet's exact historicity in order to claim a very high value for it, and you'd think that a lawyer who did argue along such a line would be making his point not *qua* lawyer but *qua* commentator. Indeed, being a lawyer might be an actual handicap in some ways: e.g. if it made the commentator too literalistic about a passage which needed an imaginative response.

This is perfectly fair criticism, except that I myself agree with C. S. Lewis (and many others) that one cannot really regard the Gospels or the Acts as "great poetry", but must approach them as basically historical writings. And in this case a lawyer may, perhaps, have a certain role to play.

13

Perhaps, too, I might add that I should welcome a poet giving us what insights he can on the New Testament, although I should expect them to be somewhat marginal. After all, few theologians have any professional qualifications as poets, and in an amateur way even a lawyer may not be completely disqualified. When I was young, writing poetry (if I may dignify it by that name) was my favourite pastime.

The fundamental characteristic which I presume all academics have in common is their dedication to the quest for truth. This quest will necessarily take many different forms. In chemistry or physics, for example, it may involve a long series of empirical experiments in a laboratory; in pure mathematics or philosophy, the rigorous pursuit of logical thought; and in history, the painstaking and imaginative sifting of evidence, whether documentary or oral, direct or indirect. My concern in this book, however, is with theologians and biblical scholars, whose work may be said to span not only that of the philosopher but also, and primarily, that of the historian. The fundamental problem, therefore, is that of the sifting and assessment of evidence; and here it is obvious that there are marked differences between scholars, periods and schools of thought. These differences show themselves in the degree to which the scholar concerned does his utmost to approach the evidence with an open mind, to put on one side his preconceived ideas, and to allow new evidence, or a new appraisal of old evidence, to make him revise his hypothesis or change his opinion. But there can be no doubt that fashions and trends of thought—whether within his own particular discipline or in the general attitude of his contemporaries—normally exert a very considerable influence, conscious or unconscious, on almost anyone.

Now from one point of view I think it would be true to say that theologians and biblical experts will stand comparison with scholars in any field of studies in the rigour of their critical approach to their subject. There can certainly be no documents in the whole course of human history which have been subjected to the dissection, discussion and minute analysis which have been devoted to the four Gospels. Yet it is also true that an academic from another discipline who browses at all widely in the writings of contemporary theologians and biblical scholars is astonished, at times, by the way in which they handle their evidence, by the pre-suppositions and *a priori* convictions with which some of them clearly (and even, on occasion, on their own admission) approach the documents concerned, and by the positively staggering assurance with which they make categorical pro-nouncements on points which are, on any showing, open to question and on which equally competent colleagues take a diametrically opposite view. It is possible, indeed, that these characteristics of a great deal of theological writing today strike a lawyer even more forcibly than they do other academics,[3] since lawyers are predisposed by their training to accept the propositions that documentary evidence should, as far as possible, be allowed to speak for itself; that an honest attempt should be made to sift and assess oral testi-mony and not to jump to any premature conclusions that it is mutually contradictory; and that circumstantial evidence may, on occasion, be exceedingly persuasive. Absolute cer-tainty can, of course, seldom be reached in any evaluation of historical evidence or the conclusions to which such evidence leads; but no one, in point of fact, demands this degree of cer-tainty in any other aspect of his daily life.

Obviously enough, testimony may be false as well as true, worthless as well as convincing; so a lawyer, and especially a judge, is always face to face with the problem of how to evaluate evidence and distinguish the reliable from the mis-leading. He will inevitably decide that the testimony of some witnesses cannot be trusted, or even that it is made up of a tissue of lies; but when he believes that a witness is honest and sincere he must accord his testimony the respect which it deserves. Even a trustworthy witness may, of course, suffer from a lapse of memory; and experience shows that a number of completely honest witnesses to a single event will

[3] But cf. in this context not only C. S. Lewis (*supra*) but A. N. Sherwin-White, *Roman Society and Roman Law in the New Testament* (OUP, London, 1963), and Dorothy Sayers, *The Man Born to be King*.

never in practice describe it in identical terms, since each of them will have seen it from a somewhat different angle and will have noted and remembered, or failed to note or remember, different details. It is the duty of a judge not only to weigh evidence against evidence but also to interpret the testimony of each witness in accordance with the meaning he intended, rather than the interpretation that may be put upon it by counsel for the other side.

II

In regard to documentary evidence, in particular, certain rules have been evolved down the centuries as to how this should be construed and interpreted in courts of law. Most of these rules are largely a matter of common sense; they govern the way in which documents as diverse as an Act of Parliament, on the one hand, or a private will or contract, on the other, should be interpreted; and some of them could with advantage, I believe, be much more consistently applied in the field of biblical studies. So it may be worth while to mention a few of these rules as they are set forth in a standard legal text book such as Odgers' *Construction of Deeds and Statutes*[4], together with some of the relevant *dicta* of a number of eminent judges.

Rule I in Odgers states categorically that "The meaning of a document or of a particular part of it is to be sought for in the document itself."[5] This means, of course, that "the intention of the parties must be discovered, if possible, from the expressions they have used" and that it is not permissible to impose on these expressions a subjective inference about the intention behind them. But while the cardinal rule is that a lawyer has no right whatever to suggest that clear and unambiguous words do not mean what they say, where the words are *not* clear and unambiguous he must resort to Rule II—that "The intention [of the parties] may prevail over the

[4] Fifth ed., by Gerald Dworkin (Sweet & Maxwell, London, 1967).
[5] Ibid., p. 28.

16

words used."[6] Even so, this does not allow a lawyer to give free rein to his own ideas about the intention of the parties; on the contrary, Lord Cottenham has explained this rule by saying that

> if the provisions and expressions be contradictory and if there be grounds appearing from the face of the instrument, affording proof of the real intention of the parties, then that intention will prevail against the obvious and ordinary meaning of the words. If the parties have themselves furnished a key to the meaning of the words used, it is not material by what expression they convey their intention.[7]

This is tantamount to saying that it is always the words or the intentions of the parties for which documentary evidence exists which must prevail; not a series of subjective conjectures as to the words they ought to have used, or the intentions they might have had.

Rule III decrees that "Words are to be taken in their literal meaning" wherever this is possible or appropriate. This is a salutary rule, but not one which can be pressed to extremes; for the subject matter of a document may show that the words

> have a meaning different from their plain, ordinary or popular meaning, if they are used in connection with the usage of some trade or profession and have thus some special, technical meaning. They may even be used in a special or peculiar sense on a particular occasion if this construction would effect the intention of the parties as collected from the document. Also if the plain, ordinary meaning of the words would lead to some absurdity or inconsistency with other expressions in the document, this plain, ordinary meaning may be modified in order to avoid the absurdity or to render the different parts of the document consistent.[8]

[6] Ibid., p. 31.
[7] *Lloyd* v. *Lloyd* (1837) 2 My. & Cr. 192, at p. 202.
[8] Odgers, op. cit., p. 36.

17

As Jessel, Master of the Rolls, put it: "The grammatical and ordinary sense of the words is to be adhered to, unless that would lead to some absurdity, or some repugnance or inconsistency with the rest of the instrument, in which case the grammatical or ordinary sense of the words may be modified, so as to avoid that absurdity and inconsistency, but no further."[9] So where the words cannot be construed in their literal, ordinary meaning, then some other meaning which is discoverable from the document itself, if this is at all possible, must be accorded them—and in such cases all the relevant circumstances may be taken into account.

This leads directly to Rule IV: "Literal meaning depends on the circumstances of the parties." In other words, where the meaning of the words used gives rise to genuine doubt, then "extrinsic evidence is admissible, not to construe the deed, but to translate for the court the terms used by the parties."[10] As Lord Blackburn put it:

in all cases the object is to see what is the intention expressed by the words used. But from the imperfection of language it is impossible to know what that intention is without inquiring further and seeing what the circumstances were in reference to which the words were used and what was the object appearing from those circumstances which the person using them had in view, for the meaning of words varies according to the circumstances in respect of which they were used.[11]

And this, in its turn, leads naturally enough to Rule VII: "Therefore the deed is to be construed as a whole;"[12] for the deed "must be read and interpreted as a whole in order to extract the meaning of any particular part or expression". As Lord Davey put it: "the words of each clause should be so interpreted as to bring them into harmony with

[9] *Re Levy, ex. p. Walton* (1881) 17 C. D. 746 at p. 751.
[10] Odgers, op. cit., p. 39.
[11] *River Wear Commissioners* v. *Adamson* (1877) 2 App. Cas. 743, at p. 763.
[12] Odgers, op. cit., p. 55.

the other provisions of the deed if that interpretation does no violence to the meaning of which they are naturally susceptible."[13] Even so, however, a court must not "deviate from the force of any particular expression unless it finds from other parts of the deed some expression which shows that the author could not have had the intention which the expression used in its literal form would imply".[14]

All this represents what might be termed the very stock-in-trade of the lawyer, and determines the principles he will instinctively follow when he sets about the task of trying to interpret a document. But it seems to me a very far cry from the way in which many theologians treat the Bible. It is, of course, perfectly true that the Bible is very different from an Act of Parliament, a contract or a will. It comprises a collection of different documents of a very heterogeneous nature; it includes poetry as well as prose, allegories as well as plain statements of fact. Clearly, then, the way in which any particular passage should be interpreted must necessarily depend, to a considerable extent, on the nature of its style and contents. But it is usually (although by no means always) clear enough whether a passage is intended to be taken in a straightforward, a poetical or an allegorical way, and whether words should, prima facie, be accorded their plain meaning or have been used in some special or technical sense. Time after time, moreover, a word, phrase or mode of expression used in one passage is used again, and in this case in an unambiguous way, in another part of the same document—or else can be interpreted in the light of circumstances, or by reference to a background, for which there is also documentary evidence.

But some theologians seem to me to pay singularly little attention to any such canons of interpretation. Instead, they betray a positively bewildering variety of approach. There are still a few, no doubt, who adopt a rigidly literalistic mode of construction and take little or no trouble to try to understand the meaning of the passage concerned in

[13] [1900] A.C. 260, at p. 269.
[14] Odgers, op. cit., p. 56.

the light of the circumstances in which it was written and the purpose the author had in mind—however much these circumstances, or this purpose, can be inferred from the document itself. There are others who make a genuine and painstaking attempt to understand what the author of the document himself meant by the words he used, but then feel perfectly free to re-interpret this meaning in the most radical way in the light of their own outlook and convictions. On occasion they will not only confidently assert that the traditions on which an author has relied cannot be regarded as representing historical events (a point to which we must return later) but even that the author has himself "invented" incidents to illustrate the teaching he is trying to inculcate—although they often add a pious rider to the effect that they are not, of course, making any imputation of deliberate falsehood. Many of them, indeed, seem to accept or reject biblical evidence on what appears to be a purely subjective basis. They will not only quote, but also treat as authoritative and decisive, a passage which suits their thesis, yet they will completely ignore other passages which run counter to their argument. Again, they often appear to take singularly little trouble to interpret the document as a whole, and reject the elementary presumption that an author is intrinsically unlikely to have contradicted himself. Instead, they seem positively to swoop, on occasion, on contradictions which do not—or do not necessarily—in fact exist. Their attitude as a whole is often distinctly ambivalent—as can be seen in its most extreme form, perhaps, when a theologian expounds a verse or passage of Scripture clause by clause, as though each component part were divinely authoritative, in the pulpit on Sunday, and then dissects it in a most radical way, and in a very different spirit, in the lecture theatre next day.

III

So much for the rules and principles accepted by lawyers

in regard to the interpretation of documents. But I can imagine many of my theological friends saying that, while rules such as these may perhaps be applicable to the determination of what is the real meaning of some phrase or argument in one of Paul's letters, they are largely irrelevant in trying to determine whether some incident recorded in the Gospels, or some statement attributed to Jesus, is in fact historical. These principles may perhaps help us to determine what the Evangelist himself was trying to say—although less so, the theologian would probably add, than in the case of a Pauline epistle, because of the dependence of the Gospels on still more primitive oral or written sources—but they would have no relevance to the problem of whether the incident or saying concerned can really be regarded as an authentic record of what Jesus himself did or said.

Nothing I have so far written has much bearing on this question, except for a few fragmentary remarks about the fundamental problem of the evaluation of evidence in general. Whatever may be true of a historian's assessment of evidence, the problem is complicated, from a strictly legal point of view, by the rules which govern the admission of "hearsay" evidence and expressions of a witness's opinion—for clearly a great deal of the evidence to be found in the New Testament comes under one or the other of these two categories. The rule against hearsay evidence means that "assertions of persons other than the witness who is testifying are inadmissible *as evidence of the truth of that which was asserted.*"[15] But it is important to note that evidence of a statement made to a witness by a third party does not always, or necessarily, come under this rule against the admission of hearsay evidence, even in a court of law. "It is hearsay and inadmissible when the object of the evidence is to establish the truth of what is contained in the statement. It is not hearsay and is admissible when it is proposed to establish by the evidence, not the

[15] Rupert Cross, *Evidence*, (Third ed.; Butterworths, London, 1967), p. 380.

21

truth of the statement, but the fact that it was made."[16] There are, moreover, a large number of exceptions to the rule against hearsay evidence, and it is noteworthy that the general objection to such evidence is today being progressively lessened, now that almost all civil litigation takes place before a judge sitting without a jury; for a judge, unlike a jury, is regarded as capable of assessing the weight that should properly be accorded to any evidence which may be adduced.

The further rule which normally insists that a witness must speak to facts which he has observed or are within his personal knowledge, not to his opinion about these facts, seems to have grown out of the rule about hearsay. It is clear, however, that there "has always been an undefined borderland between fact and opinion" and that many apparent statements of fact are merely disguised expressions of opinion.[17] Evidence which consists of the opinion even of non-experts is, moreover, admissible in certain cases; "expert" evidence is frequently admissible; and the decision as to whether a witness is qualified to give evidence of his opinion as an expert is left to the discretion of the judge, so a witness who is allegedly an expert "need not be an expert or specialist in the professional sense".[18] Even so, an American judge has said that, where "the facts from which a witness received an impression were too evanescent in their nature to be recollected, or too complicated to be separately and distinctly narrated", then he may state his opinion or impression.[19] Similarly, it is not always true that a witness must not be questioned as to his belief or persuasion, but only as to his knowledge of some fact; for this does not apply to questions of persuasion or belief "founded on facts within the actual knowledge of the witness". In other words, no hesitation has been felt in English courts "in admitting statements by witnesses which

[16] *Subramaniam* v. *Public Prosecutor* [1956] I W.L.R. 965, at p. 969.

[17] G. D. Nokes, *An Introduction to the Law of Evidence* (Fourth ed.; Sweet and Maxwell, London, 1967), p. 163.

[18] Ibid., p. 178.

[19] Cross, op. cit., pp. 367 f.

are a compendious mode of summarising a sequence of inferences, based upon perceived facts".[20] In a trial counsel will, of course, examine and cross-examine witnesses, and compare or contrast one bit of evidence with another; then, finally, the judge or jury will decide whether this witness or that is reliable or unreliable, and how much weight should be accorded to the testimony of each. Circumstantial evidence may, moreover, often be more persuasive than direct testimony, since it may be far more difficult to fabricate.

But a theologian or historian may well repudiate any comparison whatever between his studies and the processes of litigation in a court of law, where the rigid canons of evidence applied bear little relation to those probabilities which men ordinarily accept as the basis of thought and action, and on which he himself feels justified in basing his assumptions.[21] After all, he may say, must not an accused person be acquitted by a court unless his guilt can be *conclusively* proved—even if, by all ordinary standards, there is an overwhelming probability that he is guilty? Surely this is an impossible criterion to apply in everyday life—or, for that matter, in historical research?

This in fact, however, represents a considerable overstatement of the legal position. To begin with, the standard of proof demanded of the prosecution in a criminal trial is considerably more exacting than that required of the parties in civil litigation. In the former case the prosecution must satisfy the jury or magistrate concerned of the guilt of the accused "beyond reasonable doubt", while in the latter it is sufficient for one of the parties to show a "preponderance of probability". In the words of Denning J. (now Lord Denning, Master of the Rolls) in *Miller* v. *Minister of Pensions*,[22] the degree of cogency which the evidence must reach in a criminal case before the accused can be convicted

[20] P. A. Landon, as quoted in Cross, op. cit., p. 359.
[21] Including, of course, historical assumptions, without which scarcely any history could be written.
[22] [1947] 2 AER 372.

is well settled. It need not reach certainty, but it must carry a high degree of probability. Proof beyond a reasonable doubt does not mean proof beyond a shadow of doubt. The law would fail to protect the community if it permitted fanciful possibilities to deflect the course of justice. If the evidence is so strong against a man as to leave only a remote possibility in his favour which can be dismissed with the sentence 'Of course it is possible but not in the least probable', the case is proved beyond reasonable doubt; but nothing short of that will suffice.

This is something very different from *conclusive* proof. Then, turning to the degree of cogency which evidence must reach in order to discharge the burden of proof in a civil case, he said that that, too, "is well settled. It must carry a reasonable degree of probability, not so high as is required in a criminal case. If the evidence is such that the tribunal can say: 'We think it more probable than not', the burden is discharged, but if the probabilities are equal it is not."

But this, surely, is strikingly similar to the sort of evidence for which the historian habitually looks. Often, indeed, he may be totally unable to solve some problem on the basis of the available evidence—except, perhaps, by what he hopes is "inspired guesswork" or the exercise of trained intuition. Frequently, again, he will have to be content, or reasonably content, with a preponderance of probability. But sometimes, at least, he will decide that, on the evidence, there is no reasonable doubt—even if he feels compelled to add, with Lord Denning, that this need not mean that there is no "shadow of doubt".

IV

Obviously, again, this question of the standard of evidence required is a somewhat two-edged weapon. It is clearly applicable in principle, I should have thought, to the attempt to determine whether some incident or saying attributed to Jesus in the Gospels is, or is not, authentic; but it can be applied in two very different ways according to the basic presuppositions with which the scholar concerned approaches the question. If, for example, he takes the view that the Gospels were at least intended as an honest account of what the current tradition attributed to the historical Jesus, that this tradition can be shown (at least in part) to go back to a very early date, and that there are clear indications that much of it (again to speak with caution) must be regarded as authentic, then he will, presumably, apply the principles outlined above, or some adaptation of them, on the basis that the account should be accepted as prima facie reliable unless there is evidence to show that the opposite is the case.[23] But if he is firmly committed to the view that nothing in the record can be accepted as even probably true unless each detail can be shown to be authentic by a stringency of proof which, in the nature of the case, must almost always be impracticable in such circumstances, then the results he will reach by the application of these principles will be very different.

Unhappily, it seems to be all too common for scholars (or, indeed, the public at large) not only to approach the Gospels with firmly held presuppositions, but to let these presuppositions give a very subjective slant to what should be a purely objective evaluation of evidence.[24] It is true that no human being can approach any investigation with complete objectivity, for we are all to some extent influenced by the age in which we live, the training we have received, and the opinions we have formed. But there is a vast difference between the man who genuinely does his best to be objective, and who tries to give full weight to any evidence which seems to go against the point of view he would naturally embrace, and the man who holds certain preconceived ideas so strongly that he is prepared to impose

[23] The emphasis we find in the Johannine writings on valid testimony seems to me significant in this context.

[24] Many examples of this will be given in the successive chapters of this book.

them on all the available evidence and accept, reject or interpret it accordingly.

This may seem so obvious that it scarcely needs to be said. But even the most minimal acquaintance with the writings of New Testament scholars reveals the fact that some of them, as C. S. Lewis asserts, approach the evidence with the firm conviction that all that savours of the supernatural or the miraculous must necessarily be discarded as unhistorical, or at least explained as either a misunderstanding of some quite natural event or a pictorial representation of some spiritual truth. But to approach the evidence in this way seems to me not only to prejudge one particular issue but to invalidate the whole proceeding.[25] Equally, of course, there are those (of whom I must confess myself to be one) who approach the New Testament with a predisposition to regard its authors as not having been left to their unaided resources, but having been given divine help in what they remembered, the traditions they accepted, and the teaching they gave – a predisposition which could, of course, be equally inimical to an objective evaluation. Which of these two approaches is preferable must, self-evidently, depend upon the empirical criterion of where the truth happens to lie. But neither of them represents an objective appraisal of the evidence as such; and it should not be beyond our power to make a genuine attempt to lay aside our preconceived ideas and assess the evidence as objectively as possible, rather than to impose our own beliefs upon it.

Clearly, if the evidence as a whole seems to lead to certain conclusions, then these conclusions may legitimately influence, to some degree at least, the way in which we evaluate the component parts of this evidence. If, for example, certain supernatural or miraculous elements in the record rest on evidence which we find convincing, then it will certainly be somewhat easier than would otherwise be the case to accept as historical other incidents of a similar nature for which the available evidence is in itself less cogent. What must at all costs be eschewed is the attitude of mind which accepts or rejects part of the record not

[25] See pp. 12f., 15, etc. above.

because of the evidence, but in spite of it. The scholar who examines some saying or incident recorded in the Gospels with the *a priori* conviction that it *could* not really have happened will almost certainly end with the conclusion with which he began, for he will not have weighed the evidence in any way which could, even remotely, be termed "judicial". If, on the other hand, he is prepared to let the evidence speak for itself, without prejudging the issue, he may decide that it is good, suspect or inconclusive. He may then, of course, take the further step of comparing this particular saying or incident, together with the evidence which can be adduced in its support, with other parts of the available evidence, to see if they so cohere as to build up a consistent picture which he finds convincing.

I have already referred to the breath-taking assurance with which some contemporary theologians make dogmatic assertions about points which, on any showing, are wide open to discussion and debate—and on which other equally competent authorities have taken, and do take, a very different point of view. It is, of course, common enough for scholars in any field of study to argue and disagree among themselves; but it often seems to me that, should a competition in this scholarly proclivity ever be organised between the different academic disciplines, that of theology would probably come out at the top of the league. Nor is it only that theologians and New Testament scholars so often appear to bear a much closer resemblance to the barrister who argues a case than to the judge who weighs the evidence on both sides before coming to his conclusion. Even when regarded as advocates some of them seem, on occasion, to overstate their case in a way which is singularly unconvincing. Instead of inviting the jury, as it were, to consider a possible interpretation of the facts to which some of the evidence might be thought to point, they not infrequently make the most positive pronouncements that such an incident *cannot* be regarded as historical, that such a passage in the Gospels is *indubitably* expressed in symbolic or mythological terms, or that such a statement can *only* have one meaning—and all this with little or no reasoned argument, and a singular dearth of concrete evidence, to support their assumptions. We are continually told that the actual sayings and acts of Jesus are inextricably interwoven, in the Gospels, with the interpretation put upon these sayings and events by the primitive Church; but I often find myself wishing that some of the experts concerned had themselves attended an elementary course for prospective journalists in which the basic difference between news and comments, facts and theories, had been plainly and patiently explained.

The fact that I am concerned, in this book, with the attitude adopted by theologians and biblical scholars will, I hope, explain the superabundance of quotations from their writings which must—of necessity, I think—make up so many of its pages. These quotations may, admittedly, be regarded as highly selective, and are not nearly so wide-ranging as I should wish. But I have never, unhappily, learnt to read at more than a snail's pace; so the demands of a busy life inevitably preclude me from reading very widely in a discipline which is not my own. I only wish I had time to deal with the subject more adequately.

Finally, I must return to the point that the title of this book should not be pressed to extremes. I have devoted most of this introductory chapter to a somewhat detailed, and perhaps wearisome, discussion of the way in which a lawyer is trained to assess evidence, whether documentary or oral; and it will be apparent from the subsequent chapters, I think, that theologians frequently treat their evidence, whether textual or circumstantial, in a very different way. But I have not, in most cases, commented on this from a specifically legal angle, since this would have been both tedious and also, sometimes, irrelevant. As I have already remarked, my comments are not so much those of a professional lawyer as of an academic who is interested in biblical studies but himself comes from another discipline—which happens in my case to be the law.

CHAPTER TWO

The Jesus of History and the Christ of Faith

I

Unlike many of the world's religions, Christianity makes the unequivocal claim that it owes its origin to a historical person who actually lived at a specific time and place. It also asserts that he said and did certain things, died on a Roman gibbet and subsequently rose again from the dead. If it could be shown that no such person as Jesus ever walked this earth, or that the basic substance of what the Church as a whole has always believed about him has no historical foundation, Christianity as we know it would cease to be. The ethical and spiritual import of the teaching attributed to Jesus, and the inspiration of what we might then call the "Jesus myth", might, no doubt, survive; but this would not represent Christianity. It would put the Christian doctrine of the Incarnation very much on a par with one of the *avatars* of Vishnu—except only for the contrast which might still remain between the ethical implications of the one and the other.

This basic dependence of the Christian faith on history is, indeed, a matter of incredulous surprise to many Hindus. Lesslie Newbigin describes the astonishment with which a devout and learned teacher of the Rāmakrishna Mission regarded him when he discovered that the Bishop was prepared to rest his whole faith as a Christian upon "the substantial historical truth of the record concerning Jesus in the New Testament". To the Hindu it "seemed axiomatic that such vital matters of religious truth could not be allowed to depend upon the accidents of history. If the truths which Jesus exemplified and taught are true, then they are true always and everywhere, whether a person called Jesus ever lived or not".[1]

But this is quite contrary to what Christians think and believe. There is all the difference in the world, as Newbigin insists,

> between a statement about the nature of God, and a report that God has, at a certain time and place, acted in a certain way. In the latter case the occurrence is the essence of the message. The care which is taken in the New Testament to place the events recorded in the continuum of secular history is in striking contrast to the indifference which is generally shown with regard to the historicity of the events which Hindu piety loves to remember in connection with the character of the gods. There is no serious attempt to relate them to events in secular history, nor is it felt that there would be any advantage to be gained from trying to do so—even if it could be done. Their value is that they illustrate truths about God which would remain true even if these particular events had not happened.[2]

Indeed, the majority of educated Hindus do not believe that most of the *avatars* with which these "events" are connected represent anything more than mythological stories fraught with spiritual truth.

Even in the West the assertion has, of course, occasionally been made that Jesus himself was a purely mythological figure—most recently, perhaps, by John Allegro, who suggests that he was no more than a code name for the sacred mushroom. It is open to doubt, perhaps, whether even Allegro himself takes that remark altogether seriously. But however that may be, James Frazer gave expression to the attitude of the overwhelming majority of scholars when he wrote: "The doubts which have been cast on the historical

---

[1] *The Finality of Christ*, p. 50. The Hindu attitude to the Gospels is somewhat similar to the attitude many Christians take to the book of Job, for example: i.e., that it is the teaching, not the historicity, which really matters.

[2] Ibid., p. 52 ff.

reality of Jesus are in my judgment unworthy of serious attention";[3] and Otto Betz has committed himself to the statement that in recent years "no serious scholar has ventured to postulate the non-historicity of Jesus".[4]

All the same, there are a number of theologians today who concentrate their attention almost exclusively on what the primitive Christian Church thought and taught about Jesus and virtually deny that the New Testament provides us with any reliable record of what he himself actually said or did. There can be no doubt, Rudolf Bultmann has asserted, that a historical person called Jesus did really exist; and there can equally be no doubt about the existential impact he made on his followers. But it is useless to try to get back behind the message of the primitive Church and make any credible attempt to depict the life and teaching of her Master; for the Evangelists recorded traditions which had not only been moulded and fashioned by those whose whole outlook was permeated by their Easter faith, but were also deliberately (or inevitably?) expressed in a mythological form. We can, indeed, attempt to "demythologise" the proclamation and translate it into the existential idiom of the contemporary world; but it would be in vain—and even profitless—to attempt to get behind the existential impact to the historical facts on which that impact is alleged to have been founded.

Fundamentally, of course, this concentration on the "Christ of Faith" represents a reaction from the long, frustrated quest for the "Jesus of History" which had so mesmerised a succession of scholars for generations. These protagonists of the Liberal Enlightenment had firmly believed that they could get back behind the Gospels to a Galilean peasant who preached an ethic of selfless love and proclaimed the coming of God's kingdom.[5] But this attempt

[3] *The Golden Bough* (Macmillan, 1913), vol. 9, p. 412 n.
[4] *What do we Know about Jesus?* (SCM Press, London, 1968), p. 9.
[5] It was Albert Schweitzer, in his *Quest of the Historical Jesus* (1906), who rang the death knell on liberal reconstructions of a purely ethical Jesus; but his own exaggerated emphasis on an almost exclusively eschatological figure is little more convincing.

had been foredoomed to failure, partly by the preconceptions with which they approached the material available to them and partly by the nature of the material itself. They had believed that they would be able to establish the facts about this simple teacher of righteousness, shorn of all that savoured of the miraculous or supernatural; but they found that they could not disentangle what C. S. Lewis terms the depth, sanity and *shrewdness* of his moral teaching from the "rampant megalomania"[6] of those claims which alone could have given rise to the accusations of blasphemy repeatedly levelled against him, or those inexplicable works of power which caused him to be linked, on occasion, with Beelzebub rather than Yahweh. Nor could they explain why such a harmless idealist should be hounded to death. And as for the material itself, it is abundantly clear that the Gospels do not provide us with the data for anything approaching a detailed biography of Jesus. We find no attempt whatever to describe his appearance, and no conscious attempt to depict or analyse his character. There is little chronology in the records, scarcely anything about the first three decades of his life, and even in regard to the brief period of his ministry the sayings and incidents recorded are highly selective. Nor can this be explained solely on the basis that the traditions on which the Gospels rest were themselves fragmentary, and that teaching and incidents had come to be grouped together in what might be termed a series of clusters, or units, for didactic purposes;[7] for attention has recently been called to the distinctive theological emphasis and structure of each of the Gospels.[8] It is crystal clear that these books were never intended as detached and objective records of the life and teaching of one with whom the authors had no personal involvement. They were, rather, written by self-confessed disciples to put on record, before the generation of eyewitnesses died out, the basis and content of their faith.

In the Gospels, then, we find the substance of the

[6] Cf. *Miracles* (Geoffrey Bles, London, 1947), p. 132.
[7] This is one of the major emphases of "Form Criticism".
[8] E.g., by "Redaction Criticism".

proclamation of the primitive Church, transformed as this was by their belief in the resurrection of Jesus. How, then, can we distinguish between history and interpretation? How can we get behind the glow of Easter faith to the sober realism of a quest for the historical Jesus? This, we are assured, is an impossible task. There is the so-called "tunnel" or "twilight" period, out of which the primitive teaching about Jesus emerges into the light of day only—we are repeatedly told—with the publication of the Gospels some thirty-five or more years after the crucifixion. There is the inevitable bias which so often vitiates the objectivity of those who deeply venerate an outstanding—and, in this case, unique—figure. And there is the suspicion which arises, in some minds, as a result of the alleged indifference of Paul to the importance of any knowledge of Jesus "according to the flesh". But it seems to me that all these points have been greatly exaggerated. We can trace the basic beliefs of the primitive Church right back to what is virtually the very beginning. Many of the eye-witnesses were alive throughout the whole "tunnel" period, and it is fantastic to suggest that new converts were not deeply interested in the facts about the life and teaching of Jesus, and did not continually ask them questions about him.[9] The basis of the apostolic "tradition" must have taken shape at a very early date—partly in writing, but mostly in the form of oral teaching which was committed to memory. "Source" criticism, "Form" criticism and "Redaction" criticism can all throw considerable light on how the Gospels were put together, but need not for that reason be regarded as affecting their historical reliability. To this we shall have to return again and again in this book—as, also, to the allegation of such bias as to distort the record. As for Paul, his letters were concerned with the theological, ethical and liturgical problems of the Gentile churches, rather than with the life of Jesus. Nor was he himself an eye-witness of the Galilean or Judaean ministry. But he often gives us glimpses of what he had learned about the personality

9 Cf. F. R. Barry, *The Atonement* (Hodder and Stoughton, London, 1968), p. 95; G. B. Caird, *St. Luke* (Penguin Books, 1963), p. 22.

and teaching of Jesus,[10] and to interpret II Cor. 5:16 as indicating any indifference to his life and teaching is absurd.

But, however this may be, there is no doubt that the pendulum of scholarly emphasis has swung right over from the quest for the historical Jesus to the opposite extreme; and we are often bidden to concentrate our entire attention not on the Jesus of History but the Christ of Faith, the Christ of the apostolic proclamation. It is not only impossible but virtually irrelevant, we are told, to decide how much of the Gospel record represents an authentic picture of Jesus as he walked the hills of Galilee and the streets of Jerusalem, or as he taught beside the lake, in the upper room, or in the garden. All that really matters is the existential impact he made on his first disciples, and the similar existential impact he can still make on us today when the "old, old story" is set forth—whether in its primitive dress or in some much more contemporary garb. Rudolf Bultmann has even gone so far as to state that "the salvation event is nowhere present except in the proclaiming, accosting, demanding and promising word of preaching".[11] This, as E. L. Mascall justly observes, "seems to give serious point to the gibe ... that the Christ-event took place not in the years A.D. 1–30 but every time that Bultmann enters the pulpit at 11 a.m. on Sunday".[12] Even more radical writers, such as Schubert M. Ogden, go further still, and accuse Bultmann of "retaining a mythological element by tying the Gospel to the figure of the historic Jesus and so making the Gospel still unacceptable".[13] And while Paul van Buren appears to insist on the centrality of the historical Jesus, Mascall remarks that he

provides a *soi-disant* 'Christianity' in which there is no such being as God, nobody survives bodily death,

[10] For Paul's knowledge of the life and teaching of Jesus, cf. A. M. Hunter, *The Gospel According to Paul* (SCM Press, London, 1966), pp. 58 ff.

[11] Cf. E. L. Mascall, *The Secularisation of Christianity*, p. 55, quoting *Theology of the New Testament*, I, p. 302, cited by R. H. Fuller in *The New Testament in Current Study*, p. 73.

[12] Mascall, op. cit., p. 10, again referring to R. H. Fuller, op. cit., p. 21.

[13] Mascall, op. cit., p. 46.

nobody hears us when we pray, there is no risen Saviour and nothing for us when we are dead; but only, while we are in this life, an undefined 'freedom' which is alleged to be contagious and to give us the same 'perspective' on the world as was possessed by a Galilean peasant who no longer exists.[14]

II

But, to a lawyer, this thesis seems far more sweeping than the facts—and, indeed, the writings of many theologians and New Testament scholars—would in any way warrant. For this line of argument seems to give quite inadequate weight to two basic considerations: first, that the presence of an interpretative element in the Gospel records does not necessarily preclude their historical reliability or distort the picture which they give of the central figure; and, secondly, that even the most ruthless examination of the evidence seems to demonstrate that there are a number of features in the Gospels which cannot be explained in terms of the thought-forms and preoccupations of the primitive Church —but some of which would seem, on any straightforward analysis, to bear the hall-mark of the observations of an eye-witness (no matter through how many formulations they may conceivably have come).

But first, what of the resurrection itself, since it is this event, or non-event, which is alleged to have so changed the attitude of the disciples that they could no longer think of the person or ministry of the human Jesus in other than transcendental terms? I shall be returning to this subject in much more detail in two later chapters; so it must suffice, in this context, to remark that Wolfhart Pannenberg[15] and many other scholars argue that the apostle Paul probably

[14] Ibid., p. 7.
[15] Cf. *Jesus: God and Man* (SCM Press, 1968), p. 90, A. M. Hunter, *Paul and his Predecessors* (SCM Press, 1961), pp. 15–18, and C. H. Dodd, *The Founder of Christianity* (Collins, London, 1971), pp. 167 f.

"received" the basic tradition recorded in I Cor. 15 ("that Christ died for our sins in accordance with the scriptures, that he was buried, that he was raised on the third day in accordance with the scriptures")—together with a list of the principal witnesses to the resurrection—immediately after his own conversion; and that he *must* have received it in its fulness on the occasion of his first visit to Jerusalem, about which he tells us in Gal. 1. This means that it can be traced back possibly to within two years, indubitably to within eight years, and in all probability to within some five years of the event. Not only so, but Paul specifically tells us in this passage that this was no tradition peculiar to himself but the basic teaching of all the apostles; and he also observes that nearly twenty years later, when he wrote this letter to the Corinthians, the majority of five hundred witnesses to having seen the risen Christ were still alive— to confirm or deny his statement.

Now it is true that there is no explicit reference to the empty tomb in I Cor. 15; for that we have to wait for the Gospels. But Pannenberg argues convincingly, in my view, that the evidence seems to point strongly to the fact that the tomb was empty. What Palestinian Jew of the first century, he asks, could conceivably have recorded a tradition about Jesus having died, been buried, and being "raised" if he had believed that the body of the one thus described as risen was in reality rotting in a tomb in Jerusalem? How could the apostles have made a large number of converts from the very beginning in that hostile city, primarily by preaching the resurrection, if the body had still been lying in a sepulchre to which any of their hearers could very easily have walked? Why, again, do we find no suggestion that the tomb was not in fact empty in any contemporary Jewish apologetic?

A number of different theories have, of course, been put forward down the centuries to explain how the tomb might have been empty without this necessarily involving what certainly seems to have been the belief of the primitive Church: that the human body of Jesus was miraculously changed on Easter Day into a "spiritual" or resurrection body—in much the same way, presumably, as Paul says, later in I Cor. 15, will happen to those Christians who are still alive at the parousia.[16] But these theories must not detain us now. Suffice it to say, with Michael Ramsey, that it

> seems very significant in the apostles' understanding of the resurrection that it is the return to them of the Jesus who died, the Jesus to whom the wounds still belong. Thus to believe in Jesus as risen Lord meant and still means to pledge oneself to the Cross. Therefore I find myself near to Bultmann in seeing the Easter faith as an act of commitment to the death of Jesus. But I part company with Bultmann in being convinced that the resurrection was an event; and while various factors enter into my belief in it, it was an event to which the historical evidence is relevant as showing that without the resurrection the course of known history is unaccountable.[17]

Frankly, I myself find the evidence for the resurrection completely convincing. We must, of course, discuss later in this book some of the theories which have been put forward to give a rationalistic explanation not only for the empty tomb, but also for the resurrection appearances and the dramatic change which *something* effected in the little band of bewildered, dispirited and defeated disciples. Speaking generally, these theories seem to me to constitute a classic example of not weighing the evidence but deciding the issue, on *a priori* grounds, in spite of it. Our concern in this chapter, however, is with the evangelists who, on any showing, wrote their gospels from a post-resurrection perspective. But I cannot myself follow the argument that this means that the record they give of the teaching, ministry, miracles and trial of Jesus has entirely parted company with the facts. To quote Michael Ramsey again: "Much is made in contemporary studies of the contention that the Gospels

[16] See below, p.p. 98f. and 137ff.
[17] "Christian Faith and the Historical Jesus", in *Theology*, March 1972, pp. 120 f.

give us not diaries or photographs or simple memoirs but interpretative portraits. So be it. But if the interpretations are true interpretations, then the portraits may be of much historical value. The crucial question is whether the Christian communities created the figure of Jesus whom they portrayed or whether they were themselves created by a figure of Jesus whose elusive originality their portrait has not concealed."[18] Even John Stuart Mill, to go back to a former generation, considered it useless

> to say that Christ, as exhibited in the Gospels, is not historical, and that we know not how much of what is admirable has been superadded by the tradition of his followers. Who among his disciples or among their proselytes was capable of inventing the sayings of Jesus or of imagining the life and character revealed in the Gospels? Certainly not the fishermen of Galilee; as certainly not St. Paul, whose character and idiosyncrasies were of a totally different sort; still less the early Christian writers.[19]

It seems to me perfectly clear that the evangelists at least profess to be writing history, however much an interpretative element may permeate their record. "To accuse the gospel evangelists of indiscriminately submerging historical fact in a flood of miracle-mongering to serve the interests of theological propaganda would", in G. H. Boobyer's words, "be outright injustice."[20] But this is precisely what a number of scholars dogmatically assert. Take, for instance, M. D. Goulder's view of the way in which Luke constructed his narratives. He is so carried away with his "attempt to apply the tool of typological criticism" in regard to the Acts of the Apostles, for example, that he baldly asserts that the

[18] Ibid., p. 121.
[19] *Three Essays on Religion* (London, 1874), pp. 253 f.
[20] "The Gospel Miracles: Views Past and Present", in *The Miracles and the Resurrection*, p. 39 – as quoted E. L. Mascall, op. cit., p. 273.

symbolic content of the account of the ascension is almost 100% ... The motive in St. Luke's mind for its inclusion we have often had cause to remark. It occupies a keystone place in the pattern of Luke–Acts, and stands above all in the latter book against the incarnation in the former. St. Luke, then, had overwhelming reasons for inventing a story describing the ascension if one did not already exist, and his account supplies no reasons for thinking that he did not so invent one. (The spiritual reality that the ascension story represents is, of course, not affected by this argument ...).[21]

In other words we are asked to assume that Luke would have no hesitation whatever in "inventing" the whole account of the ascension, provided only that this account would represent a spiritual reality of some sort and would form a convenient introduction to his book. The fact that the self-same evidence has led other scholars to a very different conclusion does not make Goulder put forward his views as a theory, possibly worthy of consideration. Instead, he states his opinion as though it were incontrovertible fact.

D. E. Nineham is a great deal gentler in his phraseology. Yet, in a recent article on the accounts of the nativity in Matthew and Luke, he categorically asserts that "when they tell us that though Jesus had a human mother he had God—almost literally—for a father, that is the expression of their faith that, though his was a genuinely human life, what it embodied was more than human goodness and courage, even at their highest; its quality and effects were due to direct initiative on God's part."[22] It is only fair to add, however, that in the course of correspondence with E. L. Mascall[23] he subsequently stated that he had no doubt that, by the time these stories came to be written down, the

---

[21] *Type and History in Acts*, M. D. Goulder (SPCK, London, 1964), pp. 182 f. Cf. Mascall, op. cit., p. 279.
[22] "The Meaning of Christmas", in *Theology*, April, 1970, p. 159.
[23] *Theology*, June, 1970, p. 273.

evangelists did believe in the virgin birth as this had been traditionally understood.

This last statement, unlike that of M. D. Goulder, would at least exonerate the evangelists from deliberate invention. But it equally postulates the invention of the nativity narratives, as they have come down to us, by someone else, and their acceptance by the primitive Church as a whole at a very early date. The question inevitably arises, therefore, whether Nineham was led to this conclusion on the basis of all the available evidence, or whether he reached it on *a priori* grounds in the interest of the many (presumably including himself) who "do not find it possible to accept the tradition *in toto* as sober history". This is the attitude of mind of those who start from the preconceived conviction that what may be termed "physical" miracles—such as the virgin birth, or the resurrection in any sense that involved the *body* of Jesus—simply cannot be believed, even in the case of one whom the critics themselves declare to have been unique. This viewpoint opens the door, to some degree at least, to the supernatural, but firmly denies that this can have any effect on the physical—for some reason that I, for one, cannot altogether understand.

Yet it has been justly remarked that the Gospels

give the impression of being honest documents. It has been rightly said that St. Mark never spares the Twelve, and we are left in no doubt of their slowness of heart and unbelief. The story which they tell is the reverse of a success story, and no attempt is made to cloak the decisive rejection of Jesus by those to whom he initially came. There is little attempt to iron out the discrepancies in the tradition, as anyone who has tried to construct a harmony of their narratives quickly comes to realise. Whatever deficiencies a modern historian may ascribe to the Evangelists, lack of honesty is not one of them.[24]

One is also reminded, in this context, of the pungent

[24] H. E. W. Turner, *Historicity and the Gospels*, (Mowbray, London, 1963), p. 53.

remark of R. P. C. Hanson: "Why should this large collection of fictitious material have been composed by a number
of anonymous authors within a few years of the death of
this person whose existence was historical but about whom
we can know nothing else historical in spite of four
narratives which purport to tell us about him? How could
so extraordinary an effect have resulted from so obscure a
cause?"[25] The evangelists, as Otto Betz puts it, "stand in a
double relationship to him—both horizontal and vertical:
on the one hand through the current of tradition, which
carried the words and acts of the earthly Jesus to them; on
the other through faith in the heavenly Christ, present in
the preached word, in the Holy Spirit and in the Sacraments.
The modern distinction between Jesus as a historical figure
and Christ as a historical force did not exist for them."[26]
Precisely: whatever the early Christians were or were not,
they were certainly not existentialists; so whatever the
merits of an existentialist re-interpretation of the Gospels,
it can make no claim to reproduce primitive Christianity.

H. E. W. Turner aptly terms the Gospels "kerygmatic
history", and maintains that the noun is of no less importance than the adjective.[27] Of course they include the *kerygma*
or proclamation of the apostolic Church, for it would not
have been in any way sufficient to report that Jesus died
on a cross, or even how he died on a cross, without mention
of the supreme significance of who he was and what he did.
To quote Turner again: "There were after all three crosses
on the hill of Calvary, but, for the Christian, one is the
answer to the world's need, the other two formed part of
the problem." The Christian, he says,

> could not substitute for the statement 'Jesus died on a
> cross', a more generalised proposition, that 'someone died
> on a cross', without a complete evacuation of meaning.
> His statement implies a Christology resting ultimately
> on a certain fabric of events and propositions to give it

[25] *Vindications* (SCM, 1966), p. 41.
[26] *What do we know about Jesus?* (SCM Press, 1963), p. 11; cf. also p. 7.
[27] Op. cit., p. 64.

both content and support. He would probably go on to say that 'Jesus died for our sins', and, while he may well claim that in some sense this further statement is contained within the fact, he is bound to realise that he is also setting the Cross in a special context which two equally good historians may or may not have in common. But there will also not be far from his mind the impact of the Cross both as an evocative symbol and a saving instrument, and all that has flowed from it in subsequent centuries.[28]

III

It is obvious, then, that the New Testament includes — and must necessarily include — both history and proclamation, for the Christian faith is firmly founded in history and yet transcends history. But what primarily concerns us in this context is to demonstrate that the element of proclamation and transcendence does not evacuate the records of their historical relevance and validity. The idea that the resurrection, or belief in the resurrection, should have so upset the disciples that they became wholly incapable of giving an accurate description of anything that preceded it, strikes me as bordering on the fantastic. Only the most cogent evidence could support such a strange suggestion. But far from proving their case, those who make this assertion are faced with a great deal of evidence which points decisively in the opposite direction. Bultmann's "no" to the Jesus of history, as Otto Betz emphasises, simply will not do; for "if faith is directed towards a person who appears in history, in time and space, then the historical facts cannot be a matter of indifference. The mere existence of the Gospels is sufficient evidence of that. They do not only show, as Paul does for example, the crucified and risen Christ; they go behind the cross and report the words and works of the earthly Jesus of Nazareth." Nor was this merely for edification, but because those who had not had any personal knowledge of Jesus in the days of his ministry were "filled

[28] Ibid., pp. 58 f.

with anxiety about the truth, the historical basis, of their preaching. They were fighting on two different fronts: against the Jews, to whom the reality of God's power in the sphere of history had been revealed and who thus thought and questioned in historical terms; and on the other hand against gnosticism, an ever-increasing heresy within the church in which the historical facts evaporated and the humanity of Jesus was denied."[29] So the material which we find in the Gospels has, as Turner reminds us, "a double relevance, and can be used to sketch an answer to two different questions: 'Who was Jesus of Nazareth, how did he live, and what did he teach?' and 'What significance did the Christian Church come to find in him?' ... Neither question is superfluous, but the answer to the one cannot serve for the other."[30]

It seems to me, however, that many contemporary scholars concentrate almost entirely on the second of these two questions. D. E. Nineham, for example, tells us that the early Christians "will have had little leisure, even had they had the aptitude, for antiquarian research (sic) into Christ's earthly life; nor would they have thought it worth while, seeing they did not look forward to any posterity who might be expected to profit from it."[31] Or, again:

What we have, incorporated in the gospels, is the insight into the meaning of the events described which had been given and tested in forty or fifty years of the Church's experience of Jesus as the living Lord. ... The gospels were not meant to give us an uninterpreted picture of Jesus' ministry so full and detailed that we could interpret its significance for ourselves. They were meant to admit us to that understanding of, and relationship with, Jesus which was vouchsafed to the apostolic Church. At the same time they make possible sufficient historical knowledge of the person and ministry of Jesus for us to assure ourselves that the early Christians were not making

[29] Op. cit., p. 13.
[30] Op. cit., p. 70.
[31] *Saint Mark* (The Pelican Gospel Commentaries, London, 1953), p. 18.

bricks without straw; and also for us to see the sense in which their interpretations were intended and were legitimate and to set about the task of reformulating them in terms of our own needs and experience.[32]

Here the emphasis on an element of interpretation in the records may be readily accepted, although the suggestion that the knowledge which the Gospels convey about the person and ministry of Jesus is only sufficient to prove that the early Church had *some* foundation for their beliefs (and that these beliefs stand in need of a radical re-interpretation today) represents a dogmatic assertion which appears to go far beyond the evidence. Again, the reference to "forty or fifty years of the Church's history" seems to betray a tendency to stretch the time which elapsed before Mark's Gospel, at least, was written to the furthest *possible* limits; and the emphasis on the primitive Church's conviction about the immediacy of the Second Advent, and her indifference to preserving any historical records, is, I think, distinctly exaggerated.[33] As for the remark about antiquarian research, this really borders on the ridiculous at a time when a number of the eye-witnesses must have been still alive, and very many were still available who had heard the story direct from the eye-witnesses' own lips. The attitude of scholars such as Betz and Turner, quoted above, seems to me to conform much more closely to the available evidence. As Barry puts it: "why do the scholars assume that the primitive Church had no interest in the facts of the life of Jesus?" On the contrary, "one would suppose that the converts would be asking all the time, What manner of man was he? What did he say or do? Tell us more about him."[34]

It is pertinent in this context to observe that Anthony Hanson remarks that anyone who reads Nineham's *Commentary on Mark* with care "gradually becomes aware

---

[32] "Eyewitness Testimony and Gospel Tradition III", in *Journal of Theological Studies* XI (1960), pp. 263 f.

[33] See p. 188 below.

[34] Op. cit., p. 95.

of an unexamined assumption lying behind it which profoundly affects the treatment of the material and the author's view of Christian origins. This assumption is that *virtually no trustworthy historical information can have survived the period of oral transmission.* This assumption is never brought into the open, but it is undoubtedly there all the time." As a consequence,

what look like historical details in Mark's Gospel are invariably explained on other grounds. There is a whole series of alternative explanations waiting to be used. . . . The point is that the ultimate reason why these alternative explanations are brought forward is simply the assumption I have referred to. No historical fact can possibly have been preserved for its own sake by the earlier Christians; therefore when we encounter in Mark what looks like an historical fact some alternative explanation for it must be found. This is perhaps an inevitable conclusion of the rigorous application of Form Criticism. The Form Critics have always maintained that no detail about Jesus could have been preserved by the early Church unless it had some significance for the early Church. From this it is an easy step to say that, since its significance is its *raison d'être*, this, and not its historical character, is why it was preserved. The historical character having been once detached from it, the obvious conclusion can be drawn that in fact it probably was not historical. Nineham in effect, though not explicitly, takes the last step; this is to provide a non-historical explanation for every detail. . . . The desire to find some theological significance in every detail supplied by Mark leads imperceptibly into the conclusion that Mark (or his predecessors) have invented the detail.[35]

And Anthony Hanson proceeds largely to substantiate

[35] "The Quandary of Historical Scepticism", in *Vindications* (ed. Anthony Hanson, SCM Press, 1966), p. 75.

these remarks,[36] in my view, by the evidence he examines in the rest of his paper—although it is only fair to add that Nineham himself, when discussing the "units of tradition" on which the Gospel is based, observes that

> Our basic picture of Christ is thus carried back to a point only a quarter of a century or so after his death; and when we bear in mind the wonderfully retentive memory of the Oriental, who, being unable to read and write, had perforce to cultivate accuracy of memory, it will not seem surprising that we can often be virtually sure that what the tradition is offering us are the authentic deeds, and especially the authentic words, of the historic Jesus.[37]

But in spite of this, even a cursory reading of his commentary provides many examples which support Anthony Hanson's assessment of Nineham's attitude to the text. I will quote a few examples, selected almost at random, which I have myself noticed. Commenting on the incident in which Jesus is reported as having raised Jairus's daughter, Nineham says: "The actual narrative of the miracle has many traits typical of such stories in the ancient world", and among these he lists the fact that we "know that ancient wonder-workers often used formulas in a foreign tongue, and Origen tells us that such words lose their power if translated into another language".[38] But the Aramaic words quoted by Mark here were *not* a "foreign language" when spoken; and it seems much more likely that the tradition preserved the actual words used on a historical occasion. Nineham takes the same attitude with regard to the word "Ephphatha" in Mark 7:34. Again, he quotes R. H. Lightfoot's statement that one view of the words of dereliction uttered by Jesus on the cross (also recorded in Aramaic) "assumes a narrator who, interested primarily in historical fact, reports faithfully for posterity a

---

[36] Although there is certainly some truth in P. K. Walker's complaint that Hanson has given a "partial and distorted account", in places, of what Nineham has actually said (*Theology*, Nov., 1966, pp. 508 f.).

[37] *Saint Mark*, pp. 50 f.

[38] Op. cit., p. 162.

terrible and inexplicable utterance. But all our inquiry has tended to show that there was no narrator of this sort."[39] This seems to me not only an unwarranted assumption, but also a case of somewhat blatant special pleading. One wonders whether Nineham—and Lightfoot—would apply the same argument to Paul's insertion of the Aramaic term "Abba" (Father) in two letters written in Greek to largely Gentile churches, and would deny that this is an authentic echo of the historical Jesus.[40]

When we turn to the vivid detail included by Mark in the story of the feeding of the five thousand, that Jesus commanded them all to "sit down by companies on the *green* grass" (Mark 6:39), Nineham blandly remarks that "It would be a mistake to see in these words evidence of eye-witness recollection."[41] But this detail is omitted in Matthew and Luke, which runs counter to the attitude often adopted by Form Critics that stories recorded in the oral tradition were first "polished" by the elimination of unnecessary detail, and then, in some cases, suitably embellished to give them verisimilitude. As for the incident of the Syrophoenician woman and Jesus's use of the word "dog" ("to this day the supreme insult in the East"), Nineham suggests that this may have been preserved and moulded (or even invented?) for the mutually contradictory reasons that some members of the early Church were for, and others against, the Gentile mission.[42] Yet again, he dismisses the historicity of the cursing of the barren fig-tree (Mark 11:14) chiefly because "the action ascribed to Jesus seems completely out of character", and he quotes Bundy to the effect that it is "irrational and revolting ... and lacks any sort of moral motive or justification". But this seems to betray an attitude of mind that not only fails to make any real attempt to find a "rational" explanation for the incident,[43]

[39] Op. cit., p. 427.
[40] Cf. pp. 52 and 211 below.
[41] Ibid., p. 183.
[42] Ibid., p. 200.
[43] Which can perfectly easily be interpreted as an "acted" parable of judgment, performed on an insentient object. Ibid., p. 299.

but that also rejects its historicity on precisely the opposite grounds from those so often called in aid by Form Critics—for it is difficult to believe that a community which recorded the statement of Jesus that he was "meek and lowly in heart", and Paul's appeal to the "meekness and gentleness of Christ", would have "moulded" this story in a way that appears to be so surprising and uncharacteristic. It is difficult to fault R. P. C. Hanson's quip that much of this criticism is based on the principle "Heads I win; tails you lose": [44] or Anthony Hanson's comment that "We have passed unconsciously from the principle that not every detail in Mark's Gospel is necessarily historical to the conclusion that virtually no detail can possibly be historical."[45] This sort of attitude (and many examples of it could be quoted) is singularly unconvincing to a lawyer. On these premises the whole of ancient history would be reduced to the barest minimum; but it is a singular fact that these principles seem to be applied almost exclusively to the Gospels.

John Macquarrie is almost equally cautious and negative. "My own view," he writes, "is that the Christian theologian needs to assert a minimal core of factual history if the *kerygma* is to present us with a way of life that is realistic and not culled from a dream world. This minimal core is not a short list of essential incidents or sayings, but simply the assertion that at the source of the Christian religion there was an actual historical instance of the pattern of life proclaimed in the *kerygma*."[46] This is splendid so far as it goes; but it does not seem to me to go nearly so far as the evidence warrants.

IV

What, then, is the solid historical evidence for the fact

[44] Cf. *Vindications*, p. 39.
[45] Ibid., p. 75.
[46] "History and the Life of Faith", in *The Listener*, 12 April, 1962.

that some, at least, of the incidents and sayings recorded in the Gospels are genuine records of what the earthly Jesus did and taught, rather than inventions of the early Church or "interpretations" of vague memories which have been so transformed by their inclusion and repetition in the *kerygma* that all we can do is to discern, in some measure, the reason why they were so "interpreted", and thus be enabled to reinterpret them in terms of our own needs?[47] One principle of historical criticism which is often (and aptly) called in aid is that where the teaching of Jesus "diverges from contemporary Judaism or from that of the Primitive Church or preferably from both, we can be reasonably certain that we are on firm ground"; or, again, where there is "an overlap of interest between the Gospels and the early Church, but a marked difference in the scale of treatment, we can be reasonably sure that we are on firm historical ground".[48] A very considerable list of what eminently cautious scholars would include under this heading could easily be compiled; but of this a brief selection, chosen almost at random, must suffice.

C. F. D. Moule, for example, discusses a number of features in the tradition which have survived in spite of the fact that they were in clear conflict with the attitudes and concepts of the apostolic Church. He cites from P. W. Schmiedel incidents recorded in the Gospels such as the fact that his relatives regarded Jesus as mad; that he asked the rich young ruler "Why do you call me good?"; that he said that blasphemy against the Son of Man could be forgiven, but not blasphemy against the Holy Ghost; that he affirmed that he was himself ignorant of the date of the parousia; and that he gave voice to the cry of dereliction

[47] Another way of putting this would be that the traditions were expressed in a mythological form, and that they stand in need of being "demythologised" in terms of the twentieth century.

[48] H. E. W. Turner, op. cit., pp. 73 f. But it seems to me absurd, *per contra*, to dismiss as clearly unhistorical any teaching which happens to coincide with Jewish thought, or in which the teaching of Jesus may itself have moulded that of the primitive Church.

from the cross.[49] He also emphasises the "startling radicalism" of Mark's uncompromising emphasis on love of God and love of one's neighbour, as the greatest of all the commandments, when viewed against the extreme "legalism of certain sections of devout Judaism".[50] Again, referring to Jesus's attitude to women and his relations with them, he insists that the environment of the primitive Church was not one in which this portrait of Jesus could conceivably have originated. Instead, it

> would seem to have fairly forced its way through an atmosphere still to that extent alien to it and still scarcely comprehending. Jesus, who was not afraid of earning the reputation of being a gluttonous man and a wine-bibber, a friend of tax collectors and sinners, emerges in the Gospel traditions as one who risked obloquy also for consorting with disreputable women; and the extraordinary thing is that writers who must themselves have hated and feared the very risks they are describing and who were themselves not wholly free from a repressive attitude, yet, despite themselves, succeed in presenting a strangely convincing picture of Jesus — a young, unmarried man — allowing himself to be fondled and kissed[51] by such women, without either embarrassment or acquiescence in their morals. The simplicity and surefootedness of the delineation are amazing. Jesus simply accepts these women as persons: compassionately and with complete purity and simplicity he accepts their affection while moving them to repentance. Thus he establishes at once God's judgment on their standards of life and his mercy towards them. All the quite varied traditions in all four Gospels tell the same story.[52]

[49] *The Phenomenon of the New Testament*, p. 62. Other (and, some will think, even more convincing) illustrations of traditions which are in clear conflict with the attitude and outlook of the early Church could easily be cited.

[50] Op. cit., p. 63.

[51] This is, of course, a reference to Luke 7:37 f; but the phrase as it stands is, perhaps, open to misunderstanding.

[52] *The Phenomenon of the New Testament* (SCM Press, 1967), pp. 65 f.

Moule also discusses the differences of emphasis which we find when we compare Luke's Gospel with the Acts of the Apostles as an "objective test of whether or not this Evangelist, at any rate, has thrown the whole of his Easter faith back anachronously into his narrative of what happened before Easter". The answer, he tells us, is that "Luke does not attribute to the participants in his story of the ministry of Jesus the same explicit estimate of Jesus as he attributes to the apostles when they are speaking of the risen Jesus. That is to say, he represents the contemporaries of his earthly life as speaking of him with reserve. They do not use the great Christological titles of the post-resurrection preaching." This is particularly significant in regard to Luke, since we are often told that he, of all the Evangelists, is the one who "applies the title 'Lord' ($\kappa\acute{\nu}\rho\iota\sigma\varsigma$) to Jesus during his ministry and before his death and exaltation". But this, Moule remarks, is scarcely true. The use of the word in the vocative, as a respectful address (almost equivalent to our "Sir"), is, of course, irrelevant. "But the application of the word $\kappa\acute{\nu}\rho\iota\sigma\varsigma$ in its other cases, which might, indeed, be significant, is almost entirely absent, in Luke's Gospel, from the language of the *dramatis personae*. That the Evangelist himself refers to Jesus as 'The Lord' is true, but is not relevant to his reconstruction of the scene of the ministry itself."[53]

A great deal has been written about the term "Son of Man" which Jesus is depicted in the Synoptic Gospels as so often using. It has even been denied that he ever in fact used it at all, or that he ever used it as referring to himself. But in all the contexts in which this title appears in the Gospels it is put, without exception, on the lips of Jesus himself, and Turner remarks that "their content, as well as the substitution of 'I' or 'Me' in some sources for the title, clearly indicate that the Gospels regard them as referring to Jesus himself." So he concludes that it seems exceedingly unlikely that a claim "never made by Jesus himself, and rejected by the Jews both in his lifetime and after the Resurrection", should have been imported by the Church into the

[53] Ibid., pp. 57 f.

records at a later date. Why, he asks, should the early Christians "burden themselves with awkward controversy over a title which said not more but less than our Lord meant to them, unless loyalty to his usage in the days of his flesh had seemed to compel them to do so?"[54] And an even more inescapable echo of the historical Jesus is the way in which Paul, in a letter written in Greek to a Church, few of whose members would have known Aramaic, says that because God has sent the Spirit of his Son into their hearts they, too, now pray to him as "*Abba*, Father"—using the intimate family term for father in Aramaic which seems to have been unknown as a form of address to the Almighty until Jesus himself habitually used it, and which can only have been relevant to a Gentile Church because of its sacred—and historical—associations.[55]

Otto Betz, moreover, insists that "even the 'new quest of the historical Jesus' gives the impression of being constricted, both for dogmatic reasons and because it binds itself too exclusively to the methods of form criticism. . . . The 'new quest' therefore leaves a divided impression: the wall between the proclaimed Christ and the historical Jesus has been broken down, but the field that lies behind the wall is being traversed with half-closed eyes." Did the Church really have a creative influence to the extent that Bultmann's analysis suggests? he asks.

Is the outline of the activity of Jesus given first by Mark and then largely taken over by Matthew and Luke simply a free invention? Does it not in fact follow the stages of Jesus' life? The 'methodological scepticism' with which form criticism is to be applied would seem to be by no means infallible and calls in its turn for a sceptically critical eye. Its insufficiency is shown merely by the fact that there are quite different judgments among form critics about the authenticity of any given saying of Jesus . . . in the course of which many a form-critical judgment

[54] Op. cit., pp. 87 f.
[55] Cf. Gal. 4:6; and Rom. 8:15.

as to the genuineness of a particular passage falls victim to an acuter logic."[56]

Incidentally, my own experience over several years in the Middle East—where admission to the Azhar University was, until quite recently, dependent on the candidate having committed the whole of the Qur'ān to memory, and where learning by heart is still widely practised—makes me inclined to give considerable weight to the emphasis placed by Harald Riesenfeld and Birger Gerhardsson[57] on the leading role played by oral tradition in the early Church. In their view this tradition was memorised, and regularly recited, as "the sacred word". It is noteworthy in this context that G. B. Caird writes:

It is now generally agreed that the form critics overstated their case. . . . They ignored the presence of eyewitnesses of the ministry of Jesus among the first generation of Christians. They drew questionable parallels between oral tradition in other cultures, where the period of transmission is reckoned in centuries, and oral tradition in the primitive Church, where the period is reckoned in decades. They attributed incredible powers to the community, not recognizing that creative work is rarely produced by committees. They forgot that Jesus cast much of his teaching into poetic form and, as a rabbi, expected his disciples to memorize it. They assumed that the early Church could not distinguish its own teaching from that of Jesus, when in fact we know that Paul was meticulously careful to do so (1 Cor. 7:10 and 25).[58]

Betz, too, insists that "in the few places where Paul refers to a saying of the Lord a similar saying is to be found in the Synoptic Gospels; and, further, the apostle makes a clear

[56] Op. cit., pp. 18 f. – together with footnote references to T. W. Manson, etc.
[57] *Memory and Manuscript. Oral Tradition and Written Transmission in Rabbinic Judaism and Early Christianity*, Uppsala, 1961.
[58] *Saint Luke*, p. 22.

distinction between his own opinion and a saying of the Lord which has been passed down."[59]

Betz considers it certain that Jesus was baptised by John the Baptist and that he continued John's preaching. The Baptist, moreover, was clearly linked in both eschatological expectation and rigid asceticism with the desert community of Qumran, where a postulant was not accepted into full membership or admitted to the sacred meal until after a trial period of three years.

> Jesus, however, ate with the publicans and called one of them away from tax-collecting to become one of his disciples (Matt. 9 : 9–10). This unusual association with sinners, so shocking to the devout Jew, must be accounted as an especially characteristic mark of the historical Jesus. And it was precisely this behaviour which almost inevitably brought Jesus into conflict with the regulations about outward purity which were so scrupulously observed by Pharisees and Essenes alike (Mark 7 : 1–23). Nor did Jesus baptize. There was nothing of the ascetic about him.

Nor, indeed, of the legalist, for "he set himself, provocatively and in a sovereign manner, above the laws of sabbath observance wherever they interfered with his actions. That, too, is certainly historical. For the Palestinian Christians kept the sabbath in the Jewish way; they had therefore no reason to make up stories in which Jesus broke the regulations about the day of rest.[60]

Again, Betz argues that we can "certainly know that the historical Jesus proclaimed the coming of the Kingdom of God and preached repentance". Indeed, his whole work was eschatologically determined.

> In Qumran they taught that all the elect must be loved, while those rejected by God were to be hated (*Community Rule* 1.3–4); but Jesus forbade hate in general, even

[59] Op. cit., p. 22, where a number of examples of each of these phenomena is given.
[60] Ibid., pp. 32 f.

hate of an enemy, demanding intercessory prayer instead of curses (Matt. 5:44).... He saw the movement of repentance not, as they did in Qumran, as reversion to a radically interpreted Law but as a return to the open arms of the Father. God had more pleasure in the home-coming of a single sinner than over the faithfulness of many righteous (Luke 15). The fact that Jesus confronted men with God and forced them to decision cannot, as we have seen, be counted as at all unique, since this is also true of the preaching of John the Baptist and the men of Qumran. What is new is that the decision for the rule of God is a glad one: Jesus compares it with the behaviour of a labourer who finds a treasure in a field and sells all that he has in order to possess it, or with the joy of a merchant who willingly gives all his worldly goods in return for a splendid pearl (Matt. 13:44–46).[61]

It may, of course, be argued that all this was part of the primitive *kerygma*; but the question remains as to where the early Church got this teaching, if not from Jesus himself? It is significant, in this context, that Betz can assert that "no one doubts that most of the parables as they are presented in the Synoptic Gospels are genuine, and in the 'new quest' Jesus the parable-teller receives special attention."[62]

V

Much more could be said to this effect. E. Käsemann, for example, quotes the famous saying of Jesus in Matt. 11:12 and 13 about the Baptist, and comments:

Who but Jesus himself can look back in this way over the completed Old Testament epoch of salvation, not degrading the Baptist to the position of a mere fore-runner as the whole Christian community ... were to do, but drawing him to his side and—an enormity to later Christian ears—presenting him as the initiator of the

[61] Ibid., pp. 39 and 41 f.
[62] Ibid., p. 48.

new aeon? But who then is this, who thus does justice to the Baptist and yet claims for himself a mission higher than that entrusted to John? Evidently, he who brings with his Gospel the kingdom itself.[63]

Perhaps the most inescapable element in all the Gospels is the authority with which Jesus both acted and spoke. The Old Testament prophets could confidently affirm that the "Word of the Lord" came to them, and that it was the message of Israel's covenant God which they proclaimed. But it seems clear that it was characteristic of the historical Jesus that he said "Amen, amen I say unto you." Thus C. H. Dodd, when discussing the trial of Jesus, writes:

> The evangelists, I conclude, John and the Synoptics alike, take the view that Jesus was charged with blasphemy because he spoke and acted in ways which implied that he stood in a special relation with God, so that his words carried divine authority and his actions were instinct with divine power. Unless this could be believed, the implied claim was an affront to the deepest religious sentiments of his people, a profanation of sanctities; and this, I suggest, is what the charge of 'blasphemy' really stands for, rather than any definable statutory offence. . . . Whether or not Jesus had put himself forward as Messiah, the implied claim was messianic at least, perhaps rather messianic plus.[64]

Moule, indeed, not only affirms that "the figure which emerges from the most radically critical attempt at reconstruction is the figure of one whose teaching and message were of the very same quality as attaches to the figure of the apostolic proclamation", but also that "The Jesus retrieved by the most careful criticism (and it is, I think, perverse to assert that such critical reconstruction can accomplish nothing) is no longer the rationally accept-

[63] See *Essays on New Testament Themes*, p. 43.
[64] "The Historical Problem of the Death of Jesus", in *More New Testament Studies* (Manchester University Press, 1968), p. 99.

able moralist of the Liberal Protestants, but a 'catalyst'—a person whose very presence precipitates a crisis of faith and forces 'existential' decision." In an extremely interesting lecture, he says,

> W. Marxsen argues that what he calls the 'Christus-kerygma', the confessional proclamation about Jesus as Christ, ought to be tested by the 'Jesuskerygma'—the proclamation which critical scholarship is able to attribute to Jesus himself during his ministry. Otherwise, we have absolutely nothing to connect us with Jesus. And if the apostolic proclamation of Jesus as Christ is so tested ... we find that the 'Christuskerygma' is saying, about the *death* of Jesus, what the 'Jesuskerygma' says about the whole ministry, namely, that it brings men into the presence of God.

In a similar vein, Moule continues, O. Cullman "points out that what the apostles remembered of Jesus' ministry included his own interpretation of it, however much and however often this had, at the time, been misunderstood. In a sense, the post-Easter *interpretation* was only a *re-discovery* of what had been there in the teaching of Jesus himself."[65]

Michael Ramsey, in his article on "Christian Faith and the Historical Jesus" to which I have already referred, says that the message of Jesus was

> not about himself. He is absorbed in the sovereignty, the purpose and the presence of God. Yet the implied claims recur. It is Jesus who will accept or reject men in the future judgment (Matt. 7:21-22). It is for Jesus that the renunciations of discipleship are made (Mark 8:37). It is Jesus's death that will bring deliverance (Mark 10:45) and be the ground of a new covenant (Mark 14:24). His authority was quite unlike that of the Rabbis.... So the mission of Jesus both struck at the religious security of Judaism and avoided involvement in political Messian-

[65] Op. cit., p. 46.

ism. It led to such resentment by both the Pharisees and the party of the high priests that they plotted to destroy him. Of this there is no historical doubt. Nor can there reasonably be doubt that Jesus saw his coming death as lying within the divine purpose as part of his mission. . . . Such is the picture of the mission of Jesus which the Gospel traditions provide as credible history. The picture seems to make sense in relation to its environment, while its originality makes it hard to think it could be the product of that environment. It seems also that the inevitable reading-in of post-resurrection interpretation does not obliterate the traces of a primitive perspective. Above all, it seems that the traditions, belonging as they do to the Church's preaching and teaching, bear the impress not only of a theology but of a person, a person in whom authority and self-effacement were uniquely blended. While the mission of Jesus was a puzzle until the death and resurrection unfolded its meaning, it is hard to see how the resurrection could of itself have created Christianity. . . . It was the impression of the whole person, the teaching, the death, the resurrection, which led the apostles to the conclusion that Jesus is no less than Lord, Son of God, the image of invisible deity, the Word who was in the beginning. Monotheists as they were, they could worship him without idolatry; and worship him they must.[66]

VI

It is also noteworthy in this context that scholars from other disciplines often view the hypercritical attitude of theologians, and some of the conclusions to which this attitude leads them, with tolerant—or even exasperated—amusement. To digress from the Gospels to the Pentateuch for a moment, I well remember attending a few classes in elementary Hebrew, just after the Second World War, in which my teacher (himself a highly critical scholar) spent almost as much time in tearing the documentary theory to

[66] *Theology*, LXXV No. 621, March 1972, pp. 123–5.

pieces as he did in tackling the text. No reputable phil-
ologist, he asserted, could possibly accept the idea that the
editor of the Pentateuch had pieced together, sometimes
in one verse, passages cut out with a pair of scissors, as it
were, from a number of documents dating from very
different periods: it was far more likely that the solution of
some of the problems could be found in variations of
vocabulary and idiom coming from different geographical
areas. But theologians still substantially held to the theory,
he asserted, for want of an acceptable alternative. Similarly,
when we turn to the Gospels, we find that an ancient
historian of the standing of A. N. Sherwin-White considers it

> astonishing that while Graeco-Roman historians have
> been growing in confidence, the twentieth-century study
> of the Gospel narratives, starting from no less promising
> material, has taken so gloomy a turn in the development
> of form-criticism that the more advanced exponents of it
> apparently maintain—so far as an amateur can under-
> stand the matter—that the historical Christ is unknow-
> able and the history of his mission cannot be written.
> This seems very curious when one compares the case for
> the best-known contemporary of Christ, who like Christ
> is a well-documented figure—Tiberius Caesar. The story
> of his reign is known from four sources.... These
> disagree amongst themselves in the wildest possible
> fashion, both in major matters of political action or
> motive and in specific detail of minor events. Everyone
> would admit that Tacitus is the best of all the sources,
> and yet no serious modern historian would accept at face
> value the majority of the statements of Tacitus about the
> motives of Tiberius. But this does not prevent the belief
> that the material of Tacitus can be used to write a history
> of Tiberius.

In the light of this statement it would seem that New
Testament critics are, on any showing, excessively sceptical
in their approach to the Gospels, and that there is no
justification whatever for the common assumption that,

wherever there is any real or apparent discrepancy between the New Testament and some non-Christian source, the latter must always be preferred. In point of fact, moreover, Sherwin-White asserts that the reason why "the degree of confirmation in Graeco-Roman terms is less for the Gospels than for Acts" is almost entirely due "to the differences in their regional setting. As soon as Christ enters the Roman orbit at Jerusalem, the confirmation begins. For Acts the confirmation of history is overwhelming. Yet Acts is, in simple terms and judged externally, no less of a propaganda narrative than the Gospels, and liable to similar distortions. But any attempt to reject its basic historicity even in matters of detail must now appear absurd. Roman historians have long taken it for granted."[67]

If, moreover, the material we find in the Gospels must all be traced to the preoccupations and teaching of the apostolic Church, then there are certainly some exceedingly strange omissions. Why, for example, do we find so very little about the Gentile mission? Why is there such a curious silence about the vexed question of circumcision? Why, again, is there so little in the Synoptic Gospels about the Person and work of the Holy Spirit? It is scarcely surprising that Caird says that one of the weaknesses of the more extreme Form Critics is that they "failed to notice that many of the questions which, on the evidence of the Epistles, were hotly disputed in the apostolic age are not dealt with in the recorded teaching of Jesus, so that the Church cannot be accused of reading its own concerns back into the gospel tradition."[68] As C. K. Barrett puts it: "Mark then has at most scattered hints of what future life in the Church will be ... Paul has at most hints of what the historical Jesus was like."[69]

It is also interesting to note the view of such an eminent archaeologist as W. F. Albright on the Gospels. "There is

---

[67] *Roman Society and Roman Law in the New Testament*, pp. 187 ff.

[68] Op. cit., p. 22. But this is not, of course, to deny that the selection of material and mode of presentation were not influenced by what seemed relevant and significant.

[69] *Luke the Historian in Recent Study*, pp. 55. (Cf. Turner, op. cit., p. 103).

no fundamental difference in teaching," he asserts, "between John and the Synoptics; the contrast between them lies in the concentration of tradition along certain aspects of Christ's teachings, particularly those which seem to have resembled the teaching of the Essenes most closely." And he adds:

> There is absolutely nothing to show that any of Jesus' teachings have been distorted or falsified, or that any vital new element has been added to them. That the needs of the early Church influenced the selection of items for inclusion in the Gospel we may readily admit, but there is no reason to suppose that the needs of that Church were responsible for any inventions or innovations of theological significance. Whether the [Fourth] Gospel was edited by John the Presbyter of Papias ... or whether some other reconstruction is more probable, we may rest assured that it contains the memories of the Apostle John.[70]

Similarly, my colleague Duncan Derrett, in his detailed examination of the New Testament from the point of view of an expert in Oriental law, clearly regards the parables and incidents recorded in the Gospels as going back to Jesus himself, and as a true reflection of his life and teaching.[71]

Time and again as I read the New Testament, moreover, I light upon phrases, or whole passages, which seem to me to bear the imprint of an eye-witness's observation. This has, of course, frequently been noted. E. L. Mascall, for example, refers to the story of the man born blind in John 9

---

[70] Memories, that is to say, interpenetrated by reflection and theological insight. Cf. "Recent Discoveries in Palestine and the Gospel of John", in *The Background of the New Testament and its Eschatology*, ed. W. D. Davies and D. Daube, pp. 170 f.

[71] J. Duncan M. Derrett, *Law in the New Testament*, (Darton Longman and Todd, London, 1970), *passim*. It is noteworthy that Derrett originally obtained a doctorate in history, and it is largely as a historian that he now works professionally in a faculty of law. I am grateful to him for several suggestions.

and says: "when one reads the chapter in a perfectly straightforward way, one can hardly avoid being struck by the vivid impression of eyewitness reporting and by the extremely convincing characterisation of the persons involved."[72] Similarly, William Temple took much the same view of the Johannine account of how Mary Magdalene, when she went to the tomb early on Easter morning and found that the stone had been rolled away, ran and called Peter and John; of how they set out together and then both broke into running; of how John, the younger, got to the tomb first, peered in, but lingered outside; of how Peter then arrived and, characteristically, blundered straight in, followed by John; and of how they both saw the linen clothes lying there "and the napkin, that was about his head, not lying with the linen clothes, but apart, wrapped into one place". Much the same has repeatedly been noted about the incident, probably not originally part of John's Gospel, in which the scribes and Pharisees brought to Jesus the woman who had been caught in the act of adultery. Indeed, Dorothy Sayers goes so far as to remark that, to anyone accustomed to the imaginative handling of documents, the internal evidence of John's Gospel bears out the claim that it represents the direct report of an eye-witness. "The Synoptists, on the whole, report the 'set-pieces'; it is St. John who reports the words and actions of the individual unrepeated occasion, retrieving them from that storehouse of trained memory which, among people not made forgetful by too much pen and ink, replaces the filed records and the stenographer's notebook ... All through, in fact, the Gospel of St. John reads like the narrative of an eye-witness ..."[73]

It is illuminating to contrast this with the "apocryphal gospels", which were written at a distinctly later date than the canonical Gospels. B. Harris-Cooper, in the Preface to his *Translation of the Apocryphal Gospels*, says that "All who read them with any attention will see that they are fictions and not histories, not traditions even, so much as

[72] Op. cit., pp. 240 f.
[73] *The Man Born to be King*, pp. 33 f.

legends. . . . Before I undertook this work I never realised so completely as I do now the impassable character of the gulf which separates the genuine Gospels from these." Similarly, J. B. Phillips observes:

Probably most people have not had the opportunity to read the apocryphal 'gospels' and 'epistles'. . . . I can only say here that in such writings we live in a world of magic and make-believe, of myth and fancy. In the whole task of translating the New Testament I never for one moment . . . felt that I was being swept away into a world of spookiness, witchcraft and magical powers such as abound in the books rejected from the New Testament. It was the sustained, down to earth faith of the New Testament writers which conveyed to me that inexpressible sense of the genuine and the authentic."[74]

VII

It is in the light of an examination of the available evidence along these lines, in as objective and critical a way as I am capable of, that I am convinced that the historical reliability of a great part of the New Testament records of the life and teaching of Jesus can be substantiated by the most rigorous historical and critical analysis. Nor can I believe that the interval between the events and the emergence of the Gospels was nearly long enough for the processes postulated by the more extreme Form Critics to have taken place— or, indeed, that these processes would not have been kept in constant check by the presence of eye-witnesses and the authority accorded to the apostolic tradition. Stephen Neill, as I see it, did not overstate the position when he wrote:

The Jesus Christ whom the Christian meets when he comes to the Holy Communion, who is made present to him in the proclamation of the Gospel in Christian worship, to whom he speaks when he prays, who speaks

[74] *The Ring of Truth*, (Hodder and Stoughton, London, 1967), p. 95.

to him through the Holy Spirit, is the same Jesus who was born at a specific time and place in history, who lived a human life, who spoke certain words, did certain deeds, and suffered certain things, of which we have clear though far from complete knowledge.[75]

But the absolutely decisive point, for Christian faith, is the resurrection; so it is the evidence for this that we must examine in much more detail. If, on analysis, that evidence proves convincing, then surely this unique event—when taken together with the staggering claims which Jesus certainly seems to have made (and which, had they not been true, would unquestionably have constituted the blasphemy with which the Jews charged him)—can only be regarded as the divine *imprimatur* on his claims about himself, his relation with the Father and the significance of his death on the cross.[76] And if this be accepted, then the cumulative evidence brings me face to face with one in regard to whom my normal scepticism of the miraculous is displaced by a willingness to believe that the accounts of his virgin birth and "mighty acts" are in no sense impossible or incredible. Not only so, but if God did in fact break into human history in this unique way—not only to provide the supreme revelation of his nature, character and claims, but also to restore man to fellowship with himself—then I should find it intrinsically unlikely that the indispensable record of what he did, and what it means, would have been left to the unaided vagaries of human memory and fanciful interpretation; so I do not find it difficult to accept the claim that the New Testament writers were aided and guided in what they wrote by the Holy Spirit. Does this, then, automatically disqualify me, in precisely the same way as an *a priori* conviction that "miracles" can *never* happen and that the "supernatural" simply does not exist, from dealing with the evidence in the way which should characterise the approach of a lawyer or a judge? I do not think so. To the best of my ability I try to examine the

[75] Foreword to Heinz Zahrnt, *The Historical Jesus* (Collins, 1963).
[76] Cf. chapter 5 below.

evidence as a whole without imposing on that evidence my preconceived ideas; and it is the weight of the evidence, where it can be objectively tested, which leads me to certain conclusions which make it reasonable, as I see it, to accept the substantial accuracy of the records in those other points in which a similarly stringent objective corroboration is not available. And this, it seems to me, is an authentically "legal" approach.

CHAPTER THREE

The Resurrection — I

ITS BASIC HISTORICITY

I

A brief reference has already been made, in the preceding chapter, to the centrality of the resurrection in any consideration of the evidence for the validity of the Christian faith. Of this centrality there can really be no question whatever; for it is the joy and inspiration of the resurrection —giving rise, as it did, to what the early Church could describe only as a new birth to a living hope[1]—which permeates the *kerygma* through and through. Indeed, it is not too much to say that there would never have been any preaching of Jesus at all except as Risen Lord. It was his resurrection which was regarded as the conclusive proof of his deity[2] and as the cornerstone of the faith; for Paul, in an epistle from which I have already quoted and which is indubitably his, could unequivocally state that "If Christ has not been raised, then our preaching is in vain and your faith is vain"—and add that if God did not in fact raise Christ to life, then he himself (and, by implication, the other apostles too) would be no better than "lying witnesses for God". As Gerhardt Ebeling put it:

> Paul does not mean, if the resurrection of Jesus is untenable, then this one article of faith, faith in the resurrection of Jesus, is untenable. But rather, faith as a whole would be finished. It would be senseless. And this is the unanimous witness of the early church. When

[1] I Pet. 1:3.
[2] Rom. 1:4.

Christian faith speaks about its basis, it points with monotonous regularity to the crucified Jesus, of whom it is known that he is risen. This Easter witness is the germ of the Christian confession of faith, and has remained its constitutive core.[3]

About the centrality of the message of the resurrection, then, there is no room for debate. It is how that message should be understood and interpreted which is the focal point of theological controversy regarding the resurrection today. Is the resurrection to be regarded as a historical fact, or a beautiful myth; and, in either case, what sort of "historical fact", or what variety of "myth", is involved? Is it to be interpreted in purely subjective terms, or does the available evidence point decisively to some objective event? In what, indeed, does the "available evidence" actually consist; how is it to be evaluated; and how can we assess its implications? Here the approach of contemporary theologians is just about as varied, and even contradictory, as it could possibly be, as the following summary will reveal. The subject is so vast that it will be necessary to divide it into two, and to devote this chapter to the basic historicity of the resurrection and the next to a more detailed discussion of the biblical evidence.

II

It will be convenient, I think, to take Rudolf Bultmann as our starting point.[4] "But what of the resurrection?" he writes. "Is it not a mythical event pure and simple? Obviously it is not an event of past history with a self-evident meaning." So he proceeds to ask whether the resurrection narratives and every other mention of the resurrection in the New Testament can be understood "simply as an attempt to convey the meaning of the cross? Does the New Testament, in asserting that Jesus is risen

[3] *The Nature of Faith*, trans. R. G. Smith (Collins, London, 1961), p. 60.
[4] Cf. *Kerygma and Myth: A Theological Debate*, edited by H. W. Bartsch and trans. R. H. Fuller (SPCK, London, 1953), Vol. I, pp. 38–44.

from the dead, mean that his death is not just an ordinary human death, but the judgement and salvation of the world, depriving death of its power? Does it not express this truth in the affirmation that the Crucified was not holden of death, but rose from the dead?"

The answer to these questions which Bultmann himself gives is an emphatic affirmative.

> The cross is not an isolated event, as though it were the end of Jesus, which needed the resurrection subsequently to reverse it. . . . Cross and resurrection form a single, indivisible cosmic event which brings judgement to the world and opens up for men the possibility of authentic life. But if that be so, the resurrection cannot be a miraculous proof capable of demonstration and sufficient to convince the sceptic that the cross really has the cosmic and eschatological significance ascribed to it.

He admits, however, that it is undeniable that the resurrection is often regarded in the New Testament as a miraculous proof—and he cites in this context Acts 17:31 (where we are "actually told that God substantiated the claims of Christ by raising him from the dead") and the resurrection narratives. But he quietly dismisses both the "legend of the empty tomb" and the appearances of the risen Christ (which, he asserts, "insist on the physical reality of the risen body of the Lord") as "most certainly later embellishments of the primitive tradition". He also gratuitously asserts that "St. Paul knows nothing about them." Even so, he is compelled to admit that there is "one passage where St. Paul tries to prove the miracle of the resurrection by adducing a list of eye-witnesses (I Cor. 15:3–8)". But about this he first comments that "this is a dangerous procedure"; then quotes Barth to the effect that "the list of eye-witnesses was put in not to prove the fact of the resurrection, but to prove that the preaching of the apostle was, like the preaching of the first Christians, the preaching of Jesus as the risen Lord"; and then concludes that

> the difficulty is not simply the incredibility of a mythical

event like the resuscitation of a corpse (*sic*)—for that is what the resurrection means, as is shown by the fact that the risen Lord is apprehended by the physical senses. Nor is it merely the difficulty of establishing the objective historicity of the resurrection no matter how many witnesses are cited, as though once it was established it might be believed beyond all question and faith might have its unimpeachable guarantee. No; the real difficulty is that the resurrection is itself an article of faith, and you cannot establish one article of faith by invoking another. You cannot prove the redemptive efficacy of the cross by invoking the resurrection. For the resurrection is an article of faith because it is far more than the resuscitation of a corpse—it is the eschatological event.[5] For, quite apart from its credibility, the bare miracle tells us nothing about the eschatological fact of the destruction of death. Moreover, such a miracle is not otherwise unknown to mythology.

Point after point in this argument is, of course, wide open to question and debate. Why, for example, does Bultmann categorically identify the resurrection, as traditionally accepted, with the mere "resuscitation of a corpse", and how does he come to imagine that this identification follows of necessity from the fact that the risen Lord could be "apprehended by the physical senses"? He is certainly correct in his insistence that the resurrection is "far more than the resuscitation of a corpse—it is the eschatological event"; but why, one wonders, does he blandly assume, without any adequate argument, that an eschatological event can have no historical foundation? Why, again, does he completely ignore the cogency of the evidence which is available in the New Testament—and pre-eminently in I Cor. 15—by insisting that such a miracle is incredible, is "not otherwise unknown to mythology", and can be only an "article of faith"—which it would, of course, cease to be if the available evidence represented an "unimpeachable

[5] i.e., an event connected with the doctrine of the "last things" or the end of the world.

69

guarantee" (which is, obviously enough, not the case). As for his reference to Barth, we shall later let Barth speak for himself.

To Bultmann it is "abundantly clear that the New Testament is interested in the resurrection of Christ simply and solely because it is the eschatological event *par excellence*. By it Christ abolished death and brought life and immortality to light (II Tim. 1:10)." Nor does Paul only say "In Christ shall all be made alive"; he also speaks of rising again with Christ in the present tense, just as he speaks of dying with him. "It is not simply that we *shall* walk with him in newness of life and be united with him in his resurrection (Rom. 6:4 f.); we are doing so already here and now." In this resurrection life Christians, moreover, "enjoy a freedom, albeit a struggling freedom, from sin (Rom. 6:11 ff.)". Here it is noteworthy, in passing, that while Bultmann chiefly expatiates in this passage on the present experience of Christians, he certainly does not specifically deny the hope of a future resurrection; on the contrary, his words, if taken at their face value, would appear implicitly to affirm it. But the fact remains that, for Bultmann, *faith in the resurrection is really the same thing as faith in the saving efficacy of the cross*, faith in the cross as the cross of Christ." And this faith, he insists, can come only through "the way in which the cross is proclaimed. It is always proclaimed together with the resurrection. Christ meets us in the preaching as one crucified and risen." Indeed, he gratuitously adds that Christ meets us there "and nowhere else. The faith of Easter is just this—faith in the word of preaching." To ask how this preaching arose historically, he asserts, would be utterly wrong. "The word of preaching confronts us as the word of God. It is not for us to question its credentials."

But this, it seems to me, is to lapse into pure obscurantism. In point of fact, moreover, Bultmann is not by any means content to follow his own counsel and leave it there. Instead, he continues: "If the event of Easter Day is in any sense an historical event additional to the event of the cross, it is nothing else than the rise of faith in the risen

Lord, since it was this faith which led to the apostolic preaching. The resurrection itself is not an event of past history." The only reason he gives for this categorical statement is that all that historical criticism can (in his opinion) establish

is the fact that the first disciples came to believe in the resurrection. The historian can perhaps to some extent account for that faith from the personal intimacy which the disciples had enjoyed with Jesus during his earthly life, and so reduce the resurrection appearances to a series of subjective visions. But the historical problem is scarcely relevant to Christian belief in the resurrection. For the historical event of the rise of the Easter faith means for us what it meant for the first disciples— namely, the self-manifestation of the risen Lord, the act of God in which the redemptive event of the cross is completed. We cannot buttress our own faith in the resurrection by that of the first disciples and so eliminate the element of risk which faith in the resurrection always involves. For the first disciples' faith in the resurrection is itself part and parcel of the eschatological event which is the article of faith.

So the conclusion of the whole matter for Bultmann is that "Through the word of preaching the cross and the resurrection are made present: the eschatological 'now' is here. . . . In the word of preaching and there alone we meet the risen Lord." But the preaching of the cross, on this view, concerns a historical event, while in the preaching of the resurrection we move from history to "mythology"—in spite of the fact that he insists, as we have seen, that the cross and the resurrection form a "single, indivisible cosmic event". The first stands in need of no "de-mythologizing", while the second, in his view, most certainly does.[6] Yet he

---

[6] In other words, he regards the "unhistorical resurrection" of Christ as the significance of the "historical crucifixion of Jesus" (the unity of the two being that of the event and its meaning). Cf. Hans-Georg Geyer in *The Significance of the Message of the Resurrection for Faith in Jesus Christ*, ed. by C. F. D. Moule (SCM Press, London, 1968), p. 113.

is emphatic that our redemption itself "is not a miraculous supernatural event, but an historical event wrought out in time and space.... The agent of God's presence and activity, the mediator of his reconciliation of the world unto himself, is a real figure of history. Similarly the word of God is not some mysterious oracle, but a sober, factual account of a human life, of Jesus of Nazareth, possessing saving efficacy for man." Then he somewhat equivocally adds: "All these are phenomena subject to historical, sociological and psychological observation, yet for faith they are all of them eschatological phenomena. It is precisely its immunity from proof that secures the Christian proclamation against the charge of being mythological." But this does not, it seems, extend to the resurrection—which was, in point of fact, the very centre of the Christian proclamation. A lawyer instinctively recoils, moreover, from a theological faith which seems to glory in its complete "immunity from proof". It is one thing to say that faith must inevitably go beyond what can be conclusively proved to any reasonable enquirer; but it is quite another to demand that faith must have no evidence whatever on which to rest.

It is tempting to turn straight from Bultmann to one who is far more sceptical, not only about the historicity of the resurrection of Jesus, but even about any basic belief in life beyond the grave. Such is the conclusion to which Lloyd Geering comes in his recent book *Resurrection: A Symbol of Hope.*[7] In his view the progress of thought in the early Church was not from the concept of the risen Christ to a belief in a general resurrection but "almost the reverse of this. First there arose the concept of restoration to new life, understood in a variety of contexts; this led to a conviction about the resurrection of some or all of the dead at the end of the world; in the light of this conviction, the first Christians came to make their important affirmation that Jesus had been raised from the dead." This assertion, however, seems to me to run directly counter to a great deal of

[7] Hodder and Stoughton, London, 1971. Cf. pp. 7 f.

the available evidence, for the early Church appears in fact to have made the resurrection of believers depend on the resurrection of Jesus, not vice versa.[8] But the fact that Geering professes to base his conclusions on a very detailed (if singularly unconvincing) examination of the biblical evidence makes it more logical to postpone any discussion of this very controversial book until the next chapter. So we must now turn to Barth and Künneth, for both Barth and Künneth discuss Bultmann's thesis in considerable detail.

III

Barth[9] is uncompromisingly insistent on the centrality of the resurrection.

It is impossible [he asserts] to read any text of the New Testament in the sense intended by its authors, by the apostles who stand behind them, or by the first communities, without an awareness that they either explicitly assert or at least tacitly assume that the Jesus of whom they speak and to whom they refer in some way is the One who appeared to His disciples at this particular time as the Resurrected from the dead. All the other things they know of Him, His words and acts, are regarded in the light of this particular event, and are as it were irradiated by its light.

Up to this point Bultmann would, no doubt, largely have agreed (except for the thought behind the words "at this particular time"); but scarcely so when Barth immediately continues: "Whatever they proclaim in His name, the power of their message, derives from the fact that it was conveyed and entrusted to them by the man Jesus after He was raised from the dead. . . . Not only their faith in Him,

---

[8] Cf. I Cor. 6:14; II Cor. 4:14; I Thess. 4:14; etc.

[9] Barth's own views have, of course, ripened considerably down the years on this subject. The following summary represents, in general, what may be termed the "new Barth".

or their preaching of Him, but the recollection which concretely created and fashioned this faith and preaching, embraced this time, the time of the forty days."[10] And he adds that, whatever our own interpretation of "this later history" of Jesus and of the "Easter story" may be, "we can at least agree on one point. For the New Testament this later history is not just an appendix or afterthought to the main theme. It is not peripheral in the New Testament, but central; not inessential or dispensable, but essential and indispensable. And it is all this, not in a different sense, but exactly in the sense in which the New Testament takes it."[11]

Next he turns to Bultmann who, he says, demythologises the event of Easter by interpreting it as "the rise of faith in the risen Lord, since it was this faith which led to the apostolic preaching". But this, Barth asserts, "will not do. Faith in the risen Lord springs from His historical manifestation, and from this as such, not from the rise of faith in Him."[12] So we come face to face, at the very outset, with a fundamental conflict of views—in which the evidence, as it seems to me, is wholly in favour of Barth.

For Bultmann, he emphasises, the great

eschatological event includes the death of Jesus, the faith of the first disciples, their preaching, the Church, the sacraments and the Christian life. But the resurrection, understood as the allegedly objective fact of the resurrection of the man Jesus who died on the cross, of His return to life in this world during the forty days, is not a part of this eschatological event. It is a 'nature-miracle', a 'miraculous proof', and as such it must be 'demythologised', like so much else in the New Testament. It is a mistaken objectifying of a concept of the Christian understanding of existence which needs to be translated back into the reality because it cannot be accepted as an event in time and space and cannot therefore be recognised in its supra-temporal context and character. An 'Easter

[10] *Church Dogmatics* III 2, (T & T Clark, Edinburgh, 1960), p. 442.
[11] Ibid., p. 443.
[12] Ibid.

event' in this sense can be regarded only as an objectifying of primitive Christian Easter faith in terms of the
mythical world-view of the time, and it is no longer valid
for those who have ceased to hold this view. The real
Easter event, which belongs to that eschatological occurrence, is the rise of the Easter faith of the first disciples.
This was not based on any event in time, but only on the
supra-historical, supra-temporal act of God.

But here, Barth remarks, Bultmann is aware that he himself is on the verge of relapsing into mythology, if indeed
he has not already done so.[13] In direct contradiction to
Geering, moreover, Barth insists that the apostolic community "was not interested in any resurrection or actuality
of resurrection in general, but in the resurrection of this
man, and the resurrection of all men inaugurated by it".[14]

If we take what seems to be Bultmann's view—that the
recollection of the forty days "is a genuine memory of Jesus
only to the extent that it was in this history and time that
the disciples made up their minds about Him and about
His death in particular" and, in so doing, "drew far too
heavily on the mythical world-view of their age" – then this,
Barth insists, must mean that

> Jesus Himself is at work during that history and time
> only in the faith of the disciples. The 'self-declaration' of
> the 'Resurrected' is staged in the minds of the disciples
> and nowhere else. Nothing happened between Him and
> them. There was no new, and in its novelty decisive and
> fundamental, encounter between Him and them to give
> rise to their faith. They alone were engaged in this
> history. He was not. They were quite alone. To be sure,
> they had their faith, which had come into being through
> an 'act of God', whatever that may 'signify'.

But their faith had no object distinct from itself, no ante-

[13] Ibid., pp. 444.
[14] Although this, too, seems to be somewhat of an overstatement: cf.
references in the Gospels to the resurrection of the just.

cedent basis, on which to rest. "Jesus Himself had not risen. In its simple and unqualified sense, this statement is quite untenable."[15] But on this Barth unequivocally comments:

> For our part, we maintain the direct opposite. The statement is valid in its simplest sense, and only in that sense is it the central affirmation of the whole of the New Testament. Jesus Himself did rise again and appear to His disciples. This is the content of the Easter history, the Easter time, the Christian faith and Christian proclamation, both then and at all times. This is the basis of the existence of the Church and its sacraments. This—if we may call it so—is the 'eschatological event' in its manifest form.

The disciples were not alone with their faith. "It was established, awakened and created by God in this objective encounter." And he gives us the clue to the violence which Bultmann's exegesis does to the texts of the New Testament when he observes: "Bultmann is an exegete. But it is impossible to engage him in exegetical discussion. For he is also a systematic theologian of the type which handles texts in such a way that their exegesis is always controlled by a set of dogmatic presuppositions and is thus wholly dependent on their validity."[16] Precisely—although the same charge could, I think, be brought, although in a much lesser degree, against Barth himself.

Barth also criticises Bultmann's thesis on a number of other grounds which are relevant to our subject. He questions the proposition "that an event alleged to have happened in time can be accepted as historical only if it can be proved to be a 'historical' fact ... by the methods, and above all the tacit assumption, of modern historical scholarship".[17] Again, he challenges the assertion that there is a modern world-picture, "shaped for good or ill by

[15] Ibid., p. 445.
[16] Ibid., p. 445.
[17] Ibid., p. 446.

modern science", which is so binding upon us "as to determine in advance and unconditionally our acceptance or rejection of the biblical message"; and he equally challenges the corresponding assumption that we, today, "are compelled to reject a statement simply because this statement, or something like it, was compatible with the mythical world-view of the past". Have not Christians always, he asks, been eclectic in their world-views—and this for very good reasons?[18] He asserts, moreover, that "Bultmann is splitting hairs when he calls the literal resurrection a 'nature-miracle'. Far from helping us to understand it, this is merely an attempt to discredit it."[19]

Barth himself is quite unequivocal about the nature of the resurrection appearances. "It is the fact that the risen Christ can be touched," he writes, "which puts it beyond all doubt that He is the man Jesus and no one else. He is not soul or spirit in the abstract, but soul of His body, and therefore body as well. . . . It is impossible to erase the bodily character of the resurrection of Jesus and His existence as the Resurrected. Nor may we gloss over this element in the New Testament record of the forty days, as a false dualism between spirit and body has repeatedly tried to do";[20] and he remarks that we "misunderstand the whole matter, and fall into Docetism at the crucial point, if we refuse to see this". But he insists that

it is equally important to note that the man Jesus appeared to them during these days in the mode of God. During this period they came to see that He had always been present among them in His deity, though hitherto this deity had been veiled. They now recalled those preliminary manifestations of glory which they had already witnessed during His earthly life, but with unseeing eyes, and which now, in the light of what took place in these days, acquired for them the particular import

---

[18] Ibid., p. 447.
[19] Ibid., p. 451.
[20] Ibid., p. 448, cf. below, pp. 137 ff.

which they had always had in themselves, though hidden from them.[21]

[Incidentally, this seems to me a much more convincing interpretation of a number of passages in the Gospels than the suggestion of most contemporary critics that the disciples were so blinded by their Easter faith that they adapted—or even invented—traditions about the historical Jesus in such a way as to depict him in a quasi-celestial light for which there is no historical basis]. But now, Barth continues, "they actually beheld His glory. During these forty days the presence of God in the presence of the man Jesus was no longer a paradox. . . . He had been veiled, but He was now wholly and unequivocally and irrevocably manifest." And he cogently insists that for the disciples "this was not a self-evident truth, nor a discovery of their own, but a conviction which went utterly against the grain. This is made abundantly clear in the resurrection narratives, where the disciples begin by doubting and even disbelieving. But their doubts and disbelief are soon dispelled, never to return. They are definitely overcome and removed in the forty days."[22]

But the primary concern of the New Testament, he tells us, is with the fact to which reference is made in a hymn which probably belongs to the most primitive Christian tradition: "He was manifested in the body, vindicated in the spirit, seen by angels, preached among the nations, believed on in the world, taken up in glory."[23] It is this stupendous fact, he suggests, which enables us to understand why the evidence for the resurrection "can only be fragmentary and contradictory, as is actually the case in the New Testament".[24] The forty days to which he has referred more than once are, for example, not to be taken literally but typically.

[21] Ibid., pp. 448 f.
[22] Loc. cit.
[23] 1 Tim. 3:16.
[24] Op. cit., p. 452.

The narratives are not meant to be taken as 'history' in our sense of the word. . . . True, these accounts read very differently from myths. The Easter story is differentiated from myth, both formally and materially, by the fact that it is all about a real man of flesh and blood. But the stories are couched in the imaginative, poetic style of historical saga, and are therefore marked by the corresponding obscurity. For they are describing an event beyond the reach of historical research or depiction. Hence we have no right to try to analyse them or harmonise them. This is to do violence to the whole character of the event in question.

All we can say is that there "can be no doubt that all these narratives are about the same event, and that they are agreed in substance, intention and interpretation".[25]

In much the same way, he regards the stories about the empty tomb and the ascension as "indispensable if we are to understand what the New Testament seeks to proclaim as the Easter message. Taken together, they mark the limits of the Easter period, at one end the empty tomb, and at the other the ascension." True, "the empty tomb and the ascension are alike in the fact that they are both indicated rather than described; the one as an introduction, the other as a conclusion; the one a little more definitely though still in every general terms, the other much more vaguely." But "there are reasons for this. The content of the Easter witness, the Easter event, was not that the disciples found the tomb empty or that they saw Him go up to heaven, but that when they had lost Him through death they were sought and found by Him as the Resurrected. The empty tomb and the ascension are merely signs of the Easter event." Yet both signs are, he insists, so important that we can scarcely say that they might equally well have been omitted. "The empty tomb is not the same thing as the resurrection. It is not the appearance of the Living; it is only its presupposition. Hence it is only the sign, although an indispensable sign. Christians do not

[25] Ibid., p. 452.

believe in the empty tomb, but in the living Christ. This does not mean, however, that we can believe in the living Christ without believing in the empty tomb." Is it a legend, he asks? What matter? In either case it is "the sign which obviates all possible misunderstanding. It cannot, therefore, but demand our assent, even as a legend. Rejection of the legend of the empty tomb has always been accompanied by rejection of the saga of the living Jesus, and necessarily so. Far better, then, to admit that the empty tomb belongs to the Easter event as its sign."[26] And precisely similar considerations, in his view, apply to the ascension, for "again the ascension—Jesus' disappearance into heaven—is the sign of the Resurrected, not the Resurrected Himself." "Heaven", he points out, is the sum of the inaccessible and incomprehensible side of the created world, so there is no sense in trying to visualise the ascension as a literal event. "The point of the story is not that when Jesus left His disciples He visibly embarked upon a wonderful journey into space, but that when He left them He entered the side of the created world which was provisionally inaccessible and incomprehensible, that before their eyes He ceased to be before their eyes."[27]

There can be no doubt whatever, then, that Barth believes that the Jesus of the Gospels did, in actual fact, rise again from the dead. In this sense, therefore, the resurrection was a historical fact, although it transcends mere history. Not only so, but he takes the New Testament evidence much more seriously that Bultmann does. Yet he continually hesitates as to whether this piece of evidence or that is to be taken in a literal or symbolical sense. He is emphatic that the resurrection itself is *not* a mere symbol of the disciples' faith, as Bultmann asserts; on the contrary, their faith was awakened only by the fact of the resurrection. And in this, as it seems to me, the evidence points strongly in his favour. Yet this fact, he feels, was so transcendental that we cannot come to any precise conclusion about the nature of the evidence for it which is presented to us in the

[26] Ibid., pp. 452 f.
[27] Ibid., pp. 453 f.

New Testament. But in reaching this conclusion he seems to be influenced not so much by the evidence itself as by his own dogmatic presuppositions about the relationship betweeen faith and historical proof, the transcendental and the mundane—a subject to which we must return later.

IV

W. Künneth[28] is equally emphatic that the resurrection was an actual fact, and considerably less guarded in his assessment of the relevant evidence. There are "certainly notable relations between the resurrection of Jesus and history", he asserts, although "the concept of 'historicality' cannot grasp the essence of the resurrection witness, which points rather to something that transcends history."[29] This is because

no matter how important the historical relationships may be in detail, when the resurrection message is looked at in its essential character it does not exhaust itself in history but points decisively beyond the sphere of history. . . . Therefore the definition of it as a historical event involves an untenable shift of emphasis, in which the deepest meaning of the message is the very thing which cannot be validly expressed. If the resurrection of Jesus were to be understood as a merely historical happening, then it would stand among other historic events and other miracles which were played out on the stage of history. Such a comparison, however, fundamentally destroys the uniqueness of the resurrection and thus fails to grasp the basic newness of the witness to the resurrection. . . . In rejection of the 'historical' thesis we have first of all in a general sense to stress the resurrection's transcendence of history, i.e. its superiority to history. Here the dialectical attack on making the

[28] See *The Theology of the Resurrection*, trans. J. W. Leitch (SCM, London, 1965), from which the following quotations are taken.
[29] Op. cit., p. 33.

resurrection into mere history is justified—because the assumption from which the historical approach sets out, that the resurrection is an objectively ascertainable object of knowledge and accessible to impartial observation, is then seen to be fundamentally incorrect. The resurrection of Jesus is actually not a point on the historical plane to which we could conceivably have an objective relation. The historian's way of looking at it 'from outside' enables him at best to observe certain points at which it has entered history and left its mark upon it, yet the proper interpretation of these things is denied him because he sets out from a false presupposition. The significance of the real content of the resurrection witness, however, does not lie within the range of the historian's vision.[30]

But Künneth is crystal clear that the "existentialist interpretation" is quite inadequate. For Bultmann, he asserts, revelation in general "is not a thing that once happened 'somewhere and sometime', but the decisive point is, how I have to interpret the revelation event for myself today." So the cross and resurrection of Jesus are "not to be understood as past acts of salvation; but they become present phenomena, 'inherent parts of my self-understanding', to which I stand in a contemporary relationship." It is under the spell of this postulate of existentialist philosophy that Bultmann concludes that "The Easter faith is not interested in the historical question" and that the resurrection of Jesus is "myth" when considered as "a nature miracle like the resuscitation of one who is dead". But in this context, Künneth insists,

we must certainly ask: Is this Easter faith of which Bultmann talks still necessarily bound to the quite definite revelational fact of the resurrection of Jesus— and that, too, as the sole ground of faith and as the content of faith? Does he hold to the event of the resurrection, quite apart from its result in the succeeding

[30] Ibid., pp. 30 ff.

resurrection faith? From Bultmann's standpoint, the answer to that question can only be, 'No.' ... Thus despite all the will to truth that attends the existentialist philosopher's efforts, the result is a masked alteration of the very substance of the Christian resurrection message —masked by the use of biblical terms. Despite all the outward marks of a legitimate Christian theology, we have here in actual fact a philosophical reinterpretation of the Christian faith, a metamorphosis of the theological content of the resurrection reality. Bultmann's kerygma is then at all events no longer identical with the kerygma of the evangelists and apostles.[31]

Again, Bultmann has a wholly inadequate concept of revelation. "Wherever revelation is cut off from its moorings in history," Künneth insists,

we find a tendency to reduce it to general 'truths of reason.' What Bultmann, precisely in view of the results of liberalism, seeks to avoid is directly provoked in the course of his own 'interpretation'; rejecting the category of the 'historically past, unique, completed' in favour of the 'presently actual, summoning to decision' leads necessarily into the sphere of that conception of religion and of revelation which belongs to idealism and mysticism. Bultmann is not able to rescue the decisive 'once for all' by means of his principles and methods, but ends, against his will, in a philosophical metaphysic of timelessness. Thus the 'resurrection of Jesus' is reduced to a timeless symbol, to the ideogram of a general truth.[32]

But the whole witness of primitive Christians to the resurrection, Künneth argues, stands in irreconcilable antithesis to Bultmann's attempts to reinterpret it.

It is not that the experience created in the consciousness by the kerygma is the origin of faith, which can then

[31] Ibid., pp. 44 and 45.
[32] Ibid., p. 46.

argue back to some unknown and indistinct historical 'X' standing behind the message; but on the contrary the past perfect resurrection of Jesus is the unique reality which produces faith. The increasing separation of revelation from its moorings in history—here it must not be overlooked that while revelation is more than history, yet it does not become existent without history—leads to the triumph of a new form of *gnosis* divorced from history.[33]

Künneth then proceeds to examine the modern tendency to equate the message of the resurrection as witness to a myth. The meaning of the concept of "myth", he says, is "distinguished on the one hand from historical reality and on the other from the mere play of fantasy or poetic invention. Myth suggests non-historicality, but certainly not for that reason something unreal." On the contrary, "Reality is the mark of myth as opposed to fiction."[34] For myth, in fact, springs from a threefold root: from the inherited memory of pre-history; from the impression caused by the experience of the "numinous"; and from the creative power of the human spirit. So myths arise not only from the unfolding of a primitive consciousness going back to pre-history, not only as reactions to experiences, but also as the act and product of the spirit.[35]

Künneth himself, however, is unequivocal that this "tendency to understand the resurrection of Jesus from the point of view of the mythical must nevertheless be judged to be inappropriate when seen in the light of ultimate principles." It is true that the resurrection "utterly shatters the bounds of our earthly thinking and representation." Yet the records of it come to us in the form of human speech, and this "sets our proclamation the task of making clear what is 'really' meant by these earthly 'words, pictures, similes, representations, concepts', what the 'substance' of revelation in these 'earthen vessels' in actual fact is. The

[33] Ibid., p. 47.
[34] Ibid., pp. 47 f.
[35] Ibid., pp. 48–50.

task is, to transpose the biblical message into our way of thinking and our framework of ideas without its content being lost. This work of translation, however, has nothing to do with demythologising in Bultmann's sense, since the Christian message is anything but a myth. It is simply a question of the fundamental fact that God's revelation in itself is beyond contemplating and thinking out, and is accessible to us at all only in pictorial language. 'Now we see in a glass darkly'."[36] Even Bultmann cannot escape, for all his "demythologising", from retaining picture language. To Tillich, it seems, the "word of the resurrection of Jesus would in the first instance be a symbol for something transcendent and unconditional", for which "myth" serves as an appropriate vehicle. But Künneth insists that "To myth belongs the timelessness of pre-history and proto-history; it is the symbolic expression, in the religious-historical field, of the *revelatio generalis*." In contrast to this, the message of the resurrection has to do precisely with a *revelatio specialis*. "The purport of the resurrection of Jesus is not a powerful symbolic expression of a general condition, of a timeless background of being, but the strict once-for-allness and uniqueness of a concrete event which interrupts as it were the course of time and therefore, as a completed act, cannot be fitted into the general scheme of mythological ideas."[37]

Another reason why the concept of myth is inappropriate to the resurrection of Jesus is that in the birth of myths the decisive part is played by the creative mind of man.

Myth is the expression of anthropocentric religion. To combine myth and the resurrection of Jesus therefore manifestly represents a fundamental misunderstanding. ... The word of the resurrection of Jesus does not seek to be a symbolic expression of the religious movement of the soul, but rather the proclamation of a reality which is not at the disposal of man in himself, of which

[36] I Cor. 13:12.
[37] Ibid., pp. 54–7.

he cannot be even mythologically aware, and which must first be told him.[38]

Equally, Künneth asserts, it is "superficial and unfounded to say that the study of the history of religion has shown the dependence of the resurrection of Jesus on mythology. On the contrary, it is precisely the comparison with the history of religion that gives rise to the strongest objections to any kind of mythifying of the resurrection of Jesus." In this context he quotes Harnack's statement that there is "no tradition that leads to the assumption that in the circles from which Peter and the first disciples came, or among the pious Jews of that time in Palestine, such a myth was known at all, far less had any place in their religion". The "special character of the spiritual atmosphere of Israel as distinct from the syncretistic world around", Künneth insists, "calls for primary consideration. Its whole outlook stands in contrast to mythological assumptions."[39]

Another argument which sharply distinguishes the resurrection from "the customary formulation of myths and processes analogous to it" is, moreover, the "relatedness of the resurrection of Jesus to history". The resurrection of Jesus is concerned with an event which happened to a quite definite historical person, an event which "exists only in the peculiar concreteness of this relatedness to history or it does not exist at all. On this point every analogy which relates it to nature cults or vegetation rites breaks down, adapted as these are to the constantly recurring rhythm of nature." Indeed, the "very concern of the Christian witnesses to confirm as far as possible the factuality of the resurrection of Jesus disproves the assumption that this confession is to be explained by their acceptance of a myth about a dead and resurrected god." It is clear that Paul in I Cor. 15 emphasises that the evidence for the resurrection is well attested, that many eye-witnesses were still alive when he wrote, and that anyone could go and question them. This was precisely why he gives such a "list of

[38] Ibid., p. 57.
[39] Ibid., pp. 58 f.

critically sifted and accredited witnesses". The message of the resurrection of Jesus, Künneth continues, is accordingly "passionately interested in the concrete and completed reality of the event—an attitude totally foreign to the mythical frame of mind". So this message, in contrast to all the multifarious myths which abound, is

> not concerned at all with a 'deity' who dies and comes to life again, but with the man Jesus of Nazareth. . . . Thus the decisive point for a comparison with the mythical analogies—the theme of a dying and rising 'deity'—is missing from the start. The unique thing about the resurrection message is the raising of a man from the dead, of which nothing whatever is said in the myths. Moreover, it is significant that while the myths do speak of a dying, they never testify concretely to a death by crucifixion.

Similarly, the resurrection of Jesus is "no autonomous natural process, but a sovereign act of God, which has no parallel in mythology".[40]

Yet again, while "Greek thought, living as it does in the realm of mythology, sets in the centre the mystical union with the divine", the primitive Christian confession of the resurrection "knows nothing of any such mystical deification and enjoyment of immortality, but proclaims on the contrary that Christ died and rose for the sins of the world".[41] And this message, when proclaimed in the centres of heathen religions, was "not by any means felt to be a new, but fundamentally similar myth: on the contrary, it was recognised and rejected in its offensive otherness." The message of the resurrection "did *not* appear to the contemporary world to be one of the customary cult legends", but rather in terms of strict exclusiveness. "One alone is the Kyrios. Here every analogy fails. This witness, in contrast to the tolerance of the whole mythical world, comes with

[40] Ibid., pp. 59–61, quoting in part from Harnack and in part from Kittel.
[41] Ibid., p. 61.

an intolerant claim to absoluteness which calls in question the validity and truth of all mythology."[42]

Here again, as it seems to me, the evidence is overwhelmingly against those who—like Bultmann, Geering and a multitude of others—speak of the traditional doctrine of the resurrection of Jesus as having close affinities with "nature miracles" or the various mystery religions which flourished in the Middle East both before and after the time of Christ. I have referred to this subject at rather more length elsewhere,[43] and have relied heavily on B. M. Metzger's essay on "Mystery religions and early Christianity".[44] There are, of course, certain superficial parallels between the mystery religions and the world faith which was destined to replace them, but there are far more fundamental contrasts; and the evidence, as I see it, is such as to distinguish the doctrine of the resurrection as essentially different and *sui generis*.[45]

Bultmann, moreover, points to the three storeys—earth, heaven and hell—by which in his view the New Testament's picture of the world is marked as "mythical", and insists that Paul's Christology is built on this three-fold division of the universe. On this hypothesis, therefore, it is possible "to understand the idea that a heavenly being comes down from heaven to earth, lives upon it, enters after death into the realm of the dead under the earth, is resurrected, i.e. rises up again from the grave and the realm of death under the earth and by an 'ascension into heaven' returns to the 'upper' world and sits on the throne of the Lord of the universe 'at the right hand of God'." Bultmann then dismisses this, Künneth asserts, "as a thoroughly naive idea bound to a primitive picture of the world". So, for Bultmann (to say nothing of John Robinson and many others), the "mythical world-picture" of the Bible is "past" for modern man, and therefore the "mythological talk" in

[42] Ibid., p. 62.

[43] *Christianity and Comparative Religion* (Tyndale Press, London, 1970), pp. 36 ff.

[44] In *Historical and Literary Studies* (E. J. Brill, Leiden, 1968).

[45] I shall refer in the next chapter to the question of the "three days" between burial and resurrection in this context.

which that past world-picture indulges has "become incredible".[46]

To this line of argument Künneth makes a number of objections. First, that modern research has made Bultmann's own standpoint appear thoroughly antiquated. Secondly, that the resurrection of Jesus is in essence "not a declaration made with an eye to the world-picture or the study of world structure", but "belongs to the sphere of man's relation with God, which natural science can neither affirm nor deny." Thirdly, that to "make the transcendent revelation and the reality of God immediately understandable, without any use of immanent ideas and concepts", is necessarily impossible, and therefore "all speech is ultimately pictorial and all talk of God anthropomorphic." Fourthly, that this is why "the witness to the resurrection stands on the one hand beyond all questions of world-picture, while on the other hand its linguistic form bears the stamp of ideas that were originally connected with a world-picture." Fifthly, that the "concepts 'resurrection', 'ascension', 'session at the right hand of God'—figures of speech rooted in the immanent—must not be confused with the 'substance' itself". Sixthly, that it must be seriously asked whether biblical thought "was in actual fact so bound up in the space-time pattern of the world-picture of antiquity that it could think and speak even of the reality of God only in these limited categories"[47]—and the answer must be an emphatic "No". The classical example of the way Christians, centuries before Bultmann, interpreted the language of the Bible in such contexts can be seen from the fact that Luther, who still adopted the pre-Copernican world-picture, "was convinced that heaven 'as the place of God' is 'not a place in the spatial sense', that Jesus' 'ascension into heaven' is not a spatial event, and that Jesus' 'exaltation' certainly cannot mean a localising of his body in heaven, but on the contrary the formula '*dextra Dei ubique est*' ('the right hand of God is everywhere') is

[46] Op. cit., pp. 63 f.
[47] Ibid., pp. 66–69.

the decisive answer of faith to all questions raised by the world picture."[48]

But it is time to draw this present discussion to a close. Quotations could, of course, have been given from many other theologians; but it seemed preferable to concentrate primarily on a very few writers (who may, perhaps, be regarded as sufficiently typical of different points of view) and to give a reasonably comprehensive summary of their views, rather than rely on exceedingly brief, and therefore highly selective, quotations from a variety of scholars. We are concerned in this chapter, of course, only with the basic historicity of the resurrection, not with the more detailed consideration of the New Testament evidence which must necessarily follow.

V

To the historian, the one indisputable fact is the decisive change which supervened in the attitude, faith, behaviour and message of the little band of disciples. So the first and basic problem is how this dramatic change can be accounted for and explained. Can it be dismissed as no more than a profound change of mind, a radical re-assessment of the significance of the life and death of Jesus; or can it be explained only on the basis of the "appearances" of the risen Lord which the disciples indubitably claimed to have had, and for which evidence is available from an exceedingly early date? Next, how are these appearances themselves to be explained? Were they purely "subjective", or does the evidence suggest that they represent real, "objective" encounters with the Jesus who had been crucified? Even so, would this necessarily sub-stantiate his "resurrection", or merely that he was still alive? Anyway, what does the phrase that God "raised him from the dead" really mean? Does it imply that something had happened to the body which had been laid in the tomb? Was the tomb really empty, or are the stories of the

[48] Ibid., p. 69.

empty tomb a mythological addition to the primitive tradition? And even if Jesus did rise again, in some object-ive sense of that term, can this properly be regarded as a "historical event"? Or does it, rather, constitute a special form of history which is not subject to ordinary methods of historical enquiry—and is this, perhaps, substantiated, in part at least, by the host of alleged contradictions in the New Testament narratives and the addition to the primitive tradition of elements that can only be regarded as mythological?

The existentialist view of the resurrection has, I think, been adequately epitomised in quotations from Bultmann. According to this view the resurrection is "historical" only in the sense that the apostles' re-assessment of the cross (and their new-born faith in the total significance of Jesus and his mission) is a historical fact. But Ulrich Wilckens pertinently insists that "it is quite impossible that disciples of Jesus should have reacted to the catastrophes of his death by the conviction suddenly dawning upon them that he had been raised from the dead—which had never previously been asserted in Israel of any mortal." So the "so-called hypothesis of the subjective vision must be excluded as an explanation."[49] Similarly, when Bultmann describes the "Easter event" as the "self-attestation of the risen Lord", Hans-Georg Geyer insists that this is to speak "of the event by which a basis is provided for faith, but by that very token not of the question of the way in which faith arose".[50] In contrast, Geyer quotes Barth's affirmation that "this event of the forty days, and the act of God in this event, was the concrete factor in its externality, its objectiv-ity, not taking place in their faith but in conflict with their lack of faith."[51]

In cold historical fact, as Bultmann sees it, Jesus never rose again except in so far as that phrase can be meaning-fully used of his abiding significance and challenge. But it

[49] *The Significance of the Message of the Resurrection for Faith in Jesus Christ,* ed. C. F. D. Moule (SCM Press, London, 1968), p. 61.
[50] Ibid., p. 113.
[51] Ibid., p. 119.

is *possible*, he would apparently concede, that some of his first disciples had purely subjective "visions" which convinced them that Jesus was in some sense still alive. For the rest, as has been somewhat caustically remarked, the "Christ-event" is true today not because it actually happened nearly two thousand years ago (except that there was a person Jesus of Nazareth who died on a cross), but because it takes place every time Bultmann and his confrères enter their pulpits and proclaim their message.[52] And with the existentialists can be classified, in this context, those liberal scholars (such as Strauss, Renan, Schmiedel and others) whose view of the resurrection is, indeed, radically different, but who interpret it in terms of visions, wishful thinking or some form of hallucination or psychological (or, indeed, pathological) experiences which convinced the disciples that their Master was still alive. But it seems to me extremely difficult to regard any such theory as an adequate explanation of all the available evidence.

To begin with, it is only certain types of persons who are prone to hallucinations or experiences of that sort. But, unless the New Testament records have no foundation whatever except the vivid imagination or deliberate invention of the Church (and virtually no one seriously postulates so extreme a view), the witnesses to resurrection appearances can scarcely be reduced to one or two psychological types. Such experiences are, moreover, always highly individualistic, since they arise from the subconscious minds of the persons concerned. But we have the clear testimony of Paul that in this case over five hundred persons, on one occasion, had precisely the same "hallucination" at the same time, and that this happened on other occasions to smaller groups. Again, such experiences commonly concern an occurrence which is regarded with some degree of expectation and desire; but here the evidence—unless, indeed, a large number of different details have been woven into the records with almost diabolical cunning—points strongly to the fact that the disciples were disconsolate and dispirited, plunged in the gloom of dis-

[52] See p. 34 above.

appointed hopes, and expecting nothing of the sort. As John Robinson has put it, after a full acknowledgment of the shattering of the disciples' hopes by the crucifixion and death of Jesus: "And then IT happened. It came to them —or rather, as they could only describe it, HE came to them ... Jesus was not a dead memory but a living presence, making new men of them."[53]

This theory also fails to explain the slowness of the disciples, even after some of these "hallucinations", to grasp the fact that Jesus was still alive; the way in which the appearances, so far from reflecting the disciples' own spiritual ideas, "led them beyond themselves into utterly new and unexpected apprehensions of truth"[54] and the dynamic power of the resurrection in the life of the early Church, in its proclamation, and in the survival of the Church and its preaching, against heavy odds, all down history. As Geoffrey Lampe puts it: "Unless something extraordinary happened to convince them that against all their expectation God had reversed his apparent verdict on Jesus, I cannot imagine that they would later on have taken immense risks to assert in public that a man who had been condemned and hanged was no less than God's Messiah."[55]

As for the concept of visions, S. H. Hooke has pertinently remarked that one weakness of this interpretation of the resurrection appearances is that what stands out in a vision and is remembered in detail is precisely what is seen, whereas for the most part no attempt is made in the New Testament accounts to describe the form of the risen Lord (as is done, for example, in the visions in Revelation). "The emphasis all lies not on *what* they saw, but on *whom* they saw. It was not an object of sense-perception that they 'saw', but a Person, a Presence that removed their fear, and

[53] Quoted by E. Mascall in *The Secularisation of Christianity*, p. 147.

[54] Cf. *The Resurrection of Christ*, by Michael Ramsey (Geoffrey Bles, London, 1946), p. 48.

[55] *The Resurrection*, by G. W. H. Lampe and D. M. MacKinnon (Mowbrays, London, 1968), pp. 30 f.

flooded their consciousness with joy."[56] Even in the case of Paul's experience on the Damascus road—which can, in my view, be regarded as a "vision" much more justly than can the experiences of the "forty days"—it is significant that Paul himself clearly distinguished the appearance of the risen Jesus "from visions of a mystical sort which he had at other times. He sometimes experienced 'visions and revelations of the Lord' and in one of these he was caught up to the third heaven (II Cor. 12:2). He was careful to attach small importance to these experiences and to be reticent about them. But he speaks in a totally different manner about the claim that, at the beginning of his discipleship, he saw Jesus."[57] And here Geoffrey Lampe is, I think, equally emphatic. Paul, he insists, "was absolutely convinced that Jesus, who had been sentenced to death at the instigation of Paul's own friends for reasons which he thoroughly approved, had encountered him with shattering effect". He also "believed that many others before him had encountered the living Jesus". Lampe can, indeed, describe these encounters as "an experience of vision"; but he immediately qualifies this as "an objective, compelling and convincing revelation". The people from whom the tradition originated, he says,

> were absolutely convinced that there was an encounter, which they hadn't dreamed up for themselves, between the objective presence of Christ, 'outside' themselves, and their own selves. That happened. I think you have got exceedingly strong historical evidence for that, evidence which is very early indeed because the tradition had come to Paul himself from the first Christians. He actually mentions names, and appeals to the witness of people still alive who had had that experience. Above all, what impresses me is the experience of Paul himself, which we have got at first hand. He couldn't say much

[56] *The Resurrection of Christ* (1967), p. 142. Cf. *Resurrection and the New Testament*, by C. F. Evans, (SCM, London 1970), p. 173.
[57] Michael Ramsey, op. cit., p. 41. Cf. Künneth, op. cit., p. 84.

about it. I don't think he could describe what happened; but he knew that somehow or other he had met the Lord.[58]

This brings us to quite a different form of the "vision-theory"—namely, that the resurrection appearances were not hallucinations or auto-generated "visions", but visions imparted by God himself to assure the disciples that Jesus was indeed alive. As Theodor Keim put it, the appearances were not the "chance-play of visions", but rather a form of veritable "telegram from heaven", which was given to the disciples by Christ's "own impulsion and by the will of God".[59] This is closely analogous to B. H. Streeter's view that the spirit of Jesus survived and was able to convey to the disciples the certainty of his presence with them,

possibly showing Himself to them in some form such as might be covered by St. Paul's phrase 'a spiritual body'; possibly through some psychological channel similar to that which explains the mysterious means of communication between persons commonly known as telepathy; or possibly in some way of which we have at present no conception. On such a view the appearances to the disciples can only be called visions, if by visions we mean something directly caused by the Lord Himself, veritably alive and personally in communion with them.[60]

But here Künneth is more clear-cut, and insists that

the Risen One is neither a phantasy, nor a theophany, but the appearance of a new, living mode of existence. The appearance expresses the connection between life beyond death and life within history. That is why the Risen One stands before the disciples as the one who bears the marks of his wounds. . . . The Risen One is in

[58] Op. cit., pp. 7, 18, 21.
[59] Michael Ramsey, op. cit., p. 49.
[60] *Foundations* (Macmillan, London, 1912), p. 136.

fact precisely *not* God himself in some kind of disguise, but Jesus of Nazareth, raised and exalted by God. With that, all the decisive pre-suppositions for any identifying of the appearances with prophetic revelations or spiritual visions fall to the ground.[61]

The repeated references which a number of theologians make to the appearances of "the Risen One" provoke Willi Marxsen to expostulate that Paul himself does not use that phrase, but confines himself to the claim that God had revealed "his *Son*" to him, and that he had "seen *Jesus* our Lord".[62] The belief that "Jesus' resurrection had actually taken place is therefore founded for Paul *not* upon a happening of something which he considers to have taken place; on the contrary, it is a process of deduction." In historical terms, he insists, *"it can only be established* (though quite reliably) that witnesses, after the death of Jesus, claimed that something had happened to them which they described as seeing Jesus, and reflection on this experience led them to the *interpretation* that Jesus had been raised from the dead."[63] But Ulrich Wilckens convincingly replies that when Paul says "he appeared to me also" it follows unambiguously that he whom he too has seen "is regarded as *he who has risen,* and whom he has to preach as an apostle like 'the others'. The preaching of the *raising* of Christ as an act of God, exercised upon Jesus who was dead, is confirmed by the appearances, which can be specified, of this Christ. There is no doubt that this is the function of the list of witnesses in the context of the argument in I Cor. 15. Thus we are perfectly justified in speaking of the appearances of the risen Christ."[64] Similarly, Gerhard Delling insists that "it was the Jesus who was buried, who was also raised."[65]

[61] Op. cit., p. 85.
[62] Gal. 1:15 and I Cor. 9:1.
[63] *The Significance of the Message of the Resurrection,* pp. 24 and 31.
[64] Ibid., pp. 58 f.
[65] Ibid., p. 81.

VI

Marxsen's emphasis on what might, at first sight, appear to be a distinction without a difference springs, of course, from his view that the traditions about the empty tomb are unhistorical and unimportant—a subject which falls within the scope of my next chapter. There is, in my view, excellent evidence that the empty tomb is not a late accretion but part of the very earliest apostolic tradition. Indeed, Alan Richardson remarks that the "notion that the resurrection of Christ was a purely 'spiritual' affair, while his corpse remained in the tomb, is a very modern one, which rests upon theories of the impossibility of miracle drawn from nineteenth-century physics." But to Paul, as to any other Jew of the time, "a merely 'spiritual' resurrection would have appeared unintelligible. Unlike the Greeks, the Jews did not think of a man as being made up of a body and a soul; a man was a living body. If Christ was raised from the dead, he must have been raised in the body. Thus, Paul cannot conceive of those who are risen in Christ as existing in a disembodied state: they have a 'spiritual body'."[66]

Scholars such as Geoffrey Lampe argue strongly—but, in my opinion, unconvincingly—against this view. Lampe is fully assured that "the Resurrection was an event in the external world: that Jesus was actually raised from the dead." It was, indeed, "the decisive event in the history of the world: the focal point in God's dealings with his creation."[67] But he does not himself believe that this had any connection whatever, in historical fact, with the story of the empty tomb. He concedes that "the question of historicity is finely balanced, and one can't afford to be dogmatic about it. Certainly not negatively dogmatic, and I think not positively dogmatic either."[68] But he then proceeds to argue strongly, not only against "a fully corporeal presence of Jesus after his death," but also (though less emphatically)

---

[66] *An Introduction to the Theology of the New Testament* (SCM, 1958), p. 196.
[67] Op. cit., pp. 30 and 90.
[68] Ibid., p. 18.

against any belief "that the physical body of Jesus had been transformed in the grave into a spiritual body, and that it was no longer there at Easter because it had been changed into another substance which did not exist spatially".[69] He admits that it is possible that this was what Paul himself believed, but considers it improbable.[70] But while he does, of course, support this view by arguments—against the weight of the evidence, as I see it—from the epistles and from the Gospel traditions,[71] he seems to allow the "finely balanced" scales of historical enquiry to be heavily weighted by a theological consideration which appears to him basic. The fact that "Christ's Resurrection is the assurance that we too shall rise from the dead" implies, he says, "that his Resurrection was not different in kind from what we may hope for through him". If however his body

> was raised physically from the grave and did not see corruption, or if his body was transformed after death into something different, in such a way that in itself it was annihilated, then he did not experience the whole of our human destiny. His entry into life beyond the grave was different from what we may hope may be our own. For it is demonstrable that our bodies of flesh and blood will be dissolved, and that in whatever mode of existence we may be raised from death it will not be by either the resuscitation of this mortal body or its transformation.[72]

But the transformation of this mortal body into a body like his resurrection body[73] is precisely what Paul says *will* happen to those who are still alive at the parousia; so why should not the gulf between the dead and those still alive at the parousia have been bridged, as it were, in the case of one who was only very recently dead, whose body had not

[69] Ibid., p. 46.

[70] G. B. Caird, on the other hand, insists that it is essential to the argument of I Cor. 15 that the body of Jesus should have undergone such a metamorphosis. See p. 138 below.

[71] See below, pp. 122–125, 138–140.

[72] Ibid., pp. 58 f. Cf. also 97.

[73] Phil. 3:21.

decomposed, and whose resurrection not only signified the conquest of death but heralded the beginning of a time when the material would be taken up, and transformed, into the spiritual? But this is mere speculation, as is Lampe's theological contention: the question of the historicity of the empty tomb must be decided not by theological speculation but on the evidence.

This evidence, moreover, is not concerned exclusively with the biblical statements on the subject, which must be considered in my next chapter, but with what D. M. MacKinnon refers to as "the apparent inability of the opponents of the early Christian preaching to silence the message of the Resurrection once for all by producing Christ's remains".[74] The argument that no one was interested in the tomb, or that the place of burial was not known,[75] seems to me scarcely to merit serious reply. The Jewish leaders must have known, or could very easily have discovered, where the body was buried; and the proclamation that Jesus had died, been buried and then been raised from the dead must, at the very least, have aroused in Jewish ears a questioning about what had happened to the grave and its contents.[76] No one today, I think, seriously suggests that the apostles stole the body and then proceeded to foist a miserable deception on the world. Such a view would be incredible, both in psychology and ethics —as Hugh Schonfield, in his strange book *The Passover Plot*, implicitly agrees. But his own attempted reconstruction is equally untenable.[77] If, however, the body had been moved by orders of the Chief Priests or the Roman Governor, then it is inconceivable that they would not have nipped the dangerous Christian "heresy" in the bud by making the facts known. The most detailed attempt to

[74] Ibid., p. 84.

[75] *Pace* Lampe, op. cit., pp. 52 f. See below, p. 121. For those who suggest that the bodily resurrection of Jesus was a false inference from Jewish presuppositions as to what a resurrection must mean, this argument is still more untenable.

[76] Cf. pp. 120 ff. below.

[77] See my book *Christianity: the witness of history* (Tyndale Press, London, 1969), pp. 64 ff.

face up to the problem of whether the tomb was in fact empty is, I think, that of Kirsopp Lake, while the theory which seems most popular today is usually attributed to Venturini; but there are a number of decisive objections to Lake's theories, while Venturini's thesis has been dismissed as untenable even by Strauss, and would involve making Jesus himself a deceiver and his disciples either fellow-conspirators, bemused simpletons, or a mixture of both. I will not, however, repeat what I have discussed at some length elsewhere.[78] It is fashionable[79] today to pour scorn on any discussion of the series of extremely unconvincing attempts which have been made, down the ages, to explain away the tradition of the empty tomb—either on the ground that it is clearly impossible to establish conclusively that no rationalistic interpretation *could* be true,[80] or on the diametrically opposite ground that the resurrection appearances stand in need of "no external confirmation".[81] But no lawyer, I think, would fail to recognise the cogency of the evidence about the tomb—or, indeed, the fact that the evidence for the resurrection consists in a number of different strands which must be taken together, not in isolation.

VII

There remains the phenomenon that many of those who are firmly convinced that the resurrection, in the traditional sense of a genuine rising from the dead, did in fact "happen" are none the less unwilling to refer to it as a "historical event". This seems to me to spring from a number of heterogeneous factors which differ widely from one writer to another. They are all of them, no doubt, of importance to the theologians concerned, but vary greatly in their significance for a lawyer.

[78] Ibid., pp. 61–5, 84–108.
[79] *The Significance of the Message of the Resurrection*, p. 9.
[80] Robinson, op. cit., p. 47.
[81] Lampe, op. cit., p. 102.

First, there is the distinction—largely German in origin —between what may be termed in English "ordinary" history and "salvation" history, or history as this can be established, point by point, by the investigations of a historian using the normal tools of his craft, and supranatural events, or "primal history", which transcend such investigation. Take, for example, the statement that "Christ died for our sins." Here the first part of the statement, that Christ died, can be investigated—and, indeed, established —by precisely the same methods as can be used in regard to the death of Alexander, Caesar or Napoleon; but the addendum that he died "for our sins" is a statement which must be examined and evaluated by totally different methods and criteria. So, too, with the resurrection. Whether the tomb was empty, whether the disciples were transformed by some encounters they claimed to have had, and whether the initial Christian proclamation and the subsequent history of the Church can be convincingly explained on any other basis, can all be submitted to historical investigation: but the actual resurrection of Christ and his exaltation to God's "right hand" (however, precisely, each of these phrases is to be interpreted) lie beyond the scope of such methods. This is perfectly true. But it does not alter the fact that H. F. von Campenhausen could categorically (and, in my view, cogently) declare that "for all its contemporary, vivifying reality, the resurrection is still an actual event of the historical past, and as such it was handed down, proclaimed and believed. And so the proclamation of it cannot evade the historical question, and cannot in any circumstances be withdrawn from the testing of historical investigation."[82] Similarly, Alan Richardson asserts that "here is historical testimony in abundance, and it demands historical explanation";[83] and Ulrich Wilckens agrees that it is "not methodologically permissible to deny that this question belongs to the province of the historian as such, and to reserve it to the realm of pure matters of

[82] In Stephen Neill, *The Interpretation of the New Testament, 1861–1961* (London, 1964), p. 286.
[83] *History, Sacred and Profane*, (SCM, London, 1964), p. 197.

faith".[84] The debate between those who assert that "there is only one history" and those who make a distinction between ordinary history and "salvation history" (which concerns events which are "supra-historical", because they are discernible only by faith) has been discussed in some detail by G. G. O'Collins, who himself concludes that while the resurrection "is a real, bodily event involving the person of Jesus of Nazareth", it is still not "of such a nature that it can properly be called historical".[85] But this represents a distinction which seems almost meaningless to a lawyer. As Geoffrey Lampe cogently puts it:

> That Jesus was raised by God and exalted as the Lord of glory is not a statement which the historian as such has any grounds either for affirming or denying. It lies outside his province. It is an assertion that is possible only to faith. But faith makes this assertion on the basis of certain things which are recorded as having actually happened at Easter. The claims which Christian faith makes are an interpretation which it puts upon these happenings; and the historian has every right to investigate the records of these happenings and to pronounce upon the probability or otherwise that they did in fact occur. If the result of the enquiry were to be that it is exceedingly improbable that any part of the record is true, then the Easter story becomes a myth and not a part of history (and hence not a part of 'salvation history').[86]

It seems probable, indeed, that one motive for making this distinction between ordinary history and supra-history, however it may be expressed, has been the desire both to avoid the impression that the fact of the resurrection can be conclusively proved to the sceptic (which is, of course, not the case) and to enable the believer to escape into a realm, as Richardson puts it, "where the critics cease from

[84] In *The Significance of the Message of the Resurrection*, p. 61.
[85] In *Heythrop Journal*, 1966 and 1967.
[86] Op. cit., p. 33.

troubling and the faithful are at rest".[87] But this flight from reality is not likely to commend itself to a lawyer, and we shall attempt in the next chapter to make a more realistic approach to, and assessment of, the relevant evidence.

Yet again, it seems to me that, on occasion at least, theologians hesitate to affirm the historicity of the resurrection largely because there is no direct evidence as to the act of rising again from the dead. Presumably, indeed, this was something which was not susceptible to being seen or described by an eye-witness, even if one had been present; and it always seems to me significant that no attempt is made to describe it in any of the canonical Gospels.[88] Incidentally, one might well speculate how the critics would have castigated any such alleged testimony had it been included in the New Testament records. But they cannot have it both ways; and the hesitation they often show towards circumstantial or inferential evidence[89] seems to me wholly misplaced. How many facts of history—or, for that matter, how many adulteries or murders—can be proved by the testimony of unimpeachable witnesses to having actually seen the event or act concerned? Some of the best and most convincing evidence is, in reality, based on a combination of testimony and virtually inevitable inference, or on a concurrence of circumstances which are often much less open to fabrication than the memory of some fallible witness. And this is particularly cogent in regard to the case in point, where the supra-natural breaks in on the natural, and the eternal world impinges on the world of space and time. This, as we have seen, is precisely why theologians such as Barth and Künneth hesitate to regard the resurrection itself as "historical", although they stoutly maintain that it has relations and repercussions which can only be so described.

[87] Op. cit., p. 134.

[88] This is fully accepted by most commentators. But Evans comes as near as he can to a contrary view. Cf. op. cit., p. 87.

[89] Cf. for example, Geering, op. cit., pp. 19, 31 f; Evans, op. cit., pp. 180, 182.

The point at which we must end this present chapter is to say, with John Robinson, that

> If the appearances had been merely psychic phenomena, one would expect the sense that Jesus was alive to have grown progressively less vivid once the disciples ceased to be 'in touch', and those who had not seen the evidence to be as sceptical as third parties usually are to such supposed communications from the dead—let alone to reports of miraculously empty graves. But, in fact, the conviction became only the more settled once the appearances had ceased, and those who had not seen were won to just as living a faith as those who had. Moreover, the ground of appeal even for those who had shared in the appearances was not the past experience so much as the present experience. [In point of fact, he continues,] this abiding and transforming experience, grounded, not on the reports of others, but on the first-hand awareness of the living Christ, is what made and sustained the Christian church. And the very existence of the church, not merely as the historical consequence of past phenomena but as the embodiment of a present faith, is itself a major part of the evidence for the Resurrection. Indeed, it was this present conviction, which thrills through the letters, that alone caused the other evidence to be preserved.

Yet the fact remains that, for the New Testament, the Resurrection is

> not primarily an experience, but an event. It uses the phrase 'witnesses of the Resurrection' (Acts 1:22; 4:33), not of all who can testify to its power, but only of those who were eye-witnesses of the event, or rather of the identity between the risen Christ whom they had seen and the man with whom they had companied 'during all the time that the Lord Jesus went in and out among us.'[90]

[90] *The Interpreter's Dictionary of the Bible*, Vol. 4, pp. 48 f.

There is no doubt in my own mind that James Denney was right when he wrote, long ago:

> To say that the faith produced the message—that Jesus rose again in the souls of His disciples, in their resurgent faith and love, and that this, and this alone, gave birth to all the stories of the empty grave and the appearances of the Lord to His own—is to pronounce a purely dogmatic judgment. What underlies it is not the historical evidence as the documents enable us to reach it, but an estimate of the situation dictated by a philosophical theory which has discounted the evidence beforehand.[91]

So it is to the documentary evidence that we must now turn —with the remark that the attitude with which many contemporary theologians and biblical scholars approach that evidence seems to me to approximate much more closely to that of a counsel for the prosecution than that of a judge who tries to weigh the evidence.

[91] *Jesus and the Gospel* (Hodder and Stoughton, New York, 1908), p. 110.

105

CHAPTER FOUR

The Resurrection — II

THE BIBLICAL EVIDENCE

I

In our last chapter we discussed the basic historicity of the resurrection and saw that the fundamental evidence for this lies not so much in the detailed narratives as in the complete transformation of the apostles and their message. A little band of bewildered, disillusioned and dispirited cowards was transformed, in an incredibly short space of time, into a company which no persecution could silence. Not only so, but it is clear that the basic *kerygma* of the early Church was not primarily the teaching of Jesus but rather his death and resurrection. It was this message which they felt constrained to proclaim, even in the teeth of bitter opposition. The contrast between the disciples of the Gospels, who all forsook their Master in his hour of greatest need, and the apostles as we find them in the Acts and the Epistles, defies any explanation based on wishful thinking, on any attempt to vindicate the "offence of the cross"[1] or even on some theory of dreams or visions.[2] This is, I think, particularly clear in the transformation of the Peter of Good Friday, with his triple denial (for surely no one can seriously suggest that a libellous imputation of a denial he had never made was foisted by the early Church on its leading apostle?), and the Peter depicted in Acts, visited and discussed by Paul, and (in my view) expressing his own resurrection faith, possibly through the pen of Silvanus, in

---

[1] See Geering, op. cit., pp. 73–139, etc., and 140–157.
[2] Cf. pp. 92–96 above.

the first letter attributed to him in the New Testament canon.

Now, however, we must turn to the more detailed documentary evidence and discuss this as comprehensively as space allows. This evidence primarily consists in the records[3] of the alleged appearances of the risen Lord to a number of groups and individuals and also those records which refer to the empty tomb. What was the nature of these appearances? Was the tomb really empty—and, if so, what does this mean? What happened to the body which lay within it, and what degree of "corporeality" (if any) are we to attribute to the risen Christ? To what does the evidence point in regard to what we commonly call the ascension? And how are we to regard the real or apparent discrepancies between the various traditions in relation to each of these points?

In the past a number of attempts have been made to provide a harmony of the different accounts in such a way as to eliminate any contradiction—and I have been privileged to read in typescript a new attempt of this sort, in regard to what happened on the first Easter morning, which will (I hope) soon be published.[4] But for many years now the tendency among theologians has been strongly in the opposite direction: to emphasise, exaggerate and even distort the alleged contradictions. P. Gardner-Smith, for example, asserted that "No ingenuity can make the narrative of Luke consistent with that of Mark, much less is it possible to reconcile the picture presented by the fourth evangelist with the accounts of any of the synoptic writers. Mutually contradictory narratives cannot all be true.... Nothing can be made of a jumble of contradictory statements."[5] P. W. Schmiedel, again, stated categorically that the Gospels exhibit, in this respect, "contradictions of the most glaring kind", and that their number is much greater than the mere ten enumerated by Reimarus.[6] This attitude,

---

[3] Or the traditions on which the records are based.
[4] By John Wenham, Warden of Latimer House, Oxford.
[5] *The Narratives of the Resurrection* (London, 1926), p. 60.
[6] *Encyclopaedia Biblica*, col. 4041.

moreover, pervades page after page of C. F. Evans's recent work *Resurrection and the New Testament,* to which I shall refer frequently in this chapter, and in which he dogmatically asserts that "it is not simply difficult to harmonise these traditions, but quite impossible."[7] In a much more judicial way, Michael Ramsey remarks:

> So far from disregarding historical criticism, I believe that it leads us to the radical conclusion that we cannot with certainty reconstruct an ordered plan of the Easter traditions in the Gospel narratives. But I also believe that it will be increasingly realised that our inability to do this is not surprising, and does not destroy the historical value of the traditions as congruous with the Apostolic preaching that Christ was raised on the third day.'[8]

And C. H. Dodd speaks with similar caution and moderation when he observes that the various stories "differ considerably in the several gospels, and perhaps cannot be fully harmonised".[9]

In this context there are three preliminary points which I should like to make. First, that those who have sought to construct this "harmony" have been prompted to their work primarily by a desire to defend the inerrancy of the Bible, rather than the cogency of the evidence for the resurrection, while those who have exaggerated the alleged discrepancies in the traditions have equally, I think, been influenced by preconceived ideas and assumptions of an entirely different kind.[10] But although my own inclinations are, admittedly, in favour of a positive rather than a negative approach, I shall do my best to weigh the evidence impartially and assess the credence which can be given to

[7] Op. cit., p. 128.

[8] *The Resurrection of Christ,* Preface.

[9] *The Founder of Christianity,* p. 28.

[10] As D. H. van Daalen remarks, "Traditions may serve a particular purpose in the community, but that does not necessarily mean that they were invented for the purpose". *The Real Resurrection* (Collins, London, 1972), p. 41. But this is only one of several assumptions which are often made.

it, or the criticisms which may be levelled against it, on their intrinsic merits. Secondly, it is common experience for a lawyer to note how a number of witnesses will almost invariably give accounts which differ widely from each other, initially at least, about any incident at which they have all been present. Each individual will see it from a different angle (both literally and metaphorically); will note some, but by no means all, of the relevant facts; and will usually be highly selective in what he actually remembers. To a considerable degree, therefore, minor differences in some of the resurrection stories may be regarded as actually strengthening the evidence rather than weakening it; for if a number of witnesses tell exactly the same story, with no divergences, it is nearly always a sign that they have been "coached" as to what they should say, or at least have conferred together on the subject. It will, of course, be objected that some of the discrepancies in the records which have come down to us must be regarded as going beyond the point of minor differences in detail, and must be categorised, with Schmiedel, as "contradictions of a most glaring kind" which might be held to invalidate these particular elements in the web of evidence almost completely. So it is in this context that I must make my third preliminary point: namely, that a lawyer who examines this evidence feels that he would give almost anything to be in a position to question the original witnesses and elucidate, from their own mouths, some of the problems concerned.[11] The documentary evidence we have before us is fragmentary in the extreme and, self-evidently, highly selective; so to infer that one of our authorities "did not know" some of the evidence recorded by others which he himself omits represents a wholly unwarrantable assumption. Many illuminating and largely convincing suggestions have been made—literary, theological and otherwise—as to why one evangelist concentrates on part of the evidence and another on a different part. It could only be by a process of question and answer that points like this could be finally resolved. Obviously,

[11] See above, pp. 15 f., and below, pp. 145 f.

109

this is not possible; but it is nothing short of arrogant narrow-mindedness to deny that, were it possible, many of our difficulties would probably disappear into thin air.

Only this week I came across some wise words written more than a century ago by an exceedingly orthodox commentator on the Gospel of Mark.[12] In commenting on chapter 16 he notes the "confusion which confessedly exists in this part of the gospel narrative" which is "the natural effect of the events themselves, as impressed upon the senses and the memory of different witnesses", and remarks that, seeing we have in fact "not a single but a fourfold picture", we must "purchase the advantage of this varied exhibition, by submitting to its incidental inconveniences". He then continues:

A large part of the difficulty, practically felt as to the gospels, has arisen from the error of attempting the impossible, to wit, the resolution of four landscapes into one. . . . The extent to which these harmonistic methods have been carried, has produced a natural though not a rational reaction towards the opposite extreme of denying all consistency and unity in these inspired variations of a single theme, and converting even incidental proofs of oneness into pretended proofs of contradiction. Between these extremes of error, as in multitudes of other cases, there is happily a middle course of truth and moderation, which, refusing to reject the tokens either of essential harmony or unessential variation, endeavours to account for every seeming inconsistency, and yet to leave each narrative in undisturbed possession of its characteristic and designed peculiarities.

Here many theologians will instinctively recoil from the assumption behind the words "these inspired variations of a single theme"; will regard the phrase about "essential harmony or unessential variations" as an inadequate des-

[12] J. A. Alexander, who finished his commentary in Princeton in 1858. It has been reprinted by the Banner of Truth Trust (London), 1960. Cf. pp. 432 f.

cription of the state of the evidence; and will view anyone who "endeavours to account for every seeming inconsistency" with the deep suspicion reserved for those
who engage in special pleading. Very well; but is it not a
matter of plain common sense to make a *reasonable*
attempt to resolve apparent inconsistencies in any web of
evidence before jumping to the premature conclusion that
the witnesses—or, indeed, one and the same witness—have
presented us with "glaring" and "irreconcilable" contradictions?[13] Having spent some time browsing in this subject, I
must state unequivocally that, if we must go to one extreme
or the other, I find the "preliminary exploration" by John
Wenham of the way in which the records *could* be
harmonised—with admirable logic and cogency, although
admittedly on the basis of numerous suggestions and
assumptions that only an interview with the witnesses
themselves could possibly sustain—considerably more
persuasive than the dogmatic assertions made by many of
those who seem to approach the records with a marked
bias (whether conscious or unconscious) in the opposite
direction, and who do not hesitate to make bland assumptions which are not only equally incapable of substantia-
tion, but which often seem to me to fly in the face of reason.

II

Perhaps I should give some examples of the sort of thing
I have in mind even before I turn to the evidence as a
whole. It is often assumed, for instance, not only that Luke
knew nothing of any alleged appearances of the risen Lord
in Galilee, but that he represents all the resurrection
appearances, and even the ascension (as this is commonly
understood), as taking place within the brief compass of
Easter Day). Now there is no doubt whatever that the last

[13] As van Daalen sensibly remarks, "so long as all the available evidence
can be accounted for in some way or other it would be rash to discount
any part of the evidence or reject it out of hand". (Op. cit., p. 40.)

chapter in his Gospel *could* be read in this way, and C. F. Evans is, perhaps, justified in saying that "on the most natural reading of the text the journey to Bethany follows immediately" after the incidents previously recorded.[14] But not only would this, as he remarks, "seem to involve an appearance and journey at night", but—much more formidably—it would represent a glaring contradiction (*pace* Schmiedel) of his own statement in Acts 1:4 about appearances and teaching spread over a period of "forty days" between Easter and his account of the ascension, and indeed the words he attributes to Paul in Antioch in Pisidia that the risen Lord "was seen many days of them which came up with him from Galilee to Jerusalem".[15] As Michael Ramsey pertinently remarks:

> May there not be a break before the discourse at verse 44, or before the walk towards Bethany at verse 50? In the opening verses of Acts Luke seems to correct any impression he may have left that the events all happened on the one day.... It is wrong therefore to infer that Luke's narrative excludes the possibility that there were, in fact, appearances in Galilee. Nor is Luke's own omission of any Galilean tradition difficult to explain.[16]

To this last point we must return later. But this example is sufficient, it seems to me, to show how exceedingly dangerous it is to make sweeping assumptions from the way in which such ancient and fragmentary records *could* be read. It is absurd to suggest that the same author would contradict himself in this direct and palpable way— particularly when the apparent contradiction can so easily be eliminated by the simple expedient of reading the records with a little more elasticity and imagination. And this may, I think, be highly relevant to how we should read the other records. Why need we assume that different

---

[14] Op. cit., p. 96. Van Daalen is even more emphatic (Op. cit., pp. 24 f.). (Cf. also Lampe, op. cit., pp. 47 and 49).

[15] Acts 13:31.

[16] Op. cit., pp. 65 f. *Pace* van Daalen, op. cit., p. 22.

traditions are necessarily contradictory, when they can perfectly well be regarded as complementary? Why, indeed, should any reasonable suggestion as to how they can be harmonised be regarded with such deep and instinctive suspicion?

Other illustrations of precisely the same point can be cited from the same chapter in Luke. It has often been remarked with surprise, for instance, that no account is given in the Gospels of a private interview of the risen Christ with Peter, although an appearance to Peter is put in the forefront of the list of resurrection appearances in I Cor. 15. But when Luke records that the two disciples returning from Emmaus found "the Eleven and the rest of the company" saying "It is true: the Lord has risen; he has appeared to Simon", C. F. Evans gratuitously comments that "Luke is only able to make the point by an awkward insertion at the tail end of another story, which now assumes the prominence, and at the price of following it with a story of an appearance to those who already believe, though the story itself does not fit this situation. Luke was presumably unaware of any story of an appearance to Peter alone."[17] But on what grounds, it may be asked, is this reference condemned as an "awkward insertion" in what is, on any showing, a highly compressed record? Why, moreover, should an appearance to "those who already believe" be considered superfluous? Did not their dawning faith stand in need of strengthening and confirmation, and was there not much that the risen Christ would want to say to this insignificant band of very ordinary men, to whom he was committing the all-important message of the meaning of his death and resurrection? And is it really likely that Luke, the companion of Paul, was completely ignorant of any appearance of the risen Lord to Peter?

We can find further examples of a hypercritical approach in a number of assumptions, all of which seem to me quite unwarranted, which Evans makes in his comments on this chapter. The mild remark "Thus Luke turns the awkward corner"(but why is it so "awkward"?) is only a preface to a

17 Op. cit., p. 107. Cf. Lampe, op. cit., p. 49.

series of observations such as "Luke is here *almost certainly* operating *solely* on the basis of the Markan text with its mention of Galilee, and he here gives some indication of the extent to which he was prepared to rewrite his Markan original if this was required."[18] *Sed quaere.* On the next page, in a footnote, he mistakenly asserts that "Luke expressly contradicts Matthew and John in denying that any women had seen Jesus at the tomb." But Luke 24:23 in fact states that, after the women had "failed to find his body" and had returned with the news, "some of those who were with us went to the tomb", found it empty, but did not see the risen Lord. This presumably refers to the visit by Peter and John to the tomb, not to that of the women — so I cannot see that these verses "expressly contradict" the tradition that Mary Magdalene saw the risen Lord at the tomb, or that other women saw him later that morning. Again, on the next two pages, he comments on the record of the walk to Emmaus: "In its present form the legend has become a highly artificial vehicle for a statement of the apostolic preaching as it is found later in the Acts, which is here according to the requirements of narrative distributed between the participants." But is it really so intrinsically unlikely that the risen Lord gave his disciples, both on this and other occasions, the teaching they so urgently needed about the necessity for, and meaning of, his passion? On the next page he remarks that at verse 27 ("Beginning with Moses and all the prophets, he interpreted to them in all the scriptures the things concerning himself") the narrative temporarily breaks down, "as though the two already knew that the one talking to them was Jesus the Messiah". But much the more natural explanation of the verse is that the one who had suddenly joined them explained what the Old Testament said about the Messiah, and it was only afterwards that they realised that he was in fact speaking of himself. On the next page, again, he comments on the appearance to the Ten in the Upper Room: "The fright and terror it occasions follow awkwardly after the previous assured statements that the

[18] Op. cit., pp. 92 and 103. My italics.

Lord had risen and appeared to Peter." But is this sound psychology, to say nothing else, in regard to those to whom the risen Lord suddenly appeared, in spite of closed doors, with the mystery which evidently surrounded all the resurrection appearances? Almost immediately, moreover, he adds that, in the Johannine account, "the joy is joy at the resurrection itself and at recognition, in Luke it is a joy which hardly allows belief and needs a further act of eating to confirm it." But here he fails to observe that in John the joy was consequent on the risen Lord "showing them his hands and his side", and that in Luke we read that the disciples "were still unconvinced, still wondering, *for it seemed too good to be true*".[19] And so the weary sequence proceeds, assumption and assertion following each other in rapid succession.

III

But we must turn to a much more positive examination of the relevant evidence. This must, I think, be primarily based on the tradition recorded in I Cor. 15:3 ff, which begins with the statement "that Christ died for our sins, in accordance with the scriptures; that he was buried; that he was raised to life on the third day, in accordance with the scriptures" and that he subsequently appeared to a number of specified witnesses. Now by common consent this chapter was written some twenty-five years after the event; but the apostle tells us that he had already "handed on" to the Corinthians—presumably by word of mouth—this tradition which had previously been "imparted" to him. Much more important, it seems exceedingly probable that he himself "received" this authoritative tradition, in essence at least, immediately after his conversion—which may itself be dated anything from two to five years after the crucifixion.[20] But, however that may be, he must certainly

19 My italics.
20 Cf. A. M. Hunter, *Paul and his Predecessors* (SCM Press, 1961), pp. 15–18.

have received it in full on the occasion of his first visit to Jerusalem three years later, about which he tells us in Gal. 1:18 ff.[21] It was then that he stayed for two weeks with Peter and saw also "James the Lord's brother"—and it is significant that he mentions a private interview of the risen Lord with both Peter and James in the list of appearances which he here records. This means that this particular tradition was received by Paul possibly within two years, indubitably within eight years, and most probably within five years of the event. He received it, moreover, from those who were Christians before him, so it must go back to the very beginning of the Church; and he explicitly states that it was the common message of the apostolic band.[22]

So far scholars are, today, in substantial agreement. But then we come to at least six matters of debate. First, it is not at all clear where precisely the primitive tradition ends and Paul's own comments begin. The Greek suggests that the phrase "and that he appeared to Cephas, and afterwards to the Twelve" was certainly part of the original tradition, and also—but with less certainty—the phrase "Then he appeared to more than five hundred brethren at one time." It seems obvious that the succeeding comment "most of whom are still alive, though some have died" was added by Paul to underline the weight of the evidence—supported as it was by the testimony of some three or four hundred persons who were still alive when he wrote this letter (twenty years or so after he had himself received the tradition) and who were therefore available to confirm or deny what he said. It also seems probable that Paul himself added the reference to the appearance to James (presumably on the latter's own testimony when Paul met him on his visit to Jerusalem) and "to all the apostles". But it does not seem to make very much difference precisely where the primitive tradition ends and where Paul's addenda begin. The vital points are the exceedingly early date of the tradition, the explicit testimony of Paul, and the large number of witnesses who were still alive even when he

[21] Cf. Wolfhart Pannenberg, op. cit., p. 90.
[22] I Cor. 15:11.

wrote this letter. As C. H. Dodd puts it: "No statement could be more emphatic or unambiguous. In making it Paul is exposing himself to the criticism of resolute opponents who would have been ready to point to any flaw in his credentials or in his presentation of the common tradition."[23]

The next matter of dispute concerns the appearance to Paul himself, which clearly was not part of the original tradition. It seems to be assumed by most theologians that the apostle puts his own experience on the road to Damascus completely on the same level as the appearances attributed to the "forty days"—with the obvious implications which this might be thought to have as to how he himself regarded all the resurrection appearances. But it is not at all certain that this is the necessary import of his words. As I wrote some years ago: "It is true that in I Cor. 15 Paul refers to his own encounter with the risen Christ as though it were on a par with the appearances to the other apostles; but he probably means that his experience was as real and 'objective' as theirs, not that theirs was as 'visionary' as his."[24] C. F. Evans, moreover, seems to me to make quite unnecessarily heavy weather about the phrase that it was "last of all" (or, as the N.E.B. renders it, "in the end") that the Lord appeared to Paul, too.

There is the theological-psychological question of how Paul was able to say, categorically, that the appearance of the risen Lord to himself was 'last of all'. Is this meant to be a factual statement that, as far as he had been able to discover, there had been no appearance of the risen Lord to anyone subsequently to his own—if so,

[23] "The Appearances of the Risen Christ", in *Studies in the Gospels*, ed· by D. E. Nineham, (Oxford, Blackwell, 1955), p. 28.
[24] *Christianity: the witness of history* (Tyndale Press, London, 1969), p. 99. Cf. John Robinson, in *The Interpreter's Dictionary of the Bible* (Abingdon Press, New York, 1962), IV, p. 46, where he pertinently remarks: "So far from regarding his own vision as normative, he marvels at his right to include it in the series at all". This is, presumably, partly why Paul terms his birth "monstrous" or unnatural.

117

how did he know and how was he to be sure? Or is it an expression of the Pauline 'egoism', and of a dogmatic viewpoint about his own person, that with the appearance to himself and with his call to apostleship the period of revelation was over, and what remained was the mission of the gospel to the world until the parousia?[25]

But Stephen's vision of the risen Lord, just before he died, must have been burnt deeply into Paul's memory and conscience, yet he makes no mention of it here; and it is exceedingly unlikely that he would have suggested that somewhat similar visions might not subsequently be vouchsafed to others—as in the case of the writer of the Apocalypse on the island of Patmos. May not the reason why he adds his own name at the end of this list of witnesses be partly to confirm the fact of the resurrection from his personal experience, long after the "forty days", and partly to emphasise that he, too, fulfilled the basic condition of the apostolate—"monstrous" or "untimely" though this "birth" of his might be? This seems to me the natural meaning of the phrase "last of all" in this context, and it scarcely deserves to be called "egoism". This interpretation seems, indeed, to be confirmed by the next verse, which begins: "For I am the least (or last) of the apostles." When, moreover, Evans asks whether Paul himself would have "recognised the three accounts in Acts as satisfactory versions of what 'seeing' the Lord had meant to him",[26] I should think it exceedingly unlikely that he had not recounted to Luke, time and time again, how it was that, after he had "persecuted the church of God violently and tried to destroy it", God chose to "reveal his Son" to him and in him, in order that he might "proclaim him among the Gentiles".[27] Nor can I regard the alleged discrepancies[28] between the three accounts in Acts of Paul's experience as

[25] Op. cit., p. 46.
[26] Op. cit., p. 55.
[27] Gal. 1:13 and 15.
[28] *Pace* Lampe, op. cit., p. 36, who quite unnecessarily asserts that there is a contradiction here.

giving rise to any real difficulty. It is most unlikely that Luke would have contradicted himself in this way. Taking the three accounts together, it would appear that Paul's companions saw a great light and heard the sound of a voice, but saw nothing more than this and could not hear or distinguish the words which were spoken. Paul himself, however, did actually "see Jesus our Lord"[29] (whether visually, or in his verbal self-identification) and hear his words—although it may well be that the longer account of what he said includes, in the interests of brevity, some of the explanation of that message which was given to Paul a little later by Ananias or revealed to him in Arabia. This, indeed, seems to represent another example of how "discrepancies" are, all too often, quite unwarrantably blown up into contradictions.

The next (but, in my view, minor) matter of debate concerns what Evans terms "the form-critical question of the function which such a traditional formula was designed to perform in the church. Where does its accent lie, and what was it formulated to say and do?" he asks. "If its primary purpose was to assert the resurrection of Jesus with confirmatory evidence of eye-witnesses, why was it preceded by a statement of the saving nature of the death of Christ? If it was a summary statement of the saving nature of the death and resurrection, like similar statements in the New Testament, why was a list of appearances attached?"[30] But is it not sufficient to suggest that Paul felt the need to write to the Corinthians, at some length, on the whole question of the certainty and nature of the resurrection of the dead and the future hope of believers, and that he saw fit to begin his discussion with this very primitive (and, presumably, well-known) formula, *just as it was*, with a few personal addenda? To start with the fact that Christ "died for our sins" was, moreover, a most appropriate basis for his subsequent statement that "If Christ has not been raised, your faith is futile and you are still in your sins."[31]

[29] I Cor. 9:1.
[30] Op. cit., p. 46.
[31] I Cor. 15:17.

IV

Much more important, in my view, is the statement which is repeatedly made that we find no reference whatever in this chapter to the empty tomb. For that we have to wait for the Gospel records—written as they were, in their present form, at a distinctly later date. But while it is obvious that there is no explicit evidence in this chapter, and no specific mention in this primitive tradition, of the Gospel accounts of the emptiness of the tomb, it seems clear enough that there is an implicit reference. To begin with, what Asiatic Jew of the first century could possibly have written that "Christ died for our sins" (physically, of course), that "he was buried" (physically, of course), and that "he was raised again on the third day" if he had not believed that *something* had happened to the body which had been crucified and buried? The Greeks had a vague belief in a shadowy survival of the spirits of the dead in an underworld, but this was not an understanding of the nature of man, or of the meaning of "resurrection", which would have been recognised by Jews. Not only so, but Wolfhart Pannenberg pertinently asks: "How could Jesus' disciples in Jerusalem have proclaimed his resurrection if they could be constantly refuted merely by viewing the grave in which his body was interred?" And he goes on to quote Paul Althaus's statement: "In Jerusalem, the place of Jesus' execution and grave, it was proclaimed not long after his death that he had been raised. The situation *demands* that within the circle of the first community one had a reliable testimony for the fact that the grave had been found empty." Indeed, the whole resurrection *kerygma* "could not have been maintained in Jerusalem for a single day, for a single hour, if the emptiness of the tomb had not been established as a fact for all concerned". And Pannenberg then remarks:

Among the general historical arguments that speak for the trustworthiness of the report about the discovery of Jesus' empty tomb is, above all, the fact that the early

Jewish polemic against the Christian message about Jesus' resurrection, traces of which have already been left in the Gospels, does not offer any suggestion that Jesus' grave had remained untouched. The Jewish polemic would have had to have every interest in the preservation of such a report. However, quite to the contrary, it shared the conviction with its Christian opponents that Jesus' grave was empty. It limited itself to explaining this fact in its own way, which was detrimental to the Christian message.[32]

Geering, it is true, attempts to dismiss the records of the empty tomb by quoting Maurice Goquel's statement that

> If no one thought of making an enquiry about the empty tomb, it can only have been because discussions were raised at such time and place as made enquiry impossible. Either those who affirmed that the tomb was empty lived so far away from Jerusalem or such a long time after the burial of Jesus that their statement could not be verified or else no verification was ever possible because the tomb of Jesus could not be identified.[33]

He also quotes Geoffrey Lampe's remark that "Even assuming that Jesus' grave was known, which is by no means certain, it seems very possible that neither party was interested in it, or regarded the truth of Easter as dependent on it, until long after the event."[34] But leaving aside, for the present, the question of whether "the truth of Easter" is materially dependent on this point, it seems crystal clear that the resurrection *kerygma* was proclaimed with great effect in Jerusalem from the very first, that this would inevitably have raised questions as to whether anything had in fact happened to the body which had been laid in the grave, and that this must necessarily have focused

---

[32] Op. cit., pp. 100 f. Cf. van Daalen, op. cit., pp. 17 f. and 42; but contrast p. 40.

[33] Op. cit., pp. 33 (quoting from *Jesus the Nazarene*, p. 36).

[34] Op. cit., p. 53.

attention on the tomb. To suggest that it could not be "identified", whether by friend or foe, seems to me fantastic;[35] and the fact that we do not hear more about the tomb (whether in Acts or in the Epistles)—and, indeed, that there is no record whatever of its becoming a place of pilgrimage or reverence—can, I think, most naturally be explained on the basis that everyone knew it was empty.[36] If this had not been a matter of common knowledge, can one seriously imagine that Paul, for example, would never have called the matter in question? *Pace* Geering, John Robinson insists that the tradition about the burial of Jesus in the tomb, with its circumstantial explanation in all the gospel accounts, "must be accepted as one of the most firmly grounded facts of Jesus' life".[37]

Michael Ramsey summarises this question when he asks:

Did the empty tomb have a place in the primitive tradition? It seems that although the primitive tradition as we know it does not mention the *evidence* about the empty tomb, it none the less implied the belief in it. The words of the tradition, as Paul reproduces it, seem incomprehensible unless they mean that the body of Jesus was raised up.... Died—buried—raised: the words are used very strangely unless they mean that what was buried was raised up.... In default of the very strongest evidence that Paul meant something different and was using words in a most unusual way, the sentence must refer to a raising up of the body. The most radical of critics, Schmiedel, and the most scientific of critics, Lake, agreed that *belief* in the empty tomb is implied in these words.[38]

When, moreover, Lampe remarks that had Paul "known that the tomb was found empty it seems inconceivable that he should not have adduced this here as a telling piece of

[35] Cf. Pannenberg, op. cit., p. 103.
[36] *Pace* Lampe, op. cit., p. 53.
[37] Op. cit., p. 45. Cf. also Pannenberg, op. cit., pp. 103 f.
[38] Op. cit., pp. 42 f.

objective evidence,"[39] it is Lake who provides one of the most cogent replies. "Was there any reason why S. Paul should have supplied these details had he known them? Surely not. He was not trying to convince the Corinthians that the Lord was risen: he was reminding them that he had already convinced them."[40] As C. H. Dodd insists, when the early Christians, from the first, said "He rose from the dead", they "took it for granted that his body was no longer in the tomb. If the tomb had been visited it would have been found empty. The gospels supplemented this by saying, it *was* visited, it *was* found empty".[41] Künneth, moreover, asserts that it appears to be "as good as certain that the account of the empty tomb was definitely included in the apostolic tradition", and he quotes E. Stauffer's statement that "only an uncritical critic can today still describe the news of the empty tomb as legendary. All the historical evidence and critical consideration of the sources favours the conclusion that the tomb of Jesus was empty on Easter morning."[42] Lampe, it is true, suggests that it was meditation on the fact of the resurrection which "would produce the stories of the empty tomb". But this explanation seems to me to fly in the face of the evidence; and it is difficult for a lawyer to follow him when he immediately adds: "But no deliberate falsification is implied."[43] I find John Robinson much more convincing when he not only insists that the empty tomb is "almost certainly implicit" in the "pregospel tradition", but writes: "When we turn to the gospels, their evidence on the empty tomb is in substance unanimous. There are, indeed, differences of detail which at times have been given exaggerated prominence"; but none of these "is the kind of difference which impugns the authenticity of the narrative. Indeed, they are all precisely what one would look for in genuine accounts of so confused and

[39] Op. cit., p. 43.
[40] *The Historical Evidence for the Resurrection of Jesus Christ* (1907), p. 194.
[41] *The Founder of Christianity*, p. 166.
[42] Op. cit., pp. 93, 95. Cf. also Alan Richardson, *An Introduction*, p. 196. Stauffer, incidentally, was originally trained as an ancient historian.
[43] Op. cit., p. 18.

confusing a scene. The very absence of uniformity or harmonisation tells against any subsequent fabrication or agreed story."[44]

It seems to me, then, that there can be no reasonable doubt that the tomb was empty.[45] Even so, we are left with the further question whether this has any theological significance. There are a number of theologians today who would concede the fact—or, at the least, the extreme probability—that the tomb was empty but would contest its significance. What would it matter, they argue, if it could ever be shown that the bones of Jesus are still lying somewhere in the vicinity of Jerusalem? Could this, in any valid sense, be regarded as disproving the basic fact that he had risen again from the dead? Yet even B. H. Streeter (who himself regarded the evidence for the empty tomb as historically convincing, but believed that the body must somehow have been mysteriously removed by human hands) conceded that "the discovery of the empty tomb was to some extent a factor in confirming the Apostles in their belief in the Resurrection." On this Michael Ramsey pertinently comments: "It is here that the most difficult feature of Streeter's theory appears. A mistaken inference on the part of the disciples, who ascribed to the power of God what was really an act of unknown human interference with the tomb, was partly the cause of their belief! Here indeed is something hard to believe: that a kind of 'providential falsehood' had a place in the revelation of the Resurrection to the disciples and in the historical basis of the Christian faith."[46]

Geoffrey Lampe, as we have seen,[47] would go further. Since "the dissolution of the body is most certainly part of the universal lot of man" he finds it impossible to believe that this can have been "something from which the manhood of Christ was exempt". A resurrection of his "physical body, such as is implied by the empty tomb . . ., would

[44] Op. cit., p. 46.
[45] Cf. also pp. 97 ff. above.
[46] Op. cit., p. 50.
[47] Cf. p. 98 above.

point towards a docetic Christ who does not fully share the lot of men".[48] To this the obvious answer is, I think, fourfold. First, the historical evidence points strongly to the fact that the tomb was indeed empty. Secondly, it seems to have been an integral part of the apostolic witness that the body of Jesus had somehow been "raised". Thirdly, in I Cor. 15 Paul discusses both the resurrection of the dead and what will happen to those who are still alive at the parousia. The resurrection bodies of those who have died will, he says, be quite different, although in a sense derivative,[49] from their earthly bodies. Far from being "resuscitated" they will be "clothed upon", as he puts it elsewhere, with those "spiritual" bodies which are to displace their "physical bodies" and express their personalities in a far more complete and adequate way. Those still alive at the parousia will, on the other hand, "be changed in a flash, in the twinkling of an eye", and the physical body will be transformed into the spiritual. To this Lampe would reply: "But Jesus did in fact die." He did, indeed; but the evidence points to his resurrection—partly for evidential reasons, we may suppose—representing a bridge, as it were, between the experience of those who will have already died and those who will be still alive at the parousia. He died, but his body had not decomposed; and the evidence seems to indicate that it was transformed into his resurrection body—or, in other words, that the connection between his resurrection body and his earthly body was direct, not indirect, and when he received the former the latter could no longer be found. Fourthly, this is not the only respect in which Jesus did not "experience the *whole* of our human destiny". He was tempted in all things just as we are; but, unlike us, he never sinned.

A further problem with regard to I Cor. 15 concerns the sentence in the tradition that "he was raised to life on the third day according to the scriptures"—about which a

[48] Op. cit., p. 97.
[49] Primarily, I suppose, in the sense that they "embody", for a different mode of existence, the same person – and that they are, therefore, recognisable.

great deal has been written. What Scriptures, for example, did the apostle in fact have in mind as referring to the resurrection of Jesus from the dead? The Old Testament passages to which specific reference is made in the *kerygma* in regard to the resurrection are Psalm 16:8–11 (and especially "Because thou wilt not leave my soul in Hades, neither wilt thou leave thy Holy One to see corruption")[50]; Psalm 118:22–24 (and especially "The stone which the builders rejected is become the head of the corner")[51]; and Psalm 110:1 ("The Lord said unto my Lord, sit thou on my right hand, until I make thine enemies thy footstool").[52] Psalm 2:7 ("Thou art my Son: this day have I begotten thee")[53] is also taken as a reference to the vindication of Jesus as Son of God by the resurrection. Although, moreover, Isaiah 53:10–12 is not specifically quoted in the New Testament in this context, this chapter was so central to our Lord's own interpretation of his Messianic office,[54] and so basic to the apostles' understanding of the meaning of his passion, that it seems to me overwhelmingly probable that they regarded those verses as a further reference to the resurrection. It is clear, however, that none of these verses were so interpreted in Old Testament days, and that none of them, in themselves, can reasonably be thought to have given rise to the apostles' faith in the resurrection. It was only when it actually happened, when the risen Lord opened up to them "in all the scriptures the things concerning himself", and when they reflected on the event, that they came to understand these passages in this way.

V

But what of the phrase "on the third day"? I cannot

50 Cf. Acts 2:25–28; 13:35.

51 Cf. Acts 4:11; 1 Pet. 2:7.

52 Cf. Acts 2:34.

53 Cf. Hebrews 1:5 together with Acts 13:33.

54 See Vincent Taylor, in a number of different books (*The Atonement; Forgiveness and Reconciliation;* etc.). If the Old Testament foretold the *death* of the Messiah, then all the predictions of his perpetual dominion must, presumably, be regarded as a form of implicit testimony to the resurrection.

myself understand why so many scholars insist on taking the words "according to the scriptures" as a specific reference to this last part of the total statement. It seems to me much more likely that the apostle meant that the resurrection and exaltation of Christ as such were foretold, and that he added the words "on the third day" as a matter of historical fact. It is, of course, possible, but not at all likely, that Hosea's words "Come, let us return to the Lord. . . . After two days he will revive us; on the third day he will raise us up,[55] that we may live before him" *could* have been so interpreted; but they are never in fact quoted in the New Testament in this connection. As for Schmiedel's suggestion that the date of the resurrection was deduced from II Kings 20:5 (where the prophet tells Hezekiah of the Lord's word "Behold, I will heal you; on the third day you shall go up to the house of the Lord"), this seems to me fantastic. And the only other Old Testament allusion which could, I think, be quoted in this context is the story of Jonah to which, Matthew tells us, our Lord himself made reference as a simile or type of his death and resurrection. So Evans's remark that the mention of the third day "probably had its origin in the application of the scriptures rather than a visit of the women" seems to me very wide of the mark.[56] The evidence, as I see it, points much more strongly to C. H. Dodd's conclusion that the tradition "preserves a genuine memory that on that Sunday morning his tomb was found broken open and to all appearance empty".[57]

It is, I confess, a cause of continual amazement to me to note the extraordinary ingenuity with which some theologians find the most improbable sources for words and events for which a much more plausible explanation lies close at hand. Surely much the most natural reason for the mention here of "on the third day" is that it was, in point of

---

[55] A verse like this could, clearly, be regarded by some as legitimately applicable to the resurrection: but it could not have provided a basis for a fabrication of it.

[56] Op. cit., pp. 75 f.

[57] *The Founder of Christianity*, p. 167.

historical fact, on that day that the tomb was found empty, and that the risen Lord first appeared to his disciples?[58] It is true, of course, that the Gospel records do not tell us precisely when the resurrection itself took place; and Evans's remark that in Matthew's account of the descent of the angel and the earthquake "the resurrection now becomes public" and "the soldiers, with the women, become eye-witnesses to the resurrection" represents not only an exaggeration but a palpable misstatement.[59] Presumably, however, the early Church concluded from Jesus's own predictions about his resurrection that the Lord had risen somewhat earlier on the same morning.[60] I find utterly unconvincing Evans's bald and categorical statement that a reference to Jesus having said "After three days I shall rise" *cannot* be to any public statement of his. In this context Morison's argument about the evidence for the fact that one of the accusations levelled against our Lord in his examination before the Jewish leaders must have been based on a prediction of his death and resurrection in terms of the destruction and rebuilding of the Temple is, I think, far more persuasive.[61] There are, of course, a number of occasions in the Gospels when predictions of his passion and resurrection are attributed to Jesus; but these are all dismissed by many critics, chiefly on one or both of two dogmatic grounds. The first of these, that Jesus could not have known what was going to happen (except in general terms of an impending danger and doom), depends, essentially, on the theological view which is taken of what degree of supernatural knowledge may fairly be attributed to the Jesus of the Gospels—and this is, of course, only a very special case of the broader question whether we can accept any of the predictions recorded in the Bible, whether

[58] Cf. Gerhard Delling in *The Significance of the Message of the Resurrection*, p. 80.

[59] Op. cit., p. 57. Almost everyone agrees that the stone was rolled away to let the women (and others) in, not to let the risen Lord out; and it seems tolerably clear that the stone had been moved before the women arrived. See below, pp. 143 f.

[60] Or, indeed, learnt this fact from the risen Christ.

[61] See below, p. 146.

vouchsafed to prophets, apostles or the incarnate Lord, without trying to explain them all as *ex post facto* statements of what subsequently happened. The second of these grounds is the assertion that, if these predictions had in fact been made, then surely the disciples would have expected the resurrection from the first; and it is obvious that they did not. But this, I think, overlooks the basic fact that they had a very clear-cut picture of the role that the Messiah was to fulfil, and this certainly did not include crucifixion—together with the supplementary fact that Jesus often, it seems, made somewhat enigmatic remarks which the disciples completely failed to understand, and that these predictions must clearly be numbered among them. It was only after the event that they remembered, and understood, what he had said; and this, it seems to me, is singularly true to life. Thus Michael Ramsey states that "it is likely that predictions of a rising again were made by Jesus"; that "besides the three 'formal' predictions there are other more allusive ones"; and that these "are mysterious, elusive: the more so because Jesus made predictions in other kinds of imagery too."[62]

Little space need be given to the theory espoused by Geering and a number of other writers that the resurrection on the third day is a reflexion, in part at least, of some of the mystery religions. "A Sumerian reference to the descent of Inanna into the underworld states that the goddess remained there for three days and three nights", he writes, and it is also recorded that "the death of Osiris was celebrated on the 17th of the month and his 'discovery' or 'resurrection' was on the 19th day." Again, the "counterpart of the Adonis cult in Rome was that of Attis, whose untimely death was celebrated every spring in a three-day festival, in which, on the third day, he was found."[63] On this I need only remark here that S. H. Hooke justly emphasised the "immunity of the Jew to the influences of the Mystery cults"; insisted that "between the eternal, immortal, invisible and only wise God, and the dying and rising gods of

[62] Op. cit., pp. 38 f.
[63] Op. cit., pp. 89, 90.

the Mystery cults, there was a great gulf fixed"; and remarked that it is deeply significant "that the first Christian community was wholly Jewish and that the first great original Christian thinker was a Jew"—and it was he, of course, who recorded this tradition. Not only so, but in the case of Osiris we are told that "after his consort Isis had sought and reassembled thirteen of the fourteen pieces into which his body had been dismembered by his wicked brother ... through the help of magic she was enabled to re-animate his corpse." The contrast between this and the testimony of the apostolic church to the resurrection of a historical person, whom they had known and to whose resurrection they could give personal testimony, is obvious. It is also significant, B. M. Metzger remarks, that the evidence for the commemoration of the *Hilaria*, or the coming of Attis back to life, cannot be traced back beyond the latter part of the second century A.D., and in the case of Adonis, again, the only four witnesses that refer to his resurrection date from the second to the fourth century of the Christian era—while the tradition about the resurrection of Christ on the third day can, as we have seen, be traced back to well before the middle of the first century. So, if borrowing there was by one religion from another, it seems clear which way it went.[64]

The insistence "on the third day" in the New Testament records emphasises, moreover, the distinction between the resurrection and any idea of a mere spiritual survival. It was not that the deathless spirit of Jesus could not be killed, but that on the third day, by human calendars, he was "raised" from the dead. As Denney puts it: "The third day was the first day of the week, and every Sunday as it comes round is a new argument for the resurrection. The decisive event in the inauguration of the new religion took place on that day—an event so decisive and so sure that it displaced even the Sabbath, and made not the last but the first day of the week that which Christians celebrated as holy to the Lord. The New Testament references to the first day of the

[64] See, in this context, my book *Christianity and Comparative Religion*, pp. 36 ff., together with footnote references.

week as the Lord's day[65] are weighty arguments ... for a resurrection which has a place and weight among datable events."[66]

VI

Finally, Evans questions the reason why the Gospel accounts of the resurrection appearances differ so widely from the list given in I Cor. 15.[67] This must, in the nature of the case, be largely a matter of conjecture. I have already discussed the period which elapsed between the crucifixion and the appearance of our Gospels in their present form, and have made passing reference to the light which Source Criticism, Form Criticism and Redaction Criticism can throw on the way in which the traditional material on which they are based was formulated, preserved and edited.[68] It is obvious, of course, that the Gospels include an interpretative element, for a bald narration of facts without any explanation of their significance would not have met the needs of preaching the Good News to Jews and Gentiles, preparing converts for baptism, and answering the many questions which must continually have been asked. But this does not alter the fact that the Gospels were clearly intended as history, even if "kerygmatic history"; and that a great part of the material will pass the test of the most rigorous historical criticism. All the same, it is clearly possible to suggest that the Gospel writers, or those from whom they derived their material, might have embroidered it somewhat by inserting incidents and details which they themselves may have genuinely believed to be implicit in it, but which the companions of Jesus would not have authenticated.

It is at this point that we must give due weight to the force of orthodoxy, which a break-away sect needs even

[65] Acts 20:7 and Rev. 1:10.
[66] Op. cit., pp. 113 f.
[67] Op. cit., pp. 52 ff.
[68] pp. 33 ff. above.

more urgently than does its parent body. The primitive Church must have been desperately anxious to remain faithful to the apostolic tradition;[69] and I Cor. 15 itself provides direct evidence, as we have seen, that some three or four hundred witnesses to having themselves seen the risen Christ were still alive in about 55 A.D.—so a very considerable number of such witnesses must have been available throughout the whole of the "twilight period", right up till the time when the Gospels in their present form began to appear. In the meantime much of the oral teaching of the companions of Jesus must have been committed to memory, in the way common in the East even today, and some of it produced in written form. It seems exceedingly unlikely, therefore, that any major innovations would have escaped detection and censure. This does not mean, of course, that mistakes *could* not have been made or that alternative explanations of authentic traditions could not have been preserved. But it seems most unlikely—quite apart from any belief in supernatural guidance[70]—that, as long as those who had actually known Jesus survived, anyone would have ventured deliberately to introduce fictitious material, to insert wholly unauthenticated traditions, or to deny what had already been authenticated.

It would seem to follow, then, that although there are many possible explanations for the manifest differences between the three Synoptic Gospels on the one hand, and the Synoptists and John on the other—e.g. access to different witnesses and strands in the tradition, whether oral or written; the particular theological insights of each evangelist; and the methodological structure of their compositions—the discrepancies between them should not precipitately be written off as contradictions, and certainly not as crude inventions. For the rest of this chapter, therefore, I shall take the material included in the Gospels, not indeed as though it were possible to regard the evangelists as themselves standing in the witness-box and giving their personal testimony, but as statements which

[69] Cf. I Cor. 15:3; I Cor. 11:2; II Thess. 2:15 and 3:6; II Tim. 1:13 f. etc.
[70] See p. 64 above.

can be extrapolated as based on traditions accepted by a small "heretical" community as authoritative and reliable in terms of their exceedingly vulnerable situation; and I shall review this evidence to try to determine whether it is as unsatisfactory and contradictory as is often alleged today, or whether it cannot, in fact, be regarded as standing up very well to such examination.

Two initial observations may, I think, be made in this context. First, it seems to me that Evans has exaggerated the "discrepancy between the list in I Cor. 15 and the gospel narratives". It is not altogether surprising, for example, that no mention of the appearances to women is included in this brief list; partly because the testimony of women was not at that time regarded as on a par with that of men, and partly because of a natural concentration on the testimony of the apostles as of primary importance. It seems clear, moreover, that Paul's list is confined to legally competent witnesses to an ocular recognition of the risen Christ—which is one reason why stories of the empty tomb are not included. As for the private interview between the risen Lord and the heartbroken Peter, this may well have been such that he did not normally describe it in detail, but preferred to speak instead of the incident recorded in John 21:2–18. When, however, Luke makes passing mention of this first encounter with Peter, Evans remarks that he has "some difficulty" in attaching it "as an awkward pendant to his Emmaus story".[71] The reference to the appearance to the "Twelve" presumably refers either to the occasion described in Luke 24:36 ff. and John 20: 19–23, or else to the subsequent appearance described in John 20:26–29. That to the "five hundred brethren at once" may, or may not, be identical with the incident of which an exceedingly brief mention is made in Matt. 28:16–20, in which some of the participants still "doubted". Why the interview between the risen Christ and his brother James is not described is not apparent—nor, as I see it, any reason for particular comment; while the appearance to "all the

[71] Ibid., p. 53. Contrast C. H. Dodd, "The Appearances of the Risen Christ", p. 28.

apostles" may, or may not, be identical with that in Bethany recorded in Luke 24:50 ff. and Acts 1:4–11, which we commonly call the "ascension".

The second observation I should like to make is that the fact that the basic tradition recorded in I Cor. 15 was, presumably, widely known in the early Church seems to me to make it somewhat easier, rather than more difficult, to explain the way in which the different evangelists felt free to be so highly selective in the resurrection appearances which they record. To say that Matthew knew of no appearances other than those in Galilee is a misstatement, for the appearance to the women mentioned in Matt. 28:9–10 should, presumably, be regarded as taking place in Jerusalem;[72] in Mark we can only make conjectures as to how chapter 16, subsequent to verse 8, may have originally concluded; the assertion that Luke knew of no appearances outside Jerusalem is dubious in the extreme in view of Acts 1:3 and 13:31; and as for John, there is no conclusive evidence that the appearance recorded in 20:26–9 took place in Jerusalem, and no evidence at all that the "appendix" in chapter 21—concerned, as it is, exclusively with Galilee—is not authentic. It may be suggested, therefore, that the evangelists felt free to concentrate on Galilee or Jerusalem, as the case may be—whether for literary, theological or other reasons—just because it was well-known that the risen Lord appeared in both. Michael Ramsey pertinently comments that the "evidence cited by Paul appears some decades later in ampler form in the narratives of the Gospels. The appearance to Cephas is alluded to in Luke; the appearance to the Apostles is described by Luke and John; an appearance to a larger number of disciples in Galilee is described by Matthew; there is no mention of an appearance to James."[73] And Künneth remarks that "it is extremely difficult to see how the Gospel accounts of the resurrection could arise in opposition to the original apostolic preaching and that of Paul." Here "invention by the Church contrary to the apostolic witness

[72] See below, p. 145.
[73] Op. cit., p. 42.

had no place among the Church's interests, nor could it have failed to be sharply contradicted by the apostles or their pupils."[74]

VII

Three other points, not directly connected with I Cor. 15, demand brief discussion: the connection between the resurrection and ascension or exaltation of Christ; the nature of his resurrection body; and a number of other matters in regard to which the Gospel records are allegedly not only confused but mutually contradictory. About each of these subjects the most categorical statements have been made by some of the writers to whom reference has already been made in this chapter, while other scholars are much more moderate, judicious and modest in their comments and suggestions.

We have already noted that Evans and others assert that what we commonly call the ascension is depicted, in Luke's Gospel, as taking place on Easter Day[75]—in spite of the clear contradiction that this would involve between the third Gospel and Acts. But he also states that throughout most of the New Testament

the two conceptions of exaltation and resurrection jostle each other. . . . Only in the Lukan writings is a relation between resurrection and exaltation firmly established. There the resurrection has the character of an interim, limited in purpose to providing visible proofs that Jesus is alive and a programme for the future, and limited in time to forty days, when it is succeeded by exaltation in the form of a further visible and describable event, the ascension, which brings the temporary resurrection period to a close.[76]

[74] Op. cit., pp. 92 f.
[75] Op. cit., p. 58; cf. also p. 96 and Lampe, op. cit., pp. 47 and 49 f. Lampe even asserts that Luke "insists" on this.
[76] Op. cit., pp. 136 f.

But it does not seem at all necessary to go all the way with this statement, and I see no reason whatever to concur in his assertions that the combination of the ideas of resurrection and exaltation in Col. 3:1 and Acts 2:30 ff. "is not without a certain awkwardness"[77] and that "the awkwardness of the combination of these two themes remains, and the attempt to derive from the gospels a resurrection appearance which brought home the truth not only of the resurrection but of the heavenly status of Jesus, other than the *legendary* narrative of Acts 1, is not very convincing."[78] Michael Ramsey, as Evans remarks, believes that Acts 1 does not stand alone as "evidence that the disciples saw an appearance which brought home to them not only the Resurrection but also the heavenly status of their Master".[79] Elsewhere, moreover, Ramsey very plausibly suggests that Christ's "journey to the Father" was completed on Easter Day. "It is clear," he says, "that John wishes his readers to understand that the ascension took place on Easter Day. This is in contrast with the account by Luke, where the ascension is described (Acts 1:9) as happening at the close of the series of appearances during forty days. The contradiction seems puzzling. The present writer makes this suggestion. Perhaps Luke and John have different happenings in mind. John is, in 20:17, alluding to (for he could never describe) the journey to the Father's glory, a going to the Father which, though it involves historical events, is essentially beyond history. Luke is describing in a concrete picture an event whereby Jesus gave to the disciples a visible assurance that the appearances were ended. There seems no inconsistency between the truth which John is teaching and the event which Luke is recording."[80]

Later in the same book he continues:

[77] Op. cit., p. 138.
[78] Ibid., p. 141 (my italics).
[79] Ibid., p. 140, quoting from an article on "What was the Ascension?" in M. C. Perry (ed),*Historicity and Chronology in the New Testament* (Theological Collections 6, 1965), p. 135.
[80] Op. cit., pp. 86-8.

The Creeds distinguish two separate events, the Resurrection and the Ascension. In so far as it is only Luke who describes the latter event, Christian tradition derives its conception of the event from Luke's narratives. In Luke 24:50-2 Jesus blessed the disciples 'and was parted from them'. The words 'and was carried up into heaven' are textually doubtful, and it cannot be affirmed with certainty that the 'Ascension' is mentioned in these verses. But in Acts 1:9 the reference to the Ascension is clear; at the close of the forty days Jesus 'was taken up and a cloud received him from out of their sight. . . .' Besides this narrative, there are in the New Testament many references to Jesus 'going to heaven' or 'being exalted' or passing 'to the right hand of God' or 'ascending'. It is generally believed that these phrases refer to an event distinct from the Resurrection and identical with that described in Acts 1:9. It is possible however that the Apostolic writers often made little or no separation between the Resurrection and the exaltation to heaven. . . . Yet the tradition in Luke concerning the Ascension as a distinct event cannot be dismissed. There is nothing incredible in an event whereby Jesus assured the disciples that the appearances were ended and that His sovereignty and His presence must henceforth be sought in new ways.[81]

This seems to me far more convincing that Evans's assertion that, in John, "there is no place for ascension as an event closing a period of forty days of appearances" or that, in Matthew, any ascension "in the Lukan or even the Johannine sense, or any subsequent movement from Galilee to Jerusalem, would be unthinkable"[82] after the appearance in Galilee with which the Gospel closes.

This brings us to the baffling problem—which can never be solved while we live in a world of three dimensions—of the nature of Christ's resurrection body. The records point decisively to the fact that the resurrection was not a mere

[81] Op. cit., pp. 121 f.
[82] Op. cit., pp. 83 and 117.

resuscitation of the human body of Jesus, on the one hand, or the appearance of a mere "ghost", on the other. Instead, as we have seen, the evidence suggests that his human body was transformed into a "spiritual body", which could, apparently, withdraw itself from grave clothes (perhaps without disturbing them), pass through closed doors, appear and disappear, be clearly heard, and be recognised only with some difficulty; but could display the marks of his passion and invite Thomas to touch them, and could even reassure his disciples by eating before their eyes. It is quite unnecessary to conclude, with Geoffrey Lampe, that "Bodily resurrection, to which the empty tomb would be appropriate, and a raising to a new and non-material dimension of existence, to which it would not, seems to be confusedly woven together in the synoptic traditions."[83] On the contrary, the transformation of the body fits in very well with the excellent evidence for the fact that the tomb was empty; and whether the risen body can be adequately described by a reference to a "non-material dimension of existence" is largely a matter of semantics. It is noteworthy that Caird insists that it is essential to the argument of I Cor. 15 "that the body of Jesus should have undergone such a metamorphosis".[84] Similarly, Künneth states that

The Risen One reveals in the appearances his glorified existence. Constitutive for the *concept of existence,* however, is the idea of *corporeality.* Thus the appearance of the Risen One becomes a revealing of the corporeal reality of the new life. The old dispute as to whether we are to speak of a resurrection simply as such, or of a bodily resurrection, is to be dismissed as a false antithesis. The reality of the resurrection means indeed in particular also the refashioning of concrete corporeal being.[85]

Predictably, writers like Evans make a series of categorical and confident assertions. He tells us that "it does not appear

[83] Op. cit., p. 54.
[84] *Saint Luke,* G. B. Caird (Pelican, London, 1963), p. 255.
[85] Op. cit., p. 87.

likely that Paul thought of his body as the object of earthly sight";[86] that Luke gives us a "thoroughly physical presentation of the appearances of the risen Lord"[87] in which he "eats to show his humanity";[88] and that in John it is obvious that Thomas is selected "to be the vehicle of a particular aspect of the resurrection and its consequences" in a way which makes it impossible to harmonise the separate appearances or the several attitudes of the disciples.[89] But Westcott perceptively remarks that "A little reflection will show that the special outward forms in which the Lord was pleased to make Himself known were no more necessarily connected with His glorified person than the robes which he wore."[90] Yet Westcott was equally insistent that Christ's glorified body was the body that had been raised from the tomb, for "it is not that Christ's soul lives on divested of the essence as of the accidents of the earthly garments in which it was for a time arrayed. It is not that His body, torn and mutilated, is restored such as it was. . . . But in Him soul and body in the union of a perfect manhood are seen triumphant over the last penalty of sin."[91] There was thus both continuity and discontinuity. I would myself agree with W. J. Sparrow Simpson when he says that "If the Body of Christ had been cremated, His Resurrection-Appearances must have assumed much the same characteristics of physical identity as those which the Evangelists report." But in point of fact it was not cremated, but had been very recently buried—and Simpson himself accepted the empty tomb as sufficiently well attested and "indispensable for the disciples' work and the disciples' faith." In the resurrection narratives the Evangelists, he suggested, "describe the re-entrance of the glorified Body of Christ into terrestial conditions, effected for the purpose of convincing His apostles of His

[86] Op. cit., p. 66.
[87] Op. cit., p. 104.
[88] Op. cit., p. 94.
[89] Op. cit., p. 119.
[90] *The Gospel of the Resurrection*, p. 112.
[91] Op. cit., p. 10.

Resurrection, and of giving them instructions and commissions". So a body which would normally be neither visible nor tangible temporarily reassumes the "solid frame, and former appearance, and marks of the wounds, for evidential and instructive purposes".[92] But if this is correct, then there seems to be no convincing reason to reject the tradition that the risen Christ ate a piece of broiled fish.

The frequent assertion that Paul bears witness to purely spiritual visions of the risen Christ, and that then the appearances are "represented as progressively more materialistic as the gospel tradition develops", is convincingly refuted by John Robinson when he insists that the only real evidence for this thesis "is that Paul regarded all the other appearances as conforming to the pattern of his own vision on the Damascus Road. But there is little basis for such a deduction".[93] In the Gospel records "it is arbitrary to arrange the appearances in order of increasing materialisation. All the appearances, in fact, depict the same phenomenon, of a body identical yet changed, transcending the limitations of the flesh yet capable of manifesting itself within the order of the flesh."[94] This is why the common argument that Paul's teaching that "flesh and blood can never possess the kingdom of God, and the perishable cannot possess immortality" is in direct contradiction[95] to the Lucan statement that "no ghost has flesh and bones, as you can see that I have", seems to me mistaken. The phrase "flesh and blood" is a common shorthand term for ordinary human nature, while the unusual phrase "flesh and bones" seems rather to point to a certain corporeality in the body of the risen Lord. As Robinson pertinently continues: "We may describe this as a 'spiritual' (I Cor. 15:44) or 'glorified' (cf. I Cor. 15:43; Phil. 3:21) body ... so long as we do not import into these phrases any

[92] *The Resurrection and Modern Thought*, (Longmans, Green & Co., London, 1911), p. 418–21.
[93] Op. cit., pp. 47 f.
[94] Op. cit., p. 48.
[95] Cf. Lampe, op. cit., pp. 50–4.

opposition to the physical as such."[96] This "spiritual" body would certainly not have needed food; but that does not mean that the risen Christ *could* not have eaten, any more than that he could not be touched; and the evidence points strongly to the fact that he *could* be touched. Nor is it at all difficult to suggest reasons why he should ask for food. In part this may have been to put the disciples at their ease and renew fellowship with them. And had he not done so, they might well have concluded, once his visible presence had been withdrawn from the upper room, that they had merely seen a vision. But when they looked at the bones of the fish, or the plate on which it had lain, this interpretation of their experience would be impossible; they would have had convincing evidence that someone had really been there.[97]

"If the Risen Body were not objective," C. S. Lewis has robustly remarked, "then all of us (Christian or not) must invent some explanation for the disappearance of the corpse. And all Christians must explain why God sent or permitted a 'vision' or 'ghost' whose behaviour seems almost exclusively directed to convincing the disciples that it was not a vision or a ghost but a really corporeal being. If it were a vision then it was the most systematically deceptive and lying vision on record."[98] And in this context Michael Ramsey pertinently comments: "The view of a spiritual survival of Jesus held by a long line of scholars has been frankly linked with the presuppositions that we have described. These presuppositions have often been decisive in the handling of the evidence about the tomb." Precisely; and Ramsey continues: "The criticism which rejects the empty tomb as *a priori* incredible or inconsequent or crude has its roots in a philosophy which is far removed from the New Testament. For the Gospel in the New Testament involves the freedom of the living God

[96] Op. cit., p. 48.
[97] Cf. my book *Christianity*: *The Witness of History* (Tyndale Press, 1969), pp. 99–100.
[98] *Miracles* (Geoffrey Bles, London, 1967), p. 178.

141

and an act of new creation which includes the bodily no less than the spiritual life of man.[99]

VIII

I cannot here discuss all the other respects in which the Gospel narratives are alleged to be contradictory. Evans, as we have seen, asserts that "it is not simply difficult to harmonise these traditions but quite impossible." But this is largely because he seems to have a positive obsession with contradictions, and sees them, or at least suspects their presence, where the evidence does not necessarily lead to any such conclusion.

I have already referred briefly to the question of whether the risen Lord appeared to his disciples only in Galilee, or only in Jerusalem, or in both—and whether the four Gospels may not be regarded as basically complementary, rather than contradictory, in this respect. Much more could, of course, be said about the purpose which each of the evangelists seems to have had in mind and why he concentrated on some of the appearances to the exclusion of others.[100] This singular selectivity is by no means uncommon in the Gospels. Robinson, moreover, justly remarks that "it has been suggested that the appearances, first in Jerusalem, then in Galilee, and finally again in Jerusalem, correspond with where the disciples would naturally have been during, between, and again during, the festivals of Passover and Pentecost." To insist that Luke depicts the risen Christ as commanding the disciples, on Easter Day, not to leave Jerusalem involves the unwarranted assumption that Luke asserts that the words attributed to Jesus in 24 : 49 were spoken on the same occasion as those recorded in the preceding verses, instead of towards the end of the "forty days". But unsubstantiated assumptions such as this

[99] Op. cit., p. 55.
[100] Cf. Denney, op. cit., pp. 146–159; Michael Ramsey, op. cit., pp. 62 ff.; van Daalen, op. cit., p. 38; C. F. D. Moule, *The Significance of the Resurrection*, pp. 4 f.; and Robinson, op. cit., p. 47.

seem, in fact, the common coin of much critical writing. When, for instance, we turn to Matthew's account of the guard set over the tomb, of the angel who rolled away the stone, and of the appearance of the risen Christ to some of the women, Evans is not content with a comprehensive reference to a "tissue of improbabilities"[101] and to additions to the Marcan account which "are either legendary and apologetic . . . or interpret the events by a crudely literal version of the supernatural",[102] but lets his imagination prompt him to make a number of specific criticisms which are themselves wide open to question and debate. "The guards at the sealed tomb, who are found only in Matthew's version, together with the women, who because of the sealing of the tomb can now come only to visit it and not to anoint the body, become spectators of a divine miracle," he asserts. But Matthew tells us that the Chief Priests asked Pilate to set a guard over the tomb on the day after the burial, so the women could scarcely have known about this;[103] and there is no conclusive reason why they should not have come to add their "spices and ointments" (as recorded in Luke 23:56) to those hastily provided by Nicodemus (as recorded in John 19:39) on the Friday evening.[104] Nor is it at all necessary to assume, from this very concise account, that the women had already arrived at the tomb when the earthquake is said to have occurred and the angel to have rolled away the stone.[105] It is intrinsically unlikely, on any showing, that the angel would address the women, in the manner recorded, in the presence of the guards—and there are a number of ways in which the story of the earthquake, and how the angel rolled away the stone, might have

[101] Op. cit., p. 86.
[102] Op. cit., p. 82 and p. 57. Lampe, op. cit., pp. 38 and 51, is equally dogmatic. But it is important to remember that the fact that something may be recorded for apologetic reasons does not, of itself, show that it did not happen.
[103] Cf. van Daalen, op. cit., p. 20.
[104] Cf. van Daalen, op. cit., pp. 16 f.
[105] Cf. John Marsh, *Saint John* (Penguin, London, 1968), p. 633; A. Plummer, *St. Matthew* (E. Stock, London, 1910), p. 417, etc. *Pace* Lampe, op. cit., p. 51.

become known.[106] It is perfectly possible, moreover, to regard Matthew 28:2–4 as a sort of parenthesis.[107]

It seems unnecessary, again, to insist on any fundamental contradiction between the Gospels in regard to the number of angels, the position in which they were seen or the messages they are recorded as having given. It is perfectly possible to suggest that Mary Magdalene, "the other Mary" and Salome might have set out, very early, to go to the tomb; that Mary Magdalene might have run on ahead, seen that the stone was rolled away, and gone to call Peter and John; that "the other Mary" and Salome might then have come to the tomb, seen the angel and heard his message; and that a little later Joanna and other women might have come and seen two angels, as did also Mary Magdalene when she returned to the tomb. Another possible suggestion is that where only one angel does all the speaking, the presence of another may well be ignored in a summarised account; or, as William Temple remarked, that any seeing of angels involves not only the objective fact of their presence but also the subjective faculty which enables a human being to perceive it. As for the position of the angel, the account in Mark does not say that the women found the angel inside the tomb; and he might well have been "sitting on the right side", on the stone, just outside."[108] Subsequently, he and another angel might have

---

[106] It would be contrary to human nature to imagine that the guards would never have told anyone what really happened, whatever that may have been.

[107] John Wenham points out (a) that the aorist is used, in a number of N.T. verses, for the pluperfect ("had"); (b) that early chroniclers not infrequently "incorporate in a single story a number of actions and speeches which have a common theme, not indicating at all the time of occurrence" or, alternatively, jump backwards and forwards "between two or more parallel sequences of events, leaving it to the reader to understand that each item is, as it were, a flash on a cinema screen". On this view the words "And beheld" might be regarded as heralding a switch to another flash.

[108] Alternatively, the angel who originally "sat" on the stone in the Matthew story might have entered the tomb after the guard had gone. In any case, the "young man" in Mark was almost certainly an angel; and T. W. Manson says that the Greek word translated "affrighted" (AV) "implies the terror which is aroused by the supernatural".

gone inside and sat "where the body of Jesus had lain, one at the head and one at the feet," as John records Mary as finding them on her return to the tomb—for there seems to be no reason to suggest that angels must necessarily remain completely immobile. Again, the substance of what the angel or angels are recorded as having said, in each of the Gospels, may well be supplementary rather than contradictory; for the sum of all their recorded statements would represent only an exceedingly short communication.

There is, moreover, no convincing reason to deny that the risen Lord may have appeared, somewhat later,[109] to a small group of women—when, for example, they were on their way to Bethany to give their news about the tomb to the disciples, who may well have been hiding in that village. The statement in Mark that the women "said nothing to anyone" must, in any case, presumably be understood as meaning that they said nothing to anyone until they got back to their own people.[110] It is also interesting to note, in passing, that Kirsopp Lake confessed, in later life, that F. C. Burkitt's suggestion that Peter, on receiving the message from the tomb, set out towards Galilee, only to be sent back to Jerusalem by an encounter with the risen Lord, was "sufficiently attractive to make me waver in my allegiance to the Galilean hypothesis".[111] There are, in fact, a number of different possibilities.

Now, it would be absurd to assert that any of these suggestions is necessarily correct, or that the evidence in these matters points decisively in this or that direction; but it is equally (or even more) ridiculous to assert that they are necessarily wrong, and that the evidence *could not* be so interpreted. But this is just what a number of theologians do in fact state, without any qualification or peradventure whatever. There is one way only in which such problems could be satisfactorily solved, as has already been remarked: by a judicious questioning of the

---

[109] In which case this appearance might well not have been known to the two in the Emmaus story: cf. Luke 24:24.

[110] Cf. van Daalen, op. cit., p. 17.

[111] See Michael Ramsey, op. cit., pp. 69 f.

witnesses concerned. Unhappily, this is impossible; so it is surely incumbent on all who attempt to assess this fragmentary evidence to put forward their theories with becoming modesty as hypotheses which, in their view, have a certain merit, and not as *ex cathedra* statements of fact.

This is, by and large, the way in which Frank Morison[112] sets out his theories—by discussing the evidence and then suggesting the conclusions to which he believes that it leads. I am myself far from convinced by many of his conclusions, although I think that he has made out a strong case for the setting of a guard, for the dream of Pilate's wife,[113] for Jesus's cryptic statement about the destruction and rebuilding of the temple,[114] and for the seven weeks' gap between the resurrection and its first public proclamation (for it seems exceedingly unlikely that the early Church would have invented such a gap if it was not a matter of history). It is interesting to note that Evans refers to Morison's book as "an outstanding and brilliant example" of a series of "inspired guesses and hypotheses".[115] But it seems to me that Morison pays much more attention to evidence as such than does Evans, and that the latter is far more prodigal than Morison in what I feel compelled to describe, in this context, as a series of uninspired guesses and brash assertions.

To substantiate this last statement I append a short selection of quotations from this book which seem to me to come within this category. "It is *plain* that Matthew's final chapter furnishes neither reliable historical information nor early Christian tradition about the resurrection."[116] Happily, many other scholars are much less extreme.[117]

[112] *Who moved the Stone?* (Faber, London, 1930).

[113] *Pace* Evans, op. cit., p. 82.

[114] The false testimony on this point at the interrogation before the Jewish leaders seems to represent a garbled version of John 2:19 (Cf. Mark 14:58 and Acts 6:14).

[115] Op. cit., p. 128.

[116] Op. cit., p. 85 (my italics).

[117] Cf. for example R. V. G. Tasker, *The Gospel according to Matthew* (Tyndale Press, London, 1961), pp. 270 ff. And Michael Ramsey, in commenting on certain elements in Matthew which "arouse a suspicion

"Strictly speaking, there is no place in the Fourth Gospel for resurrection stories, since the ascent or exaltation has already taken place. Nevertheless, and *doubtless* in deference to Christian tradition, the evangelist supplies three, to which a fourth has been added."[118] But what objection could there be to an already exalted Lord revealing himself, as risen from the grave, to his bewildered and despondent disciples?[119] The evidence, moreover, points strongly to the fact that the Fourth Gospel ends with the resurrection, rather than the exaltation of the cross, not out of "deference to Christian tradition", but for two very good reasons: first, deference to historical fact; secondly, that had the cross *not* been followed by the resurrection, no one would have considered it an exaltation. "That only Peter and the beloved disciple, and not all the disciples, are sought out by Mary, and that these alone go to the tomb, is connected with whatever purpose the evangelist had in mind in combining and contrasting Peter and this other mysterious figure in his gospel."[120] But might it not also, conceivably, be "connected" with the consideration that this was, in fact, what actually happened? On this passage William Temple writes: "It is most manifestly the record of a personal memory. Nothing else can account for the little details, so vivid, so little like the kind of thing that comes from invention or imagination."[121] "The interrogation before the Sanhedrin . . . appears to be one of the

---

that they present Christian *midrash* rather than history", immediately adds that "the presence of embellishments such as these makes it all the more impressive that the stories retain so many signs of a truly primitive perspective". (Op. cit., p. 60).

[118] Op. cit., p. 116 (my italics).

[119] Michael Ramsey, who insists that, in John, "the note of victory resounds through the story of the passion", clearly sees no difficulty here. He remarks that "if there is Life present in Death" in the passion narratives, "there is also the note of Death still to be heard in the midst of Life" in the narratives of the resurrection, with the Johannine emphasis on the wounded hands and side of the risen Lord (op. cit., p. 82).

[120] Op. cit., p. 121.

[121] *Readings in St. John's Gospel* (Macmillan, London, 1949), p. 376. Similarly, John Robinson sees here "no marks of an incipient legend" (op. cit., p. 45).

rare instances in which Mark felt compelled to fill in a gap
in his knowledge by an implausible, theologically motiv-
ated invention."[122] But surely this is a somewhat over-
confident statement, to say the least?[123] "The parousia
expectation ... has now irretrievably collapsed."[124] But
this, in my view, is an arrogant assertion with which many
would disagree. After a careful perusal of this disappoint-
ing book one is not surprised to find Evans remark (perhaps
somewhat wistfully?) that "the principal difficulty here is
not to believe, but to know what it is which offers itself for
belief."[125]

Geering, of course, goes even further in his sweeping
assertions. "Both the literary form and the actual content
of the earliest version, viz. the Marcan, show not only that
it *definitely* contains some legendary elements, but that it
is unlikely to have had *any historical foundation at all*", he
remarks.[126] When this Gospel was written, he asserts, "it is
likely that *none* of the original Apostles were still living",
so there was "*no-one* to raise authoritative objections".[127]
But it seems exceedingly probable that, of the Twelve,
John at least was still alive; and many of Paul's "five
hundred brethren" must necessarily have been available,
and could have raised "authoritative objections".[128] "Jesus
truly died. He remains dead for all time,"[129] he positively
(or negatively) asserts. But here he would be challenged
by almost all the other theologians I have quoted. The way
in which Geering often reasons can, perhaps, be illustrated
from two statements which are separated by only two
pages. On the first of these he writes, in regard to "the
tomb pericope", "If this supposition is anywhere near the
truth ..."[130]; and on the second he concludes: "We can

[122] Op. cit., p. 145.
[123] Many scholars, in point of fact, take a different view.
[124] Op. cit., p. 165 n.
[125] Op. cit., p. 130.
[126] Op. cit., p. 56 (my italics).
[127] Op. cit., p. 57 (my italics).
[128] Cf. pp. 36 and 116 f. above.
[129] Op. cit., p. 220.
[130] Op. cit., p. 50.

summarise the discussion up to this point by saying that the literary form of Mark's tomb pericope shows *definite* signs of having developed in three stages."[131] But there are, happily, few scholars who are likely to take Geering's book very seriously.

It will, perhaps, be salutary to end with the testimony of Dorothy Sayers, who approaches the traditions primarily from the point of view of another discipline:

The playwright, in any case, is not concerned, like the textual critic, to establish one version of a story as the older, purer, or sole authoritative version. He does not want to select and reject, but to harmonise.... And in doing this, he is often surprised to find how many apparent contradictions turn out not to be contradictory at all, but merely supplementary. Take, for example, the various accounts of the Resurrection appearances at the Sepulchre. The divergences appear very great on first sight; and much ink and acrimony have been expended on proving that certain of the stories are not 'original' or 'authentic', but are accretions grafted upon the first-hand reports by the pious imagination of Christians. Well, it may be so. But the fact remains that *all* of them, without exception, can be made to fall into place in a single orderly and coherent narrative without the smallest contradiction or difficulty, and without any suppression, invention, or manipulation, beyond a trifling effort to *imagine* the natural behaviour of a bunch of startled people running about in the dawnlight between Jerusalem and the Garden.[132]

[131] Op. cit., p. 52 (my italics).
[132] *The Man Born to be King*, (London, 1943), p. 35.

CHAPTER FIVE

Sin, Forgiveness, Judgment

I

We have been concerned in the last two chapters first with
the essential historicity of the resurrection and then with a
more detailed examination of the biblical evidence on
which this historicity rests. The numerous appearances of
the risen Christ were, it seems, far from uniform; but what
was common to them all was the central fact of recognition.
It was the same Lord Jesus whom they had known and
loved who revealed himself to them as alive and risen; and
it was this which gave rise first to sheer incredulity and
then to the wondering joy which is the most unmistakable
note in the New Testament proclamation. "The emphasis
laid upon physical aspects of the Lord's risen body is not",
as Robinson insists, "in the interest of materialisation for
its own sake but of placing beyond dispute his identity: 'See
my hands and my feet, that it is I myself (ἐγώ εἰμι αὐτός;)
handle me, and see'. . . . Every appearance has at its heart
a recognition scene, in which Jesus either says something or
does something which establishes his identity."[1] And one
of the chief ways in which he did this was by displaying
the marks of his Passion. This note runs through the whole
of the apostolic proclamation. "The returning Lord cannot
appear without the marks of the nails (John 20:25), the
Lamb victorious is the Lamb standing, 'as though it had
been slain' (Rev. 5:6), and the 'living One' is by definition
the one 'who died' (Rev. 1:18; 2:8). This note of continuity
is preserved throughout the apostolic preaching."[2] As we
have already noted, moreover, the most primitive tradition

[1] Op. cit., p. 49.
[2] Ibid., p. 50.

about the resurrection which has come down to us starts with the unequivocal affirmation that "Christ died for our sins according to the Scriptures"; the "cup of blessing" of which we partake, particularly on the day when we commemorate the resurrection, symbolises the blood which was poured out, as he himself said, "for the forgiveness of sins"; and it was God's raising of Christ from the dead which, as Paul declared at Athens, gives assurance that he will one day "judge the world in righteousness".[3]

But what, precisely, does the tradition mean by the words "Christ died for our sins according to the Scriptures"? And how do theologians and New Testament scholars understand these words today? It is to this subject that we must turn in this chapter: the meaning of what we call the atonement, together with some reference, however brief and inadequate, to the nature of sin, the connection (if any) between sin and death, and the biblical teaching about judgment. And this, in its turn, makes it essential that we should discuss, in part, the nature of God as this is revealed in the Bible; his attitude to sinners and their sin; the concepts of the love of God and the "wrath" of God; the basis of our forgiveness; and the way in which such terms as "propitiation", "expiation" and "reconciliation" are to be understood.

Obviously enough, the biblical concept of sin, and especially of the connection between sin and death, has been seriously undermined, at least in popular thinking, by the widespread rejection of belief in any historical "Fall". To the secular evolutionist of the past it was, indeed, perfectly simple to explain sin as no more than a regrettable relic of animal ancestry which would be slowly eliminated by the evolutionary process. But this is scarcely a tenable theory today; and the facile optimism of the pre-War years has largely given way to a philosophy of frustration, disillusionment and despair. Whatever its origin, there can be no doubt whatever of the fact of human sin and selfishness.[4] It is true that what some would regard

[3] Cf. I Cor. 15:3; Matt. 26:28; Acts 17:31.
[4] The Bible, indeed, throws little light on the origin of evil.

151

as the Christian obsession with the individual's "sins of the flesh" has been replaced, or at least mitigated, by a new emphasis on the corporate guilt of society in its avarice, exploitation and injustice. But a deeper sense of the solidarity of humanity in sin—and in sin which is very often not deliberate, but instinctive and almost inevitable—should make it easier, rather than more difficult, to accept the biblical doctrine of original sin. The fact that the account of both the creation and the fall in the first three chapters in the book of Genesis has been given in somewhat pictorial language[5]—the only language, indeed, which could be equally meaningful for successive generations of men—should not lead us to conclude that the basic teaching of the Bible that man was created in the "image and likeness" of God, but that this image has been sadly marred and defaced by sin, can no longer be accepted. To say with John Hick and F. R. Barry that "Man has never lived in a pre- or un-fallen state, in however remote an epoch. He has never existed in an ideal relationship with God, and he did not begin his career in paradisal blessedness and then fall out of it into sin and guilt"[6], is to make a dogmatic assertion without any adequate basis.

But Barry is surely right when he says that

> original sin means something fundamental in the whole human situation, and . . . so far from being harsh and savage, it is, rightly understood, a merciful doctrine. For it means that, while we are free moral agents and responsible for the sins we commit, yet none of us is solely responsible. . . . We are all together involved in a situation into which we were born, which comes to us by inheritance—partly genetic, still more social and cultural—by which all of us are conditioned and which seems in a real sense to be working through us.

[5] The "tree of life", for example, is mentioned at the beginning of Genesis and the end of Revelation; and I can see no reason why it should be regarded as literal in the first case and symbolical in the second.

[6] *Evil and the God of Love* (Macmillan, 1966), p. 181, quoted by Barry in *The Atonement* (Hodder and Stoughton, 1968), p. 46.

He then proceeds, quite gratuitously, to assert that this does not represent a falling away from "original righteousness" and that Adam bequeathed no "taint" to his posterity; but he still comes to the conclusion that "a tendency to sin *is* inherited", that "a propensity to commit sin must be recognised as innate in all of us", that we are "all born into an inheritance in which to do good is harder than to do evil", and that behind "sins" there lies, "at the very centre of personality, the far more intractable fact of 'sin', which belongs to the constitution of human nature and is omnipresent in all human experience—though it may not always be called by that name. Sin is man's estrangement from God", from his fellow-men and from himself. But he is estranged from himself primarily in the sense that he was created to be God-centred and God-dependent; and the very essence of original sin is that we are, all of us, born essentially self-centred creatures. This can be seen very clearly in infancy, long before a child is guilty of any deliberate sin. And Barry is certainly right when he says that, although modern man may not be worrying about his sins, yet "about sin he *is* worrying, desperately. We speak of alienation from our culture; St. Paul put it in more downright language—alienation from the life of God. . . . It is sin, of which sins are symptoms, which has to be cured. And that is something that man cannot do for himself, because sin resides in his own self-centred will."[7]

It is strange, therefore, that Barry ridicules the doctrine of "total depravity". It seems that he has not in fact taken the trouble to try to understand what this doctrine really means, but has contented himself with a caricature. It is not surprising, of course, that anyone who goes no further than the nomenclature of the doctrine, and his own deductions about what it denotes, should repudiate the whole idea. But the exponents of this doctrine are themselves careful to emphasise that it does *not* mean that every man is as evil as he could be, or that he cannot do good in any sense of that term: it simply means that man's inherent corruption extends to every part of his nature and that he

[7] Op. cit., pp. 54–7.

can do nothing that is *perfectly* good—or, as a hymn puts it, that he can do "nothing free from taint of sin". And this is pungently expressed by Paul in the third chapter of his letter to the Romans.

II

What, then, of the connection, in biblical teaching, between sin and death? Of this, Christopher Evans asserts that "for Paul death was associated with sin in a way it cannot be for us", and that it "remains a stubborn fact that this close inter-connection of sin and death is not an idea which modern man can share", so the New Testament "is bound to lose something of its force here".[8] But why? Basically, death is, of course, a symbol of that alienation from God of which F. R. Barry writes so movingly, as can be seen clearly in Paul's description of living men as "dead in trespasses and sins".[9] The aptness of the symbol, more-over, is not only that life in alienation from God is not life at all, in any true sense, but also that physical death, as we now know it, not only leaves us impotent but represents a stark and radical separation from everything that makes up human life and involves human relationships. It is idle, as I see it, to speculate as to what would have been the case had man never sinned. The Bible is emphatic that God alone has inherent immortality; but the Old Testament, in Alan Richardson's words, does not encourage the senti-mental notion that death, as we know it today, is "natural", or "a necessary and beneficial aspect of the ordering of nature; on the contrary, death is evil (Deut. 30:15,19), bitter (I Sam. 15:32), horrific (Ps. 55:4 f.): in short, it is unnatural, though the Bible does not know this expression. The fact that it is all these things is in some way connected with the fact that (like sin) it is alien to the divine nature

[8] *Resurrection and the New Testament*, p. 166.
[9] Eph. 2:1.

and is no part of God's original intention in the creation."[10] But he gratuitously continues: "How this alien thing (cf. I Cor. 15:26, 'the last enemy') found an entry into God's good universe we are not told"; for we are, in fact, told in both the Old and New Testaments that "death"—which presumably means not only spiritual death, but also physical death as we now know it—is the result of, and presumably part of God's judgment on, human sin.[11] But to return to Richardson: "the real horror which attaches to death is the fact that death is the symbol in the natural order, in a fallen world (cf. Gen. 3), of rebellion and separation from God."[12] In other words, death is "something that involves the whole man. Man does not die as a body. He dies as a man, in the totality of his being. He dies as a spiritual and physical being. And the Bible does not put a sharp line of demarcation between the two."[13] As Michael Ramsey puts it:

The connection between Sin and Death ... lies deep and widespread in the Biblical attitude to man. For if man is created in the image of God, in order that he may reflect God's own attributes and live in unbroken fellowship with God, then the true and perfect relation of God and man will have no place for death. This is not to say that man was once immortal, nor is it to deny that death is natural and inevitable to man as we know him. But it is to affirm that in the true and perfect manhood death has no place.[14]

It is in this context, I think, that we should interpret the Greek word $\dot{\epsilon}\nu\epsilon\beta\rho\iota\mu\dot{\eta}\sigma\alpha\tau o$ used in John 11:33 of our Lord's emotional reaction at the tomb of Lazarus. As B. B.

---

[10] Biologists may well question this statement; but we must concentrate, in this context, on human death *as we now know it*.

[11] Cf. Gen. 2:17; Rom. 5:12 and 6:23; I Cor. 15:56.

[12] *A Theological Word Book of the Bible* (SCM Press, London, 1957), pp. 60 f.

[13] Leon Morris, *The New Bible Dictionary*, (IVF, London, 1962), p. 301.

[14] *The Resurrection of Christ* (Geoffrey Bles, London, 1945), p. 21.

Warfield put it: "What John tells us ... is that Jesus approached the grave of Lazarus, in a state, not of uncontrollable grief, but of irrepressible anger. He did respond to the spectacle of human sorrow abandoning itself to its unrestrained expression, with quiet, sympathetic tears: 'Jesus wept' (verse 36). But the emotion which tore his breast and clamored for utterance was just rage." The word is twice repeated: "He raged in spirit" (verse 33); "raging in himself" (verse 38). But why such intensity of feeling, this "inwardly restrained fury" which "produced a profound agitation of his whole being"? And the answer Warfield gives is that

> the spectacle of the distress of Mary and her companions enraged Jesus because it brought poignantly home to his consciousness the evil of death, its unnaturalness, its 'violent tyranny' as Calvin (on verse 38) phrases it. In Mary's grief, he 'contemplates'—still to adopt Calvin's words (on verse 33)—'the general misery of the whole human race' and burns with rage against the oppressor of men. . . . It is death that is the object of his wrath, and behind death him who has the power of death, and whom he has come into the world to destroy.[15]

This is important because the way in which he was to "destroy him who had the power of death", and thereby liberate men from the bondage of fearing this "last enemy", was by dying himself. As Michael Ramsey puts it:[16] "He truly died. He underwent, so both the Gospels and the Epistles tell us, the whole fact of death in all its bitterness. . . . He tasted death for sinners, making Himself one with them. He took upon Himself the reality of death in its connection with sin." This was, indeed, "the deepest point of His loving identification of Himself with mankind. He put Himself beside them, He went the whole way with them, He shared in the darkness of their self-sought

[15] *The Person and Work of Christ* (The Presbyterian and Reformed Publishing Company of Philadelphia, Pennsylvania, 1950), pp. 115 ff.
[16] Op. cit., pp. 34, 22.

purely mysterious, and brought into the sphere of cause and effect: sin is the cause, disaster the effect. At the same time they taught that Jehovah was loving and merciful, and desirous of saving His people from disaster, by saving them from sin which is the cause of disaster. Of course they did not rationalise away the 'numinous' sense of the Wrath of God, but they brought into relief the personal relation of love and mercy in which God stands towards His people, and which transcends wrath. While there is a tension, not wholly resolved, between the wrath and the mercy of God, it would be fair to say that in speaking of wrath and judgment the prophets and psalmists have their mind mainly on events, actual or expected, conceived as the inevitable results of sin; and when they speak of mercy they are thinking mainly of the personal relation between God and His people. Wrath is the effect of human sin; mercy is not the effect of human goodness, but is inherent in the character of God. When they speak of His righteousness, as we have seen, they find it consummated in a merciful deliverance of His people from the power and oppression of sin — in fact, from 'the Wrath'.

So he proceeds to argue that the way was "open for a further development in which anger as an attitude of God to men disappears, and His love and mercy are all-embracing". This, he asserts, is

the purport of the teaching of Jesus, with its emphasis on limitless forgiveness and on God's fatherly kindness to 'the unthankful and evil'. In substance, Paul agrees with this, teaching that God loved us while we were yet sinners (Rom. 5:8) and that it is His kindness which leads us to repentance (Rom. 2:4). But he retains the concept of 'the Wrath of God' (which does not appear in the teaching of Jesus, unless we press certain features of the parables in an illegitimate manner . . .); he retains it, not to describe the attitude of God to man, but to describe an inevitable process of cause and effect in a moral universe.[23]

And A. T. Hanson has devoted a whole book to the elaboration of much the same thesis, but with certain significant modifications.[24] It is noteworthy, moreover, that in his more recent article on the subject in *A Dictionary of Christian Theology* Hanson states categorically that the wrath of God "is essentially impersonal. . . . The alternative is to regard God's wrath as his personal reaction to sin or to the sinner. This always leads to a fatal dichotomy; either God is depicted as loving and angry by turns, or, still worse, the Father is depicted as just and angry and the Son as merciful and loving."[25]

One cannot but feel, however, that both Dodd and Hanson—and a plethora of other writers—"protest too much" on this issue. Hanson's enthusiasm for his thesis has even led him to make statements which are manifestly incorrect—as, for example, when he states that in the New Testament neither God nor Christ is "ever described as angry or as being angry". But we are explicitly told in Mark 3:5 that in the synagogue, just before healing the man who had a withered hand, Jesus "looked around at them with anger ($\dot{o}\rho\gamma\acute{\eta}$), grieved at their hardness of heart".[26] Hanson does, however, concede that, throughout much of the New Testament, "it is constantly implied that unbelievers are in the sphere of sin, law and curse. . . . In view of this, Dodd's statement that the concept of wrath does not appear in the teaching of Jesus seems questionable." But he immediately adds that "the essential idea of judgment as an impersonal process can be traced in much of his teaching."[27]

Here the penultimate sentence is, as I see it, much closer to the New Testament evidence than Dodd's (or Hansons's)

---

[23] *The Epistle of Paul to the Romans* (Collins, Fontana Books, 1959), pp. 49 f.
[24] *The Wrath of the Lamb* (SPCK, London, 1957).
[25] pp. 362 f.
[26] Cf. also pp. 155 f. above.
[27] *The Wrath of the Lamb*, p. 179.

more extreme statements. It might even be said that Dodd, in this context, almost depersonalises God. He does not, of course, go all the way with the Muslim view that God is so transcendent that he cannot be affected in any way by his creatures, made glad by their obedience or sad by their disobedience; for he puts a paramount emphasis on the love of God. But he seems to think that anger against sin is completely incompatible with love for the sinner. Like so many writers, he has, I think, over-reacted to a distorted doctrine. What so often seems to happen is something like this. First, some theologian isolates one aspect of the New Testament revelation and exaggerates it. Then, over-enthusiastic followers take this tendency still further, and develop it to the point of positive distortion, in their teaching and preaching.[28] Next, this distorted doctrine is caricatured, consciously or unconsciously, by those who react against it; and, finally, this caricature is held up to ridicule, and an attempt is made to expunge, or explain away, all traces of the original teaching. This is, to me, the only explanation of the vehemence of the attack on certain aspects of the atonement, which seem to me clearly biblical, made by a number of theologians whose writings I normally regard with respect and gratitude. And I must confess that it seems to me that A. M. Hunter—with, perhaps, less erudition than Dodd but with a much less doctrinaire reaction against an unpalatable concept—is far closer to a straightforward reading of the Bible when he writes:

Sixteen times in his letters Paul refers to the wrath of God. Thrice he gives the phrase in full, but generally he speaks of 'the wrath'. He says that God 'shows' wrath, or that his wrath is being revealed against human sin. Sinners are 'vessels of wrath' (or 'children of wrath'). Judgment Day is 'the Day of wrath', as Jesus is our 'deliverer from the wrath to come'.

This language repels many people today. They would

[28] It must, however, be recognized that some of the most one-sided, extreme and inadequate interpretations of the atonement have come directly from leading theologians themselves, rather than their followers.

fain hold that anger in any shape or form is foreign to God. They would like to interpret Paul's phrase in terms of some impersonal doctrine of retribution—the inevitable operation of the law of cause and effect in a moral world.

But the Bible does not take this way. No student of the Old Testament prophets can doubt that the wrath of God was for them a personal activity of God. Nor can we doubt that, though Jesus laid a new emphasis on the love of God, he found the divine reaction to evil an awful reality, and (we may add) that, as he himself approached death—witness the 'cup' saying and the Cry of Dereliction—felt the weight, without himself being the object of provocation, of the wrath of God.

The same is true of Paul and the other New Testament writers who take a graver view of God's wrath than even the Old Testament prophets. On the other hand, they have found a hope of reconciliation to God unknown to the Old Testament. 'God has not destined us for wrath, but to obtain salvation through our Lord Jesus Christ.' (I Thess. 5 : 9).

We have noted that Paul often speaks of 'the wrath' (it almost demands a capital letter) without naming God. This is not because he thinks of it impersonally, but because he finds it quite unnecessary to say whose wrath it is (cf. the phrase 'the Day', meaning Judgment Day, *Dies illa*). By 'the wrath' Paul means God's holy displeasure at sin. It is the eternal divine reaction against evil without which God would not be the moral Governor of the world. Paul thinks of it as both present and future. It is that divine aversion to evil and sin which, though active in the present time, will not reach its climax till the Judgment.[29]

Similarly, John Marsh, in commenting on the words in John 3:36 "He who puts his faith in the Son has hold of eternal life, but he who disobeys the Son shall not see life;

[29] *The Gospel according to St. Paul* (SCM, London, 1966), pp. 70 f.

God's wrath rests on him", justly observes: "The wrath of God is the obverse side of his love."[30]

But why, we must ask ourselves, do we find this seeming compulsion to argue, with learning and even passion, against what appears to be the inescapable teaching of the Bible? Two chief reasons can, I think, be identified. The first is the utterly distorted (and, indeed, blasphemous) pictures which have sometimes been drawn[31] of a God whose basic reaction to a fallen world is one of hostile anger and impending judgment, but who has been appeased in part by a sinless Jesus whose matchless love for sinners impelled him to offer himself as their substitute, to bear savage punishment in their place, and thus to propitiate God's wrath and win pardon for those who sign their names, as it were, to this transaction—or, alternatively, of a God who insists on exacting a wholly adequate (and, therefore, humanly impossible) penance for every positive sin and a sufficient work of supererogation for every failure in righteousness, and who can only be "satisfied" by the fact that the one wholly righteous man crowned a life of unbroken and vicarious merit by a supreme penance of which others might avail themselves.[32] This represents, of course, a positive parody of the character of God, an absolutely unwarranted separation between the Father and the Son, and a consequential distortion of what the New Testament means by "propitiation" (or "expiation")[33] and of the whole concept of an atonement which was, and is, not only "vicarious", "participatory" and "representative" but also, in a real sense, both "penal" and "substitutionary". Yet this cause of aversion need not, I think, prove catastrophic, for the false theology inherent in

[30] Op. cit., p. 198.

[31] Whether by their advocates, or by those who exaggerate and even parody them. See above.

[32] Cf. Geoffrey Lampe in *Soundings*, ed. A. R. Vidler (Cambridge University Press, 1966), pp. 180–9, *passim*. But it should be possible to recognise biblical truths behind their theological exaggeration or distortion.

[33] I couple these terms not because they are synonymous, for they are not; but because we find them used as alternative translations of one Greek word.

such imagery can be shown to be unbiblical (and is, in fact, often more ill-considered, apparent or even caricatured than deliberate, real or genuine), and the crude colours and clumsily etched outlines can be replaced by a truer representation. But the second reason for this aversion is much more fundamental: namely, a passionate conviction that the character of the "God and Father of our Lord Jesus Christ" is such that anything that savours of righteous indignation or penal judgment must be regarded as totally alien to him. To this the short answer is that this is not the God whom the Bible reveals—or, indeed, a God who would command our basic moral respect, to say nothing of reverence.

To a lawyer, this smacks of a philosophy of punishment which concentrates exclusively on the reformation of the criminal and leaves no place whatever for either deterrence or any concept of retribution. Of course the attempt to reform a criminal is of cardinal importance; but it may not be possible of attainment. Nor can one have regard only for the criminal as an individual; so the deterrence of others is universally recognised as a legitimate factor in penal sanctions, in the interests of society as a whole. It is only the idea of any retributive element in punishment which arouses the sort of moral aversion of which we have been speaking. Yet a punishment designed either to reform or deter which is wholly unrelated to the gravity of the offence or the way in which others are treated—or, indeed, which takes no account of the circumstances of the case or the possibly diminished responsibility of the accused—would be odious. The very fact that we instinctively say "That's not fair" about some punishments bears witness, I think, to what may justly be termed a retributive element which must be *one* of the components in any adequate theory of punishment. As C. S. Lewis puts it: the "concept of Desert is the only connecting link between punishment and justice", for there "is no sense in talking about a 'just deterrent' or a 'just cure'.... Thus when we cease to consider what the criminal deserves and consider *only* what will cure him or deter others, we have tacitly removed him from the sphere of justice altogether; instead of a person, a subject of rights, we now have a mere object, a patient, a 'case'."[34] But this is not to deny that, among men, the retributive can all too easily become vindictive.

IV

Any discussion of the wrath of God leads us, inevitably, to those New Testament verses where the Authorised or Revised versions use the word "propitiation". In the context of the atonement these are Rom. 3:25 and I John 2:2 and 4:10—to which should be added Heb. 2:19, where the A.V. quite incorrectly reads "reconciliation". In the RSV the word "expiation" is in each case preferred, while in the NEB the translation in Rom. 3:25 is "the means of expiating sin", in I John 2:2 and 4:10 "the remedy for the defilement of our sins", and in Heb. 2:19 "to expiate the sins of the people". In Romans the Greek word is that used in the Septuagint for the "mercy seat"—that is, the *place* where God welcomes sinful men on the basis of the atoning sacrifice there symbolised; but it could equally be linked with the other New Testament passages as signifying the *means* whereby this welcome is made possible. The basic idea, then, is that something has to be done about sin before a holy God can give that royal welcome to the sinner which the New Testament, in particular, makes it clear that he longs to extend.

It is not my purpose here to discuss the precise difference between the words "propitiation" and "expiation", except in the context of the 'wrath of God'.[35] On the purely impersonal view of that phrase "expiation" is, obviously, more appropriate; and it may well be that the term "propitiation"—with its primary sense, both in ordinary

[34] "The Humanitarian Theory of Punishment", in *Undeceptions* (Geoffrey Bles, London, 1970), p. 239. My italics.

[35] Strictly speaking, "expiation" is concerned only with sin, while "propitiation" brings in the additional sense that, because sin has been "covered", God's wrath against it has been "averted." For the way in which this is to be understood, see below.

language and pagan religions, of "appeasement"—may give rise to such misconceptions of the biblical teaching that it should be used only if, and when, it can be adequately explained. In many religions, beyond question, it is man who must bring some sacrifice to appease or assuage the vindictive anger, or even malignity, of an offended god. But it is clear that this is not the concept of sacrifice in the Old Testament; while in the New Testament it is God himself, not man, who provides the propitiation, and it is because of his love and goodwill to man that he does so (cf. I John 4:10). It is obvious, then, that it is not man—or even Jesus—who takes the initiative, but God himself; so there can be no question of changing a basic malignity or hostility into a grudging acceptance. On the contrary, it is the propitiation he has provided which represents the supreme demonstration of his love. Why, then, not abandon the word "propitiation" and all for which it stands, as a multitude of contemporary theologians would urge?

The answer, as I see it, is that the term "expiation", like "propitiation", stands in need of explanation if it is fully to convey the idea behind the biblical verses concerned. We have already seen that the fact that God loves men and women in all their guilt does not imply that he does not deeply disapprove of the sin which separates them from him: indeed, that he does not "hate" the sin which causes such sorrow, evil and estrangement. But he does not, of course, "hate" sinners: far from it, he loved them enough to come in the person of his Son to die for them. We must not, however, abandon the idea that God is not only implacably hostile to evil as such, but that he is also grieved and displeased with the wilful sinner; and that the love of God in such cases does not in any way exclude a holy indignation —i.e. the "wrath" of God in the true sense of that term— and just condemnation. To take any other view with regard to a Hitler, a Stalin or those who make fortunes from deliberately ruining other lives through hard drugs —to give a few random and extreme examples—would reduce God to the impersonal and the amoral. Does the "propitiation", then, have the effect of changing God's attitude to sinners? Surely the answer must be "Yes and no"—or, better, "No and yes". "No", in the sense that it is not his fundamental character or attitude[36] which is in any way changed. God is love, and it was his love which prompted him to provide a propitiation which was infinitely costly. "Yes", in the sense that he can and does now receive the sinner on a new basis and into a new relationship, for he is now "accepted in the beloved", and the sin which inevitably came as a barrier between him and a holy God has been removed.[37] If this teaching in the New Testament (as I believe it to be) can be preserved in and by the word "expiation", then so be it. Otherwise, whichever word is used—propitation or expiation—will stand in need of elucidation.

But this leads us on to three further problems. To what extent is it appropriate to use "penal" language of the atonement? How far is this "forensic" imagery a necessary and theologically valid part of the doctrine of "justification"? And should what Jesus did for us at the cross be described, in part, in "substitutionary" terms? To some contemporary theologians it is substitutionary language which is most offensive; to some it is the forensic imagery; whereas to others the idea of a penal sacrifice is an even more basic objection. This last, for example, is true (if I understand him aright) of Geoffrey Lampe. We can, of course, fully agree with him when he states that it would be grossly inadequate to interpret sin solely "in a legalistic fashion as a transgression of commandments instead of a deep violation of personal relationship"[38]—although, even here, the contrast he draws is, in a sense, more apparent than real, for the New Testament teaches that to love God (i.e. to have a personal relationship with him) *is* to keep his commandments.[39] But when he asserts that, much more

[36] Cf. in this context, Geoffrey Lampe, *Soundings*, p. 182.
[37] Cf. P. T. Forsyth, *The Work of Christ* (Hodder and Stoughton, reprinted in 1946), p. 105.
[38] *Soundings*, p. 181.
[39] Cf. I John 5:3.

serious   penal
substit   emy
of sup   like
a hang   ders
offence   r or
the pe   e a
fixed r   ma-
tion of   It is
a legal   only
of a w   ame
sort of   a
differen   ing.
Even i   ave
referred   tive
element   rom
it; all t   ent
in any adequate philosophy of punishment, alongside
"the reclamation of the criminal" and the deterrence of
others. In regard to the atonement, moreover, this is still
more misleading. It would be a gross caricature to suggest
that every doctrine of the atonement which includes a
penal element means that God has "a tariff of sentences"
for human sins and that Christ bore an exact equivalent of
the punishment due to each individual for each and every
sin. What the New Testament states is that he who himself "knew no sin was made sin (or, less likely, a sin offering) for us" and that Christ was "made a curse for us".[41] On
this A. M. Hunter justly comments that "passages like these
reveal the holy love of God taking awful issue in the Cross
with the sin of man. Christ, by God's will, dies the sinner's
death and so removes sin. Is there a simpler way of saying
all this than that Christ bore our sins and that his sufferings
were what, for lack of a better word, we can only call
'penal'?" And he adds in a footnote: "Some people
instinctively boggle at the word 'penal'—and rightly, if the
suggestion is that God punished Christ; but wrongly, if they
fail to realise that an innocent person can be involved in

[40] Op. cit., p. 187.
[41] II Cor. 5:21 and Gal. 3:13.

168

the penal sufferings of others ... because he deliberately chooses in love to identify himself with sinners."[42]

As Forsyth insists again and again, Paul does not say that Christ was made a sinner, but that he was made sin. On him "sin's judgment fell.... God did not judge Him, but judged sin upon His head. He never once counted Him sinful; he was always well pleased with Him"[43] — and never more, we might add, than when, in those hours of darkness, Jesus suffered the unfathomable anguish of experiencing that separation from fellowship with his Father which is the basic consequence of sin. For it is in this sense — alone, as I see it — that the awful "Cry of Dereliction" on the cross can be understood. Of its authenticity there can, surely, be no doubt whatever; but how is it to be interpreted? That it represents the most poignant illustration of the fact that Jesus was "in every respect tempted as we are" would, presumably, be generally agreed. But the verse continues "yet without sin" — so we cannot explain this cry in terms of doubt or loss of faith. Was it, then, a tragic mistake; a mere feeling, which had no substance whatever in fact, that his intimate fellowship with his heavenly Father had been broken? Surely not; it was that he, as the New Testament asserts, was being "made sin" for us, and "bearing our sin in his own body on the tree".[44] To bear sin or iniquity means to be answerable for it, to endure its penalty — and this is precisely what he was doing. But Forsyth insists that we should never say that Jesus was "punished", but rather that he "bore the penalty" of our sins; not that he himself was "accursed", but that he was "made a curse" for us, when he "acted in our stead".[45]

This concept of God's "curse" must, as F. F. Bruce insists, have been one of the earliest elements in Paul's thought. Before the experience on the Damascus road the

[42] Op. cit., p. 26.

[43] Op. cit., p. 83.

[44] In this context it is noteworthy that the word "tree" is used for the "cross" not only in I Pet. 2:24 but also Acts 5:30, 10:39, and 13:29. It seems inescapable that this is an echo of Deut. 21:22 f., as quoted in Gal. 3:13 (see below).

[45] Op. cit., p. 240.

statement in Deut. 21:23 that "a hanged man is accursed by God" had, no doubt, sufficed to dismiss as impossible any suggestion of a crucified Messiah. But the resurrection had proved that the crucified Jesus was far from "accursed" in himself. So "sooner rather than later Paul must have reached the conclusion ... that Jesus submitted to the death of the cross in order to take upon himself the curse which the law pronounced on all who failed to keep it completely (Deut. 27:26). The *form* of this argument was such as Paul was quite familiar with in the rabbinical schools, but no Rabbi had ever formulated the *substance* of this bold argument—that the Messiah should undergo voluntarily the curse denounced upon the breakers of God's law in order to liberate them from the curse. But in this way the doctrine of a crucified Messiah, which had been such a stone of stumbling to Paul, became the corner-stone of his faith and preaching."[46]

It is a gross distortion of this view of the atonement— or, rather, of this one aspect of its many-sided significance —to say with Geoffrey Lampe that here

The Cross is no longer the point at which the paradoxical love of God embraces men at the moment when they are supremely unlovable; it is rather the scene of an apotheosis of law and justice. It is where we see justice enthroned as God. There is still a revelation of divine love in the death of Christ, for God, in the person of the Son, undertakes, out of his own spontaneous love, to satisfy the demands of his justice; but love has to serve the ends of justice, and justice remains the higher principle.... God is justice. He is also love; but only secondarily.... Such theories exhibit two fundamental defects. They subordinate love to justice, and so resolve the principle of the gospel into that of law.... They also bring back into the gospel of reconciliation a subtle form of the idea of merit and reward. God does not reconcile sinners to himself freely and spontaneously. His favour is still proportional to desert. He does not simply accept

[46] *The Epistle to the Romans* (Tyndale Press, London, 1963), pp. 36 f.

the unacceptable on the sole condition of willingness to be accepted.... Man has still something to offer God from his own side; he need not utterly abandon his pretensions to self-justification or the idea that he may have some merit to plead. He possesses it vicariously.... He can, as it were, clothe himself with Christ's achievement as his substitute, and need not stand utterly naked in the presence of God.[47]

Here the element of distortion basically consists in drawing the picture in terms of justice versus love as almost personalised qualitites in the Godhead, and in depicting justice as the dominant feature. It seems to me much closer to the tenor of New Testament teaching to put the central emphasis on the matchless love of God, but to insist, with P. T. Forsyth, that the attributes of God "are not things within Himself which He could handle and adjust. An attribute of God is God Himself behaving, with all His unity, in a particular way in a particular situation." Thus "the love of God is not an attribute of God; it is God loving. The holiness of God is not an attribute of God; it is the whole God Himself as holy." There is no conflict here. God is love; but that love, as Forsyth insists, is holy love. "How essential the holiness of that love is to our respect for it and our faith in its unchangeableness,"[48] he exclaims. "He could not trifle with His own holiness. He could will nothing against his holy nature, and He could not abolish the judgment bound up with it."[49] That was why "the sinner's reconciliation to a God of holy love could not take place if guilt were not destroyed, if judgment did not take place on a due scale"—which, as he argues elsewhere, means a racial or even a cosmic scale. "That was what took place in the Cross of Christ."[50] Indeed, if God "had not

[47] *Soundings*, pp. 182–4. This is, no doubt, a reaction against a view of the atonement expressed in terms of "merit", "satisfaction", "punishment", etc., in a way that identifies it with ideas of supererogation and penance – or, indeed, one which uses exclusively, or excessively, juridical terms.

[48] Op. cit., pp. 117 f. and 113.

[49] Ibid., p. 112.

[50] Ibid., p. 132.

vindicated His holiness to the uttermost in that way of judgment, it would not be a kind of holiness that men could trust."[51] And Lampe's parody of this view seems to have led him—unconsciously, I feel sure—into what appears to be a scornful reflection on Paul's aspiration to be "found" in Christ, not having a righteousness of his own, but "that which is through faith in Christ, the righteousness from God that depends on faith"[52]—or, in a word, of being "accepted in the beloved". In a later paper,[53] it is true, he explains himself more clearly when he says that "it is certainly true that God sees us, as it were, in Christ and accepts us in him and not for the sake of what we are in ourselves"; but he adds that this "need not, however, and should not, mean that Christ's obedience ... is imputed to us. Righteousness, like sin, is a word which primarily denotes a relationship to God." It seems to me, however, that he is here making a distinction largely without a difference, for our relationship to God in Christ is clearly dependent on who he was and what he did.[54]

V

What seems to me inescapable is that Jesus himself, and the apostles after him, repeatedly turned to Isaiah 53 in referring to the meaning of his passion.[55] It is deeply significant, I think, that Jesus is reported as having quoted from this chapter on the road to Gethsemane,[56] and that behind his basic prediction of his passion ("the Son of Man did not come to be served but to serve, and to surrender his life as a ransom for many)[57] almost certainly

[51] Ibid., p. 136.

[52] Phil. 3:9.

[53] "The Saving Work of Christ", in *Christ for us Today*, ed. Norman Pittenger (SCM Press, London, 1968), p. 146.

[54] Cf. Rom. 5:15 ff. In this context, cf. *Paul and Rabbinic Judaism*, W. D. Davies (SPCK, London, 1948), p. 268, etc.

[55] Cf. in this context, Vincent Taylor's books on the atonement.

[56] Luke 22:37.

[57] Mark 10:45 NEB. Cf. Matt. 20:28.

lie "the ideas and language of the Suffering Servant passage in Isaiah 53".[58] We find echoes of this, moreover, time and again, in the epistles. On the statement in Heb. 9:27 and 28 ("and just as it is appointed for men to die once, and after that comes judgment, so Christ, having been offered once to bear the sins of many, will appear a second time, not to deal with sin, but to save those who are eagerly waiting for him") A. T. Hanson, for example, comments that the reference to the Suffering Servant here, in the words "to bear the sins of many", "makes it likely that Christ is thought of not as in any sense having been involved in the guilt of sin, but as having accepted the consequences of sin, become voluntarily involved in the process of God's wrath; e.g. Isa. 53:4,5."[59] In I Pet. 2:24, again, the echo of Isaiah 53 in the words "He himself bore our sins in his body on the tree" is placed beyond all question by the subsequent phrase "By his wounds you have been healed"; and the same thought almost certainly lies behind I Pet. 3:18, where we read: "For Christ also died (or 'suffered') for sins once for all, the righteous for the unrighteous."

We are compelled, therefore, to take very serious account of Isa. 53 in our interpretation of the atonement. It may, of course, be argued that we should construe Isa. 53 in terms of the atonement, rather than *vice versa*,[60] on the basis of the principle that we should, as a general rule, interpret the Old Testament in the light of New Testament teaching. And if, indeed, we knew—from explicit New Testament statements—the full meaning of the atonement, this would be a very persuasive argument. But the fact is that, while we find conclusive proof that the primitive Church regarded Isa. 53 as referring to Christ and his atoning death (cf. Acts 8:32–35), we equally find that Jesus

---

[58] Cf. F. J. Taylor, in *A Theological Word Book of the Bible*, p. 187, and Alan Richardson, *An Introduction to the Theology of the New Testament* (SCM Press, London, 1958), p. 220 (*Pace* Barrett in *New Testament Essays, Studies in Memory of T. W. Manson* (Manchester, 1959), pp. 1–18.

[59] *The Wrath of the Lamb*, p. 135.

[60] This point was put to me by Geoffrey Lampe, both in a conversation and in a letter.

and his apostles explained the meaning of that death in terms of Isaiah's prophecy. So it is to that prophecy that we must necessarily turn. And it seems inescapable that words such as "He was wounded for our transgressions, He was bruised for our iniquities; upon him was the chastisement that made us whole, and with his stripes we are healed. All we like sheep have gone astray; we have turned every one to his own way; and the Lord has laid on him the iniquity of us all"[61] carry both a "penal" and a "substitutionary" connotation—as do also the phrases in verse 8 that he was "stricken for the transgression of my people"; in verse 10 that "it was the will of the Lord to bruise him; he has put him to grief; when he makes himself (or 'thou makest his soul') an offering for sin, he shall see his offspring, he shall prolong his days"; in verse 11 that he shall "make many to be accounted righteous; and he shall bear their iniquities"; and in verse 12 that he "poured out his soul to death, and was numbered with the transgressors; yet he bore the sin of many."[62]

When we come, next, to the vexed question whether the atonement must be regarded as having, *inter alia*, a "substitutionary" element, it is extraordinary to note the contortions in which scholars become involved in order to evade or deny this. D. E. H. Whiteley, for example, says that "the death which Christ died to save us from a penal death was not itself penal.... He underwent misunderstanding, scorn, rejection, and crucifixion on our behalf, that is to say vicariously,[63] in order to save us from the consequence of our own sin. But God did not transfer to him the punishment due to us on account of our sin, as if punishment were something impersonal."[64] Would it not be far closer to biblical teaching, however, to say that what

[61] Isaiah 53:5 and 6.

[62] Quotations from RSV throughout.

[63] It is noteworthy, however, that the term "vicariously" properly includes an idea of "substitutionary". As Pannenberg puts it: a service "has vicarious character by recognizing a need in the person served that apart from this service that person would have to satisfy for himself". Cf. op. cit., p. 259.

[64] *The Theology of St Paul* (Blackwell, Oxford, 1964), pp. 130 f.

Jesus suffered should not, indeed, be regarded as a "punishment" imposed on him, but rather as God himself in Christ bearing the judgment or penalty of the sin of the world? Whiteley admits that, in what Hunter describes as Paul's "climatic statement"[65] that "For our sake (God) made him to be sin who knew no sin, so that in him we might become the righteousness of God",[66] the phrase "made sin" could mean "Made to bear the guilt of sin, treated in a penal substitutionary transaction as if he were a sinner" (notice the slant given to this interpretation by the term "transaction"). But he goes on to say that it "could also mean that in the providence of God Christ took upon himself human nature, which though not essentially sinful, is *de facto* sinful in all other cases", and concludes that the "second incarnational, participatory explanation is to be preferred"—against, I should have thought, the plain meaning of the words and the almost explicit teaching of the passages quoted above. Similarly, when commenting on Mark 10:45 and Matt. 20:28, he remarks that two interpretations are possible: "(1) Just as men are freed from slavery by the payment of a ransom, so Christ freed us from sin and from death at the cost of his own life. He died instead of (*anti*) us in the sense that but for his death we should have perished. (2) God accepted the death of Christ instead of our death in order to satisfy the demands of justice, if indeed it can be said that 'justice' is satisfied by the death of any but the sinner."[67] But here, again, he not only gives a slant to his words, but reads into the verses a quite unwarrantable polarisation between what Gustaf Aulén terms the "dramatic" or "classical" view of the atonement, on the one hand, and the "juridical" or "Latin" view, on the other.[68] Surely the most natural meaning of Mark 10:45 is a combination of Whiteley's two glosses which gives a more adequate meaning to the preposition ἀντί than does the first, and something much closer to the

[65] Op. cit., p. 26.
[66] II Cor. 5:21.
[67] Op. cit., pp. 136 f. and 144.
[68] *Christus Victor* (SPCK, 1931), pp. 20 ff.

original than the second: namely, that "Just as men are freed from slavery or debt by the payment of a ransom, so Christ freed us from both the bondage and penalty of sin by dying in our place." It is noteworthy that F. J. Taylor comments that "the use of the preposition 'for', requiring the ordinary meaning of 'in the place of the many', suggests a substitutionary idea which is elsewhere expressed by reference to what Christ bore for men (Rom. 3:24; Gal. 3:13; II Cor. 5:21)".[69] Similarly, J. A. Alexander, in his commentary on Mark 10:45, writes: "*For*, not merely for the benefit, but in the place of, as their substitute, the only meaning which the particle here used will bear in this connection";[70] and R. V. G. Tasker comments on the corresponding verse in Matt. that this "conveys the idea of substitution. Christ was to die in the place of (*anti*) many the death which they, not He, deserved."[71]

Alan Richardson may, perhaps, be taken as an example of the many theologians who make the most dogmatic and categorical assertions to the contrary. Any

notions of Christ's bearing a penalty or punishment instead of us ... have no basis in the teaching of the N.T. [he writes] When a N.T. writer says that Christ suffered for sins once (I Pet. 3:18), or quotes Isa. 53:5, 'by whose stripes ye were healed' (I Pet. 2:24), he is enunciating (as the context makes clear) the Isaianic doctrine of the saving righteousness of God, made visible and effective in the vicarious suffering of his Messianic Servant. The N.T. writers certainly regard Isa: 53, as Jesus had done before them, as predicting the sacrificial death of Christ, but they do not use it to teach a 'substitutionary' ... theory of the atonement."[72]

[69] *A Theological Word Book of the Bible*, p. 187.
[70] *Mark* (repub. by The Banner of Truth Trust, 1960), p. 294.
[71] Op. cit., p. 196.
[72] *An Introduction to the Theology of the New Testament*, p. 239. Cf. also F. R. Barry, op. cit., pp. 88, 129, 170. But contrast Barry, p. 102, where he commits himself to the exceedingly questionable statement that "There was nothing in the Jewish Scriptures to suggest a Messiah who should suffer." In point of fact the Old Testament teaching that the Christ *must*

But I doubt if this would be regarded as a valid and acceptable interpretation of the relevant documents in any court of law. It is far closer to a straightforward interpretation of Paul's thought to say, with W. P. Paterson: "It is vain to deny that St. Paul freely employs the category of substitution. . . . He does not, indeed, expressly say that Christ died in our stead (ἀντί); the phrase is 'on our behalf' (ὑπέρ Rom. 5:8, 8:32; I Thess. 5:10, etc.), or 'on account of our sins' (διά Rom. 4:25; περί I Cor. 15:3). But the idea of an exchange is unmistakeable. Christ suffers death, which is the penalty of our sins, not of His own; man is the recipient of a righteousness which he has not built up, but which is won for him by Christ (II Cor. 5:21)."[73] As P. T. Forsyth puts it: "God made Christ sin in this sense, that God as it were took Him in the place of sin, rather than the sinner, and judged the sin upon Him; and in putting Him there He really put Himself there in our place (Christ being what He was); so that the divine judgment of sin was real and effectual." Thus God made Him to be sin "so that we might have in God's sight righteousness by our living union with Christ, righteousness which did not belong to us actually, naturally and finally. Our righteousness is as little ours individually as the sin on Christ was His."[74]

Karl Barth is still more explicit. Commenting on the last few verses in II Cor. 5 he writes:

I do not see how in this context we can avoid going back to the basic meaning of καταλλάσσειν. The conversion of the world to Himself took place in the form of an exchange, a substitution, which God has proposed between the world and Himself present and active in the person of Jesus Christ. That is what is expressly

---

suffer was, Luke tells us, explained by the risen Lord both to the two disciples on the road to Emmaus and to a larger company in the upper room (Luke 24:25 ff and 44 ff). W. D. Davies, moreover, maintains that the concept of a suffering Messiah may well have been one strand in Rabbinic Judaism. Cf. *Paul and Rabbinic Judaism* (SPCK, London, 1948), pp. 274–84.

[73] Hastings, *Dictionary of the Bible*, IV, p. 345.
[74] Op. cit., p. 83 f.

stated in the verse (21) with which the passage closes. On the one side, the exchange: 'He hath made him to be sin for us (in our place and for our sake), who knew no sin. . . . Here we have it in the simplest possible form. . . . And on the other side, the exchange: He does it, He takes our place in Christ, that we (again in the simplest possible form) might be made the righteousness of God ($\delta\iota\kappa\alpha\iota\sigma\acute{\nu}\nu\eta$ $\theta\epsilon\sigma\hat{\nu}$) in Him.' It does not say simply that He was made sin and we the righteousness of God. The first is obviously the means or the way to the second. . . . To be made the righteousness of God means (as the positive complement to Christ's being made sin) being put in a place or status in which we are right with God.[75] [Later, he continues:] At this point we can and must make the decisive statement: What took place is that the Son of God fulfilled the righteous judgment on us men by Himself taking our place as man and in our place undergoing the judgment under which we had passed. That is why He came and was amongst us. . . . Because he was a man like us, He was able to be judged like us. Because He was the Son of God and Himself God, He had the competence and power to allow this to happen to Him. Because He was the divine Judge come among us, He had the authority in this way—by this giving up of Himself to judgment in our place—to exercise the divine justice of grace, to pronounce us righteous on the ground of what happened to Him, to free us therefore from the accusation and condemnation and punishment, to save us from the impending loss and destruction.[76]

"Jesus Christ for us", he asserts, signifies

His activity as our Representative and Substitute. In the New Testament the words $\dot{\alpha}\nu\tau\acute{\iota}$, $\dot{\upsilon}\pi\acute{\epsilon}\rho$ and $\pi\epsilon\rho\acute{\iota}$ are used to bring out the meaning of this activity of

[75] *Church Dogmatics IV*, ed. G. W. Bromiley and T. F. Torrance (T. and T. Clark, Edinburgh), Pt. I, p. 75.
[76] Ibid., pp. 222 f.

Jesus Christ. They cannot be understood if—quite apart from the particular view of the atonement made in Him which dominates these passages—we do not see that in general these prepositions speak of a place which ought to be ours, that we ought to have taken this place, that we have been taken from it, that it is occupied by another, that this other acts in this place as only He can, in our cause and interest, that we cannot add to anything that He does there because the place where we might do so is occupied by Him, that anything further which might happen can result only from what is done by Him in our place and in our cause. If someone gives his life a λύτρον ἀντὶ πολλῶν (Mk. 10:45), then he necessarily acts in the place and as the representative of the πολλοί, paying on their account but without their co-operation what they cannot pay for themselves. If he sheds his blood περὶ πολλῶν (Matt. 26:28), that again is an act which is to the advantage of the πολλοί, but it is his blood which is shed and not a drop of theirs.... If, according to the saying of the High Priest in John 11:50, it was expedient that one man should die ὑπὲρ τοῦ λαοῦ, this expressly involves that the people should not die, but that he should die in place of the people to save the people.[77]

But we must be careful, Barth warns us, "not to describe this event, the coming of Jesus Christ in place of us sinners, this exchange between the divine and our false human position, as an exchange only in appearance, as a kind of dressing up or masquerade...."[78] If anything is in bitter earnest it is the fact that God Himself in His eternal purity and holiness has in the sinless man Jesus Christ taken up our evil case in such a way that He willed to make it, and

[77] Ibid., pp. 230 f.
[78] Cf. here Forsyth's statement: "There can therefore be no talk of hood-winking. Atonement means the covering of sin by something which God Himself had provided, and therefore the covering of sin by God himself. It was of course not the blinding of Himself to it, but something very different." (Op. cit., p. 55.)

179

has in fact made it, His own."[79] And he poignantly concludes: "All sin, great or small, flagrant or less obvious, needed and needs to have been ... borne by Him. When He bears it, even the greatest of sins cannot damn a man. If it were not that He bears it, even the smallest would be enough to damn him utterly..... The man who is saved in the person of another, and can be saved only in that way, is obviously in himself a lost man."[80]

It is noteworthy that this "substitutionary element"—for it is, indeed, only one facet in the many-sided wonder of the atonement—is present in verses which refer to the "ransom" Jesus paid to set us free and also in verses which refer to his having been "made sin" on our behalf. In other words, it recurs in verses which use the imagery of the slave-market, the sacrificial system or what has been termed the "court of law". This seems to suggest that Gustaf Aulén has somewhat over-emphasised the difference between the "classical" and the "juridical" interpretations of the atonement. He is absolutely right, of course, when he says that one or other of these two distinct ways of looking at the work of Christ can be so emphasised, isolated and exaggerated as to make it appear that they are essentially contradictory. But the truth is that they are, in reality, complementary and interdependent. The way in which Christ gives us deliverance from sin, death, the accusing law of God and even Satan is, surely, that he "bore our sins", that he "died for us", that he was "made a curse for us" and that he thereby broke "the power of him who had death at his command". And his victorious death was followed by a resurrection life which he shares with his people through his Spirit.

The simile of the law-court recurs, in part, in the concept of justification. Rashdall, as F. R. Barry emphasises, contends that "the only way in which men can be 'justified' in

---

[79] Ibid., p. 237.

[80] Ibid., pp. 411 and 413. The biblical meaning of substitution is well expressed in the couplet from the well-known hymn:
"Bearing shame and scoffing rude,
In my place condemned He stood."

the sight of God is by *being* just"; but Barry goes on to say that "the verb to justify does not mean to make just, it means to *pronounce* just, that is, to acquit, to pronounce not guilty in a law court."[81] C. K. Barrett, on the other hand, maintains that linguistically (and in view of the Hebrew verb *hitzdiq* which lies behind it) to "justify" does mean "to make righteous", but with a recognition that "righteous" in this context "does not mean 'virtuous', but 'right', 'clear', 'acquitted' in God's court. Justification then means no legal fiction but an act of forgiveness on God's part, described in terms of the proceedings of a law court. Far from being a legal fiction, this is a creative act in the field of divine-human relations."[82] Or, as A. M. Hunter puts it:

The metaphor certainly was forensic in origin, and that meaning still survives in some of Paul's contexts, e.g. Rom. 8:32 f. But the opinion is growing among scholars that, although originally forensic, the verb on Paul's lips has for the most part become soteriological and means 'forgive' or 'pardon'. Certainly it is so in Rom. 4:6–8. Perhaps then we may settle for the meaning 'set right' with the connotation of 'forgive'. 'Justification', says Jeremias, 'is forgiveness, nothing but forgiveness, for Christ's sake.'[83]

And Hunter adds, in a footnote, that "according to T. W. Manson, *On Paul and John* (London, 1963), p. 57, justification is a *regal* rather than a *judicial* act, and means amnesty or free pardon."[84]

VI

This leads us straight into what might be called the

[81] *The Atonement,* p. 87.

[82] *The Epistle to the Romans* (Adam & Charles Black, London, reprinted with minor changes, 1962), pp. 75 f.

[83] I would respectfully suggest, however, that justification goes beyond the sense of "pardon". In non-theological language it means that sin has been not only forgiven but forgotten, and the sinner treated as though he had never sinned.

[84] Cf. *The Gospel according to Paul,* p. 21.

man-ward side of the atonement, with which I shall deal much more briefly—not, of course, because it is not exceedingly important, but because it is far less controversial than the God-ward side. It has been pointed out by a multitude of writers that those who put a major emphasis on God being reconciled to man do so against the tenor of most of the verses in the New Testament in which the word is used. As James Stewart insists, *"God is the Reconciler"*;[85] and he quotes W. N. Clarke's affirmation "That the willing God seeks to bring unwilling men to His holy fellowship is the uniform teaching of the Scriptures, and the heart of the Gospel."[86] In the central passage of all, II Cor. 5:18–20, we find a sustained appeal to men and women to respond to the initiative which God has already taken; and in Rom. 5:10, Eph. 2:16 and Col. 1:19 ff. the emphasis again is, in each case, on man (or, in Col., "all things in heaven and earth") being reconciled to God, rather than on God being reconciled to man. And the reason for this, I think, is sufficiently obvious: that it is we, not God, who need to experience a radical change of attitude. God is not "hostile" to us, whereas we are, by nature, not only sinners but "enemies" to God (Rom. 5:10). Of the sacrificial love of him who "so loved the world that he gave his only-begotten Son" there can be no doubt whatever, while we, of ourselves, cling to our own will and repudiate the love and fellowship he offers. So there is a very real sense in which it is only the message of the cross which will change our attitude: for when we see how black sin is in the sight of a holy God—so black that even he could deal with it only by carrying it to a cross; and when we come to realise something of how great is his love—so great, that he was willing to go to such an incredible length to save us from it; then, and then only, the Holy Spirit helps us to begin to hate our own way and to love God and his way. It is thus that the process of reconciliation is effected in our hearts.

So far, so good. But many contemporary theologians and

[85] *A Man in Christ* (Hodder and Stoughton, 1935 and 1964), p. 211.
[86] *An Outline of Christian Theology*, p. 325.

commentators seem here to go to the other extreme, and to deny that there is any sense at all in which God is reconciled to men. And here Karl Barth's comments on καταλλάσσειν[87] should give us pause; for the word fundamentally means bringing two parties, between whom there was previously a barrier, into unity and fellowship; and it is in this context that Barth speaks of an "exchange". This brings us back, once more, to the concept of the "wrath" of God, the "propitiation" or "expiation", and the doctrine of "justification". As we have seen, there was certainly no need for any fundamental change in God's attitude to man; it was quite the other way round. But there *was* a basic need that sin should be expiated before the God whose nature is holy love could welcome the sinner whose sin had inevitably caused him both grief and righteous indignation: that, indeed, is why the supreme demonstration of his love was that he himself provided the "propitiation". In other words, the "reconciliation" rests entirely on the divine initiative, but it is two-sided: it was man who needed to change his basic attitude to God, not *vice versa*; but there was, nevertheless, a real sense in which the obverse side of God's love—his aversion to sin —had to be removed.

It seems to me, moreover, that we find this at least hinted at even in some passages which use the term reconciliation. Thus in Rom. 5:10 the phrase used is that we have now "received the reconciliation"; while in II Cor. 5:18–21 we are told that the "ministry of reconciliation" is to proclaim, at one and the same time, that God was in Christ "reconciling the world to himself" and "not counting their trespasses against them"—and this because Christ had been "made sin" for us. When F. R. Barry says that any concept of God being "reconciled to man" is "in flat contradiction to Scripture"[88] he certainly goes too far. Thus James Atkinson shows from a detailed consideration of Rom. 5:8–11 and II Cor. 5:18–21 that

[87] See p. 177 above.
[88] Op. cit., p. 129.

on Rom. 5:9 and 10, shows how intimately the idea of being "reconciled" goes with the idea of being "justified".[96] Forsyth, moreover, insists that:

> Our reconciliation is between person and person. . . . Any reconciliation which only means change on one side is not a real reconciliation at all. A real, deep change of relation affects both sides when we are dealing with persons.[97] [So, he goes on,] there was reconciliation on God's side as well as ours; but wherever it was, it was effected by God Himself in Himself. In what sense was God reconciled within Himself? We come to that surely as we see that the first charge upon reconciling grace is to put away guilt, reconciling by not imputing trespasses. Return to our cardinal verse, II Cor. 5:19. In reconciliation the ground for God's wrath or God's judgment was put away. Guilt rests on God's charging up sin; reconciliation rests upon Christ being made sin for us. [Later, he justly adds] Reconciliation was finished in Christ's death. Paul did not preach a gradual reconciliation. He preached what the old divines used to call the finished work.[98]

In other words—and here, I think, we reach the cardinal point at issue—the cross of Christ is not only the basis on which God entreats men to accept the amnesty he offers, but also the basis on which that amnesty can be proclaimed.

As has often been said, error creeps into doctrines of the "work of Christ" not so much in what men assert, for it has innumerable facets, as in what they deny. But yet another reason is the inadequacy of our appreciation of the guilt of sin and the holiness of God. John Robinson is at his best when he emphasises the "absolute identity of the Divine love and the Divine justice". In God, he says,

> justice is a quality of His love and a characteristic of its

[96] pp. 107 f.
[97] Op. cit., pp. 75 f.
[98] Op. cit., pp. 82 and 86.

working. His love is a love of cauterising holiness and of a righteousness whose only response to evil is the purity of a perfect hate. Wrath and justice are but ways in which such love must show itself to be love in the face of its denial. If it appeared in any other form, it would be less than perfect love. It is most important to hold to the fact that justice is in no sense a substitute for love."[99]

For God is, if I may venture the expression, "all of a piece" But the concept of the "wrath of God" is linked, in the Bible, not only with that alienation or estrangement from fellowship with him here on earth which is the inevitable (and sensible) consequence of sin, but also with the "Day of Wrath" or the "Day of Judgment". And this, in its turn, is intimately connected with the concept of the parousia, or the "Day of the Lord".

VII

One of the most significant features of recent New Testament scholarship is the rediscovery of the eschatological teaching which pervades the Gospels and Epistles, to say nothing of the Apocalypse. To both Jesus and his apostles the future was dominated by the coming of the Kingdom, by the Judgment, and by the "restitution of all things". And it was Jesus himself to whom all judgment had been committed; it was he who was to "restore all things"; and it was the King alone who could and would usher in the Kingdom (in the eschatological sense of that term). This is, of course, a vast subject which is obviously beyond the scope of this chapter. But I must confess to a sense of irritation when Christopher Evans dogmatically asserts that "The parousia expectation presupposed that the world and history were of a certain kind, and were to receive a certain kind of consummation. This was already eroded to some extent in the New Testament itself. . . . It has now irretrievably collapsed, along with the view of the world

[99] *In the End, God* (James Clarke & Co., London, 1950), pp. 104 f.

187

and history that goes with it."[100] But has it? To speak for myself, this is simply not true. What, precisely, has brought about this "irretrievable collapse"? Presumably not merely the fact that we have discovered that the earth is round instead of flat, or that man has walked on the moon? Nor can I see the relevance of any particular "view of history" to an event which clearly transcends history and brings history as we know it to an end.

It is clear, of course, that many in the primitive Church believed that the Jesus who had temporarily withdrawn his visible presence would very soon manifest himself in glory. But it always seems to me that theologians are guilty of exaggeration when they allege that this is the express teaching of the New Testament writers.[101] As early as the second letter to the Thessalonians we find the explicit warning:

> Now concerning the coming of our Lord Jesus Christ and our assembling to meet him, we beg you, brethren, not to be quickly shaken in mind or excited, either by spirit or by word, or by letter purporting to be from us, to the effect that the day of the Lord has come (or, better, 'is at hand'). Let no one deceive you in any way; for that day will not come, unless the rebellion comes first, and the man of lawlessness is revealed, the son of perdition, who opposes and exalts himself against every so-called god or object of worship, so that he takes his seat in the temple of God, proclaiming himself to be God. . . . For the mystery of lawlessness is already at work; only he who now restrains it will do so until he is out of the way. And then the lawless one will be revealed, and the Lord Jesus will slay him with the breath of his mouth and destroy him by his appearing and his coming.[102]

[100] *Resurrection and the New Testament*, p. 165.

[101] Thus J. J. von Allmen, *Worship, its Theology and Practice* (Lutterworth Press, 1965), says that he has never yet found an argument which really convinces him "that the apostolic Church lived in the expectation of an imminent parousia". Cf. p. 228.

[102] II Thess. 2:1–4 and 7–8. RSV.

Now, however these verses are interpreted, they clearly teach that the "Day of the Lord" is not to come until a good deal has happened first, including a widespread apostasy; and that this "rebellion", whatever its precise nature, will be put down by what is termed, in the Greek, "the epiphany of his parousia". So here we find two of the three words most commonly used in this context: *parousia*, which means "presence," "arrival" or (especially in the papyri) "royal visit"; *epiphany*, which means "shining forth", "manifestation"—or something eminently visible; and *apocalypsis* (not itself found in this verse), which means "disclosure", "unveiling". In other words history as we know it will be wound up by what can be described only as an act of divine intervention in which the risen Lord, always present in and through his Spirit, will disclose himself in a visible manifestation.

It is, of course, equally clear that with the passing of the years, and with the death of generation after generation of Christians, this New Testament hope soon began to burn low, and the absorbing interest of the Church became that of personal immortality and individual salvation. Not that this emphasis was, in fact, ever absent: witness the parable of the shepherd who left the ninety-nine to go out in search of one lost sheep, and Paul's consuming passion "by all means to save some". But in the New Testament we find this vital question of personal salvation set against the backcloth of the Advent, the Judgment and the Kingdom; and all down the ages individual Christians, as well as extremist groups, have emphasised what has been called "this blessed hope". Nor can I for a moment see why modern man has any reason to take a different view.

This will, of course, be greeted with derision by many. So was Paul when he declared at Athens that God "commands all men everywhere to repent, because he has fixed a day on which he will judge the world in righteousness by a man whom he has appointed, and of this he has given assurance to all men by raising him from the dead" (Acts 17:30 f.)— although, in that case, it was the idea of the resurrection rather than the parousia which provoked ridicule. Similarly, again, Paul tells us that in the first century the "word of the cross" was folly to those who were "perishing"—a stumbling block or scandal to Jews, and nonsense or an absurdity to Greeks. But he still preached the cross, the resurrection and the parousia, and these doctrines were the very foundation of the Christian Church. They are just the same in the twentieth century: still derided by many, as lacking both credibility and relevance; but still the "power of God unto salvation" to those who, convicted and persuaded by the Spirit, accept them. What, too, could be more relevant to our world of war, suffering, injustice and sin than the thought that it is not, finally, the Church which must succeed in converting the world, much though she needs to gird herself to this task: in the end it will be the Lord himself who will intervene, both for salvation and for judgment. And in the context of judgment the first chapter of this same letter expressly states that there will be some who will "suffer the punishment (or 'pay the penalty'?) of eternal destruction and exclusion from the presence of the Lord and from the glory of his might, when he comes on that day. . ."[103] On this James Denney comments:

> These are awful words, and it is no wonder that attempts have been made to empty them of the meaning which they bear upon their face. . . . If the gospel, as conceived in the New Testament, has any character at all, it has the character of finality. It is God's *last word* to men. And the consequences of accepting or rejecting it are final; it opens no prospect beyond the life on the one hand, and the death on the other, which are the results of obedience and disobedience. If there is any truth in Scripture at all, this is true—that those who stubbornly refuse to submit to the gospel . . . incur at the Last Advent an infinite and irreparable loss. They pass into a night on which no morning dawns.[104]

But the dominant emphasis in the New Testament is on

[103] II Thess. 1:9 f.

[104] *The Expositor's Bible*: *The Epistles to the Thessalonians* (Hodder and Stoughton, 1892), pp. 294.

the "Good News": on life, not death; on deliverance, not bondage; on salvation, not judgment. This may, perhaps, provide a partial explanation of the fact that so many contemporary theologians tend to be "universalists", in the sense that they believe that judgment will be only temporary and purgative, and that the love of God will eventually triumph even in the hardest and most resistant hearts.[105] This is a doctrine which we should all, of course, embrace with relief and delight were it not that there are so many passages in the New Testament which—as Denney asserts so strongly—seem to preclude it. It is true that there are also a number of verses which, taken by themselves, would appear to support the universalist thesis; but they are much less numerous than those which point in the opposite direction, and it seems to me far easier to interpret these verses in a way which is not contradictory to the positive warnings and affirmations of a judgment which is eternal in its effects than it is to evacuate the latter of their almost inescapable meaning in favour of the more general statements on which the universalist relies.[106] To say this, however, is not to suggest that there is not a very real danger in attempting to harmonise all the different strands in the biblical revelation into a completely coherent and logically consistent system of theology. There are tensions, and seeming antitheses, in the full-orbed teaching of the Bible which we eliminate at our peril, for we have no right to impose an essentially human logic on spiritual truths which the Bible proclaims but does not always explain.

If, of course, one follows John Robinson and a multitude of other theologians and New Testament scholars in the belief that no confidence can be placed today in "the authority of infallible propositions of Holy Writ"[107] and that theology must be regarded, not as "a deductive science of revelation",[108] but as an inductive process of reasoning from the life and proclamation of the Church, and its understand-

---

[105] Cf. James Atkinson, in *A Dictionary of Christian Theology*, p. 352.

[106] Cf. James Atkinson, op. cit., p. 22.

[107] *In the End, God* (James Clarke, London, 1950), p. 20

[108] Ibid., p. 26.

ing of revelation, to a formulation of "such general statements about God and His relation to man as will account
scientifically for the facts under examination,"[109] then any
compassionate and good man (such as John Robinson himself certainly is) would be very much inclined to come to
the universalist conclusions for which he argues so
movingly.[110] Others, like F. D. Maurice (a theologian whose
thought seems to be much in vogue today) accord much more
authority to specific New Testament verses, but often
appear to interpret them in a way which is foreign to their
plain meaning. Thus, in a series of sermons preached in
Lincoln's Inn (which might, therefore, be regarded as
almost prescriptive reading for a lawyer), he puts enormous
emphasis on Christ's death as a vicarious and redemptive
sacrifice, but succeeds in giving passage after passage a
universalist interpretation. When preaching on the text
"He has redeemed us from the curse of the law, having been
made, or become, a curse for us", he says, for example:

> The curse which the Law pronounced upon men was
> death, death in its most odious, most criminal shape; and
> He underwent it, an actual, not a fantastic crucifixion,—
> the sentence of the rebel and the slave. Do you ask how
> this act effected the purpose of redeeming any, or how
> many were included in the benefits of it? The question is,
> indeed, most difficult, if by redemption you understand
> *in any sense* the deliverance of man out of the hand of
> God, the procuring a change in His purpose or will. . . .
> But if you suppose that it is the spirit of a man which
> needs to be emancipated, a spirit fast bound with the
> chains of its own sins and fears, then I do not see what
> proof, save one, can be of any avail, that a certain scheme
> of redemption is effectual. Appeal directly to the captive.
> See whether the announcement, that the Son of God has
> died for him, does dissolve that horror of God, that feeling
> of Him as a tyrant, the forger of bonds, the inventor of a
> curse, by which he has been possessed.[111]

[109] Ibid., p. 27.
[110] Ibid., pp. 108 ff.
[111] *The Doctrine of Sacrifice* (Macmillan, Cambridge, 1854), pp. 140 ff.

Somewhat similarly, he insists that the "propitiation" (and he prefers this translation of the word) proclaimed in Rom. 3:25 represents a "sure declaration", in the *fact* of Christ's death, "of God's righteousness in the forgiveness of sins"—and he contrasts this with "the theory of propitiation, not set forth by God, but devised to influence His mind,—of a propitiation that does not declare God's righteousness *in* the forgiveness of sins, but which makes it possible for Him to forgive sins, *though* He is righteous." He then continues:

> Those mighty words, 'That He might be just, and the justifier of him which believeth in Jesus,' are entirely stripped of their meaning by the strange interpolation of the word *yet*. They are supposed to say that God is *just*, and yet that, in consequence of Christ's offering, He *can* justify those who believe in Him.... God does not manifest His righteous will and purpose, His righteous character, in the death of His Son; but, through the agency of that death, a certain notion of justice ... is satisfied; and so a certain portion of mankind may be excused the penalty of their past ill-doings.[112]

Obviously enough, Maurice in both these quotations commends his own teaching—in which he passionately believed—by what is a caricature, or at least a distorted form, of the sort of teaching which he deprecates. There can, of course, be no question of "procuring a change" in God's purpose or will, or of anything "devised to influence His mind". On the contrary, the whole initiative is clearly God's alone. It is perfectly true, as Maurice insists, that Paul "affirms that the barrier between God and His creatures is removed by Himself, is removed freely without money and without price, and that the act of His Son in shedding His blood is the authentic declaration of that removal."[113] It is also true that God "puts away sins *because*

[112] Ibid., pp. 159 ff.
[113] Ibid., p. 155.

He is righteous, *because* He would not have the man tied
and yoked to evil, *because* He would make him His free
and true servant."[114] But this, as we have seen, does not
mean that there was not a righteous, and in no sense
"vindictive", judgment on sin which necessitated an atonement in which, as D. M. Baillie put it, "God alone bears
the cost."[115] It is thus, he explains, that the two strains of
teaching which can be distinguished right down from the
age of the Old Testament prophets "become one in their
Christian climax: the strain that tells of God's readiness to
pardon freely and abundantly, and that which persistently
speaks of the need for a costly atonement.[116] It is gloriously
true "that God loves us equally through all our sins, that
His love in no wise depends on our being worthy of it, but
is eternally seeking us for our good, and that His forgiveness
is free to all who will accept it"; but it is also true that the
forgiveness he gives "comes from the heart of a love that
has borne our sins" and is firmly based on an expiation
which has been "made in the heart and life of God
Himself".[117]

Modern man, as Baillie says, may not have much sense of
sin, but he often has a strongly developed "moral-failure
complex". This may take the form of a profound dis-
satisfaction with his own personal character and conduct, or
it may involve an obscure but poignant sense of complicity
in the evils of the society of which he is a member. And there
is no real solution "until we allow the whole situation to be
transformed by an orientation towards God. A moralist, as
such, can never forgive himself. That is where we see most
plainly the bankruptcy of the attempt to have morality
without the life of faith. The endeavour is sure to defeat
itself, because it is self-centred instead of God-centred,
which is the very root of evil." But when the consciousness
of moral failure becomes "a sense of sin against God, a
sense of having disobeyed the will of God, of having

[114] Ibid., p. 159.
[115] *God was in Christ* (Faber and Faber, London, 1956), p. 175.
[116] Ibid., p. 178.
[117] Ibid., pp. 171 and 178.

betrayed the love of God"[118] then, and then only, we can find liberation in the forgiveness which comes from the fact that Christ died to redeem us from our sins. He has liberated us from the guilt, penalty and power of sin, and made us "free indeed". He has redeemed us from meaninglessness, futility and merely traditional ways of thought,[119] on the one hand, and from lawlessness on the other.[120] He has purged our consciences from the haunting sense that we must somehow win God's favour by what we do or are, and has thus set us free to "serve the living God"[121] as sons into whose heart he has sent the Spirit of his "Only-begotten" Son, crying "Abba, Father".[122] And our redemption, in each case, was "by his blood"[123] — which can, I think, be regarded as almost a short-hand symbol, in the New Testament, for his atoning death. It was God himself who "in Christ was reconciling the world to himself, no longer holding men's misdeeds against them".[124] So Christ shed his lifeblood as our ransom, our representative, our Saviour and (when properly understood) our substitute. There was, indeed, no other way.[125] We can truly say, with Christina Rossetti:

> None other Lamb, none other Name,
> None other Hope in heaven or earth or sea;
> None other hiding place from guilt and shame;
> None beside Thee.

[118] Ibid., pp. 162 ff.
[119] I Pet. 1:18.
[120] Titus 2:4.
[121] Heb. 9:12–14.
[122] Gal. 4:5 f.
[123] Cf. Eph. 1:7; 1 Pet. 1:19; Heb. 9:14.
[124] II Cor. 5:19.
[125] F. R. Barry repeatedly questions, or caricatures, the *necessity* of Christ's atoning death. Cf. op. cit., pp. 59, 99, 106, 129.

CHAPTER SIX

The Difference in Being a Christian Today

I

Hitherto we have been concerned with the approach of various contemporary theologians and New Testament scholars to such subjects as the Jesus of the Gospels, the essential historicity of the claim that God raised him from the dead, a more detailed consideration of the biblical evidence for the resurrection appearances and the empty tomb, and such basic theological questions as sin, forgiveness and judgment. So it may be appropriate to devote a final chapter to "The difference in being a Christian today" —partly because this is, in itself, such a fundamental subject, and partly because it represents the title of a recent book by John Robinson, published only a few months ago.[1] A great deal of what he says is, moreover, very much in tune with a singularly persistent, and even clamant, note in contemporary theological thought. It may be of some value, therefore, to attempt to analyse the arguments of this book in what will approximate to a review article, although it will include a few excursions to other publications. This major concentration on a single book is, perhaps, justified by the fact that John Robinson is probably the most widely-read exponent of what has been termed the New Theology: a theology which many people find singularly perplexing— partly because it represents such a curious mixture of ideas firmly based on the New Testament and others which have no such basis, and partly because New Testament words and verses are often used in a way which would certainly have surprised their original writers.

This enigma is, moreover, epitomised in Robinson him-

[1] (Collins, Fontana Books, Redhill, 1972).

self, for he combines in an extraordinary degree a basic conservatism in his approach to the New Testament documents with an extreme radicalism in his attempt to re-interpret the message of those documents in terms of the contemporary world. Examples of the comparative conservatism of his approach to the New Testament may be found in numerous quotations in preceding chapters of this book; while examples of his radicalism will inevitably abound in this chapter. But anyone who knows him personally is impressed by his transparent honesty and goodness, and there can be few men who have suffered more from misrepresentation by the press.

In his first chapter, "The End of the Stable State", he observes that the title of his book raises two distinct yet inter-related issues: "the difference in being a *Christian* today (rather than, say, a humanist)" and "the difference in being a Christian *today* (rather than yesterday)." The second issue is, moreover, closely connected with the contemporary quandary about "identity": or the question "Who am I in relation to those around me? What is my distinctive role?" And "Who am I in relation to my past? Am I the person that I was?"[2] Creeds, codes and articles of religion have in the past, Robinson asserts, served (to borrow a phrase from the Thirty-Nine Articles of the Church of England) as a "mark of difference, whereby Christian men are discerned from others that be not". But all this now "seems to have gone. We are constantly told that on faith, on morals, on private prayer, public worship, church discipline, or the meaning of mission, people 'just don't know where they are' ".[3] So they feel that they have "lost their bearings—and that in the one area of life which they trusted would remain an island of security in a sea of change. For religion told you what to believe, what to do and what to expect."[4] But instead of "looking only to what can be salvaged from the old identities" we must "ask boldly whether distinctively Christian existence is likely in future to be characterised . .

[2] p. 11.
[3] p. 15.
[4] p. 16.

by a body of doctrine, a code of behaviour, a pattern of spirituality, a religious organisation, which is peculiar to Christians and marks them off by exclusion from others." On the contrary, he argues, our identity today cannot be the same as it was in the past; instead, our "individuality", in the sense of being "a peculiar people" separated from other men, must be virtually discarded in favour of the aphorisms that "we find our identity by losing it in identification", and that "we are *distinctive precisely as we are not distinct*".[5] In other words, to be a Christian is to be authentically human, neither more nor less—a point to which Robinson continually recurs.

Now at first sight this seems singularly alien from the teaching of the New Testament, where it is unequivocally stated that "flesh and blood" (which presumably means men and women as they are by nature) "cannot inherit the Kingdom of God". Indeed, we are told that a man cannot so much as "see" that Kingdom unless or until he has been radically changed, or "born of the Spirit", for "that which is born of the flesh is flesh; and that which is born of the Spirit is spirit". But the point at issue is not nearly so clear-cut as this might seem to indicate, for Robinson goes on to quote Bonhoeffer's statement that "To be a Christian does not mean to be religious in a particular way ... but to be a man—not a type of man, but *the man that Christ creates in us*." These last, italicised words are all too often omitted from the quotation; and Robinson pertinently adds: "That is to say, the true dimension of humanness is not what we are when left to ourselves, but what we have it in us to become when taken out of ourselves into the full potential stature of humanity in Christ."[6] And this, of course, radically changes the meaning of the quotation.

In other words it all depends, as he rightly insists, "on what it means ultimately to be human". But instead of asserting, with Robinson, that "the Christian (as indeed the Marxist) man is to be defined in terms of what he is open to. And it is in its estimate of this that the Christian faith differs

[5] p. 17.
[6] p. 18.

from a closed humanism",[7] it seems much closer to the basic teaching of the Bible to say that man was originally created in the "image and likeness of God"; that this image has been so marred that men and women, although they have not wholly lost it, are now far from being what they were intended to be; that the "express image" of God can be found only in Christ; and that part of the redemption he came to bring us is the progressive re-creation of that image in every true disciple, and its final and triumphant renewal when at last we see him face to face and are "changed into his likeness".

But we must return to Robinson and the book under discussion. Again and again his insights, and the way in which he expresses them, are singularly attractive, particularly when he confines himself to accurate and scholarly exegesis of the New Testament. The trouble is that so often he does no such thing. He has described himself as "constitutionally a both-and rather than an either-or man"; and this is continually apparent in what he writes. The consequence is that he seems, all too frequently, to combine a deep understanding with a strange "woolliness" of thought; to give great weight to some of the New Testament evidence, but largely to overlook the equally valid evidence which does not support his thesis. And this quality, which seems distressingly common in theologians, makes a lawyer positively itch to submit him to a little forensic cross-examination.

II

In his second chapter, entitled "The Way—Now", Robinson tells us that "the greatest single search that unites our distracted world" can be summed up in the words of the three Wise Men in W. H. Auden's Christmas oratorio *For the Time Being,*

> To discover how to be human now
> Is the reason we follow this star.

[7] Ibid.

"If the Christian message is to have *any* relevance," Robinson asserts with somewhat typical exaggeration, "it will be because it comes to men as an answer to that question."[8] So he proceeds to consider this under the three headings of the Way, the Truth and the Life. This is, of course, a common and wholly acceptable approach. But it may be permissible to remark that the verse from which these words are taken (John 14:6) might, perhaps, be rendered "I am the true and living way"; for it is a common Semitic usage to employ nouns in the place of adjectives, and the whole purport of both verse and context seems to be an emphatic assertion that Jesus is the only true and effective way to God, to the exclusion of all others.

First, then, the Way, since Christianity "is primarily a style of life, a pattern of living. Moreover, this is the product it has publicly to show to the world. This represents its store-front" (although he rightly adds that "behind that indeed lies a belief and at the heart of that belief an interior life").[9] This is fair enough. Christians are, indeed, exhorted by Paul to let their aims "be such as all men count honourable", and by Peter to let all their behaviour "be such as even pagans can recognise as good". But to deduce from this that distinctively Christian existence (not behaviour, be it noted) is, in Bonhoeffer's words, "essentially something secular,"[10] involves interpreting the words "essentially" and "secular" in a somewhat special way.

For myself, I completely agree that the Christian, like his Lord, must be deeply involved in the common life of his fellow men; that basically (and I emphasise this word) the "truly human is not one thing for Christians and another thing for non-Christians"; and that when one comes face-to-face with contemporary moral problems — such as civil liberties, race, questions of life and death, sex, censorship, etc. — the Christian may all too often find that his own opinion co-incides with that of some humanists more closely

[8] p. 23. My italics.
[9] p. 24.
[10] Ibid.

than with that of some of his fellow Christians.[11] But this, although extremely important, is not the fundamental issue, for true Christianity does not consist in the convictions about social questions, however vital, which seep down from a man's mind to his innermost being, but rather a transformation of heart which then has to be worked out in terms of mental convictions and daily behaviour. In other words, the movement is not from the circumference to the centre, but the other way round.

Again, Robinson is at his best when he observes: "This does not mean that Christianity makes no difference. There is—or should be—a difference of dimension in our estimate of man. In the light of Christ *both* the demand *and* the freedom of a genuinely human existence ought to appear a great deal more searching." There should, too, "be expected of Christians a morality that exceeds what can be expected (let alone enforced) in society as a whole. But it is not a different kind of morality." But when he continues: "What distinguishes a Christian is not to be moral, any more than to be religious, in a particular way, but to be a man—with the radical obedience and freedom of Jesus Christ"[12]—he seems to me to combine an emphasis on the fact that morality and religion, as God intended them to be, are for man as man, rather than for some particular class of persons (which is obviously true), with a failure to recognise (or, at any rate, emphasise) that fallen man does not, and cannot, behave or worship in that way, even if he takes Jesus Christ as his example and model: he desperately needs that transformation of his innermost self which can be effected only by the Spirit of God, and which has been made possible not so much by the life, as by the atoning and reconciling death, of that same Jesus.

Robinson next turns to a disquisition on basic moral questions, in which he seems to me to betray the same sort of ambivalence. "No responsible advocate of situational ethics denies law in favour of love or sees the two as antithetical,' he tells us. This could scarcely be bettered. But

[11] pp. 25 f.
[12] p. 26.

when he insists that law should never (it seems) "decide the moral issue", but only "safeguard" it, he goes overboard in favour of the thesis that moral choices in such matters as "sex relationships, divorce, euthanasia, gambling, drugs, reading-matter and the rest" must be left to the unilateral discretion of "the individuals concerned", and that the role of law is exclusively to safeguard these individuals against "exploitation or abuse". It is, he believes, "a cardinal insight of the gospel" that in all these things—and, it would seem, in all circumstances—the place of the law "is at the edge to protect freedom, not at the centre to prohibit it".[13]

Now almost everyone would agree that the basic function of law is to protect, rather than restrict, the proper exercise of individual rights and liberties. But it is impossible, in practice, to safeguard the rights and liberties of some members of society without imposing any restrictions whatever on the unbridled freedom of others. Robinson, as chairman of a law-reform society, does not, of course, go nearly so far as to advocate the immediate and unqualified removal of all legal controls. But he passionately believes that the above-quoted "cardinal insight of the gospel" (*sic*) must be "translated, without any illusions about the selfishness and evil of man, into the moral leadership and legislative framework of a free, responsible, seculiar society—all to the end that life can be more deeply and truly human."[14] This sounds like a recipe for utopia until one realises that Robinson, whatever he may say, does in fact labour under some rather obvious illusions about the essential "selfishness and evil of man", about what "moral leadership and legislative framework" can accomplish, and about the feasibility of a society in which its basic institutions, together with the human dignity of some of its members, need no longer be secured—in the last resort—not only by the legal restraint of others (which must, inevitably, to some extent restrict *their* freedom) but also by the use of law, in certain cases, to protect people from themselves.

Even John Stuart Mill, for example, qualified his famous

[13] pp. 26 f.
[14] p. 27.

dictum that "the sole end for which mankind are warranted, individually or collectively, in interfering with the liberty of action of any of their number, is self-protection" (that is, "the only purpose for which power can be rightfully exercised over any member of a civilised community, against his will, is to prevent harm to others. His own good, either physical or moral, is not a sufficient warrant. He cannot rightfully be compelled to do or forbear because it will be better for him to do so, because it will make him happier, because, in the opinion of others, to do so would be wise, or even right"), by explicitly limiting this principle to "those in the maturity of their faculties" (i.e. sane, responsible adults) and to members of "civilised communities".[15] And H. L. A. Hart, who seems to me to go beyond Mill in his unqualified insistence that criminal sanctions must *never* be used to uphold moral standards, takes a totally different stance from Mill's when he argues that it is legitimate for the criminal law sometimes to be used for "paternalistic" purposes (e.g. by making it difficult for even a sane, adult member of a civilised society to obtain easy access to hard drugs). He defends this departure from Mill's view (shared, as it is, by much liberal opinion today), as

due, in part, to a general decline in the belief that individuals know their own interests best, and to an increased awareness of a great range of factors which diminish the significance to be attached to an apparently free choice or to consent. Choices may be made or consent given without adequate reflection or appreciation of the consequences; or in pursuit of merely transitory desires; or in various predicaments when the judgment is likely to be clouded; or under inner psychological compulsion; or under pressure by others of a kind too subtle to be susceptible of proof in a court of law. Underlying Mill's extreme fear of paternalism there is perhaps

[15] *On Liberty.* Reprinted in *Utilitarianism, Liberty and Representative Government* (Everyman's Library no. 482, J. M. Dent, London, 1910), pp. 72 f.

a conception of what a normal human being is like which now seems not to correspond to the facts.[16]

It is noteworthy, moreover, that Mill himself found it impossible to decide whether an adult member of a civilised society might not rightly be subjected to criminal sanctions if he became a pimp or kept a gambling house. This hesitation would seem, at first sight, to run right against his basic principles; but he saw much force in the contrary argument that "if society believes conduct to be bad, it must be at least a disputable question whether it is good or bad: that being so, society is entitled to exclude the influence of solicitations which are not disinterested."[17] This means that, while the law should not prohibit a responsible adult from doing himself physical or moral injury, or two responsible adults from mutually engaging in such practices, it is distinctly arguable whether the law may not rightly be called in aid to seek to prevent the exploitation of the moral weaknesses of third parties, or the public at large, for commercial gain—or, in other words, commercialised vice.

Yet again, questions of divorce, euthanasia and abortion can scarcely be said to represent moral choices which are exclusively personal. Any lawyer or doctor is aware, for example, of the many and complex problems connected with "voluntary" euthanasia. If a patient who was in pain had the right immediately to require a doctor to give him a lethal dose, who can tell whether he would not have changed his mind at a later date? If, on the other hand, any such request is to be made in advance, what effect is this likely to have on the future relationship of the patient with his doctor? And if voluntary euthanasia is accepted as right and proper in the community at large, then who can predict the pressure of conscience likely to be felt by a sensitive person, whose care may fall exceedingly heavily on others, to relieve them of this burden?

These are only a few examples, selected almost at

[16] *Law, Liberty and Morality* (OUP, London, 1963), pp. 32 f.
[17] Op. cit., pp. 154 f.

random, to show how difficult it is consistently to banish law to the "edges" of society, or to speak in sweeping terms of moral choices which should be "taken by the individuals concerned and safeguarded by society against exploitation or abuse". I have no doubt whatever, for example, that abortion is justifiable when the life or basic health (whether physical or mental) of the mother is genuinely at risk; but a human foetus is not on a par with a tumour or a troublesome tooth—and it is an oversimplification to say with Robinson that "society should give the mother every encouragement, facility, *and therefore the real freedom*, to keep her child however unwanted; but finally the responsibility must be hers, since she has to carry it."[18] Certainly her interest in the matter is far greater than that of any other individual; but it is not exclusive. There are also the interests of the father, the doctor and nurses involved in an abortion, the foetus, the moral principle of the sanctity of life, and the indirect effects which a fundamental change of attitude in regard to euthanasia and abortion may have on society as a whole. This over-simplified approach to the whole question of morality and law ignores, moreover, the part that law may legitimately play in forming moral attitudes. Morris Ginsberg, for example, has pertinently remarked that American legislation designed to prevent and penalise racial segregation might well, if persistently enforced, "help to bring about a change in attitude, in behaviour and eventually in moral convictions".[19] And precisely the same is true, I think, of our own Race Relations Acts.

Robinson next returns to his thesis that "The aim, how to be human now (and it is an aim which is constantly expanding), should be the same for Christians and non-Christians. Of course it often isn't; and Christians have been subhumanist as well as humanists sub-Christian."[20] Now it is, of course, sadly true that Christians often behave in a way of which many humanists would be ashamed; but how, one

[18] p. 27.
[19] *On Justice in Society* (Penguin Books, London, 1965), p. 235.
[20] p. 27.

wonders, can a non-Christian even aspire to be a "new creature", or a "new creation",[21] in the way in which Paul insists is true, in principle, of those who are "in Christ"? Almost at once, however, Robinson changes into what I can only call his "Christian gear", and emphasises that Jesus insisted that the righteousness of his followers should exceed that of the Scribes and Pharisees; that they should love their enemies and "be perfect" (whether or not the Aramaic word behind this term primarily means "whole, generous, gracious") "as their heavenly Father is perfect"; and should be open to "the grace of our Lord Jesus Christ and the love of God and the fellowship of the Holy Spirit".[22] The love of God, he tells us, is "man's ultimate environment, what he is made from and what he is made for;" and the "basic difference between the Christian and the non-Christian humanist" is that, for the Christian, "love is not only what ought to be the ultimate reality but what is. Herein is love: not that we love God—or man—but that he loves us". And it is through the grace of our Lord Jesus Christ, alone, that we can find "evidence" for "such an estimate of the cosmos": that "at heart being *is* gracious— not merely good as opposed to alien or absurd."[23] This is profoundly true; but why cannot we follow the Jesus who provides this evidence a little further and speak, in a much more intimate and meaningful way, about a loving Person rather than an "estimate of the cosmos"? "The Christian way," Robinson splendidly insists, "rests upon the logic 'Freely you have received: freely give.' 'Accept one another as Christ has accepted you', and, most fundamentally of all, 'Accept yourself—for you have been accepted'.... The Christian knows what every psychologist testifies, that we learn to love not by being told to love but by *being loved*." This is excellent. But why complicate what is so delightfully simple by adding: "And it is this reality at the root of our humanness that the ultimacy of grace—or (viewed the other

[21] Or, in Bonhoeffer's words quoted above, "the man that Christ creates in us".

[22] p. 28.

[23] p. 29.

way round) the divinity of Christ—is affirming."[24] What *does* this really mean?

Robinson can, indeed, speak in personal and unequivocal terms about God, as when he tells us that *koinonia* in the New Testament means "participation in the great, encompassing, environmental reality of God, of Christ, and above all of the Holy Spirit". But he then asserts that "Real living is *koinonia*: without it life cannot be whole, human or holy. . . . To be without participation, economically or politically, is to be deprived, diminished, denied as human beings. . . . Holy community is a secular phenomenon for all men, to be celebrated where it is, wherever it is, and to be fought for where it isn't."[25] There is, of course, a great deal of truth in these observations; but, again, what do they really mean in this context?

For myself, I cannot escape the conclusion that this represents either muddled thinking or a totally inadequate interpretation of the New Testament. It is perfectly true that in this chapter Robinson is concerned with the "public marks" of the Christian "life-style" rather than its inner secrets; that it is, indeed, the calling of Christians to be fully involved in all that is authentically human, recognising—as the Epistle to Diognetus puts it—that "They dwell in their own countries, but only as sojourners; they bear their share in all things as citizens, and they endure all hardships as strangers. Every foreign country is a fatherland to them and every fatherland is foreign."[26] Precisely; but the basic reason why they are "sojourners" and "strangers", dwelling in lands which are in one sense always "foreign", is that the *koinonia* of God, Christ and the Holy Spirit is something far deeper than social justice (passionately though the Christian should fight for this) or, indeed, than any "secular phenomenon for all men". It is a unique creation of God in the hearts of those who have not only experienced a natural birth as citizens of this world, but a second birth into the spiritual family of God.

[24] Ibid.
[25] p. 30.
[26] Quoted by Robinson, at pp. 30 f.

Once more, however, Robinson changes into his essentially Christian gear. He speaks of that "baffling combination of attachment and detachment" which a Christian experiences just because he "cares more about this world than other men, and cares less: he may well give his life for it, but he will not give his life to it."[27] He tells us that Christians "are here on temporary papers: their citizenship is elsewhere. They must live their distinctive new life in the midst of this old world and its values. And between the two there is war."[28] He also brings out vividly the paradox between injunctions such as "Submit yourselves to every human institution" and "Live as free men." But here he cannot refrain from lapsing into the shibboleths of "Situation Ethics", and insists that the Christian style of life "has no absolutes but love" and is "free, supple, flexible, because it goes unerringly for the person rather than the principle".[29] Yet there are many circumstances in which an exclusive regard for "the person" may involve the breach of an abiding principle which may ultimately affect not one person but many. Which of us is in fact able to hold in balance the interests of the individual or individuals immediately concerned, of third parties, and of society as a whole—particularly when we are ourselves deeply and emotionally involved? When Robinson says (this time in *Honest to God*): "Love alone, because, as it were, it has a built-in moral compass, enabling it to 'home' intuitively upon the deepest need of the other, can allow itself to be directed completely by the situation. . . . It is able to embrace an ethic of radical responsiveness, meeting every situation on its own merits, with no prescriptive laws",[30] he is either looking at fallen humanity through very rose-tinted spectacles or indulging in a fantasy of wishful thinking. That is why the God who is love has enunciated in the

[27] p. 31.
[28] p. 32.
[29] pp. 33 and 34.
[30] p. 115. I have discussed Situation Ethics rather more adequately in my recent book *Morality, Law and Grace* (Tyndale Press, London, 1972), pp. 50 ff.

Bible—Old Testament, Gospels and Epistles—abiding moral principles with such emphasis and insistence.

III

The third chapter, "The Truth—Now", starts excellently with the unequivocal statement that "The most fundamental question about Christianity is not, Does it work? but, Is it true? And traditionally the most distinctive thing about Christianity has been not its way of life but its beliefs." How, then, can we speak of "the truth now"? "The way may change but surely not the truth, 'the everlasting gospel'. For is not Jesus Christ 'the same yesterday, today and for ever'?"[31]

Robinson solves this problem by affirming, with Kierkegaard, that the question of truth is, for the Christian, always "an existential one. His is not simply Pilate's question 'What is truth?' but 'What is my relation to truth, what is true for me?'"[32] For once, however, Robinson is acting out of character, for here he is making an either-or assertion where he should be making a both-and affirmation. For Christianity is first and foremost a historical religion, and the truth about Jesus Christ is primarily historical and "once and for all". Indubitably it must also come to us in an existential way which challenges our personal response; but this is, I believe, always and essentially secondary. It seems to me fundamentally misleading to say: "The doctrine of the Atonement ... is actually about the transformation of human relationships here and now. But it doesn't appear to be: it seems to be about some distant divine-human transaction on 'a green hill far away', of which people *begin* by asking, "How on earth could this affect me?"[33] For here Robinson—unconsciously, I feel sure—is resorting to the age-old device of using somewhat loaded phrases like "some distant divine-human trans-

[31] p. 36.
[32] p. 37.
[33] p. 39.

action", a "green hill far away", and "How on earth could this affect me?" to obscure the fundamental point that the basic purpose of the atonement was to mend the broken relationship between men and God,[34] and that it is this primary reconciliation which issues in "the transformation of human relationships here and now", not the other way round.

Robinson further confuses this issue, as it seems to me, when he interprets the Johannine statement, that the test of what is authentically and distinctively Christian is "Jesus Christ come in the flesh", as relating not only to the past but "to the Christ who is in the world as we are in the world—embodied in people".[35] As a New Testament scholar he must know perfectly well that this is not what John meant: he meant that no teaching is authentically Christian which denies the historic Incarnation. True, we have the promise of the incarnate Lord that he would not leave us orphans, but would come to us in and through the Spirit. But surely it is a misuse of this particular passage in I John 4 to make it the basis of the assertion "The starting-point still is flesh and blood, and the movement is from relationships to revelation, from experience to authority, from Christ as man to Christ as God"[36] —true though the last clause, in particular, certainly is.

It is in this context that Robinson affirms that he does not personally believe "that the word 'God' *is* finally dead. Ultimately I doubt if we can get on without it (or some other like it) for designating *and grounding* the recurrent awareness of transcendence in experience." But he adds that he is "entirely prepared to accept that we should not start with the word 'God', and I'd happily settle for a moratorium or close season on its use. After all, Jesus, for whom God-language was no problem, used it remarkably little in talking to the crowds."[37] In point of fact, however, Jesus seems to have talked a great deal about—and to—his

[34] See chapter 5 above.
[35] pp. 39 f.
[36] p. 40.
[37] pp. 40 f.

Father; so much so that Paul, writing a letter in Greek to a church which can have known little or no Aramaic, could find no better way of expressing the existential experience of one who has been "adopted" by faith into God's family than by saying that God sends into such a man's heart the "Spirit of his Son, crying 'Abba, Father' "—using the intimate family word for father in Aramaic which can only represent a vivid remembrance—passed on to Paul by the original disciples—of the habitual way in which Jesus himself (probably for the first time in human history) addressed God in prayer.

I am in complete accord with Robinson in believing that men come to God through "the man Christ Jesus", and not to Christ through "God". But it seems to me to be going too far to say, with Fred Brown, that God *is* Astonished Joy, God *is* Community, Responsibility, Fulfilment (or Freedom from Fear), or to concur in Robinson's comment "For in real meeting and giving of yourself you do encounter that to which the tag 'God' has been attached."[38] Surely it is crystal clear that Jesus—the Word made flesh, as Robinson emphasises—thought of God not as a "tag" word, or an abstract experience of what is good, right and loving, but as a living Person whom we can get to know in a personal way; and whom we often meet, it is true, in human situations, but pre-eminently in Jesus himself, as the risen, living Lord. Before we say with Fred Brown "There are more Christians outside than inside the Church",[39] it all depends, of course, on how we define the terms "Christians" and "Church" in this context. To assume that anyone who *acts*, on some occasions, in a "Christian" way has in fact experienced that repentance, faith, forgiveness and membership in his body which Christ came to give us is merely an example, I fear, of wishful thinking; but the different pictures of the Judgment Day given in the New Testament, when taken together, certainly seem to teach that "saving faith" must have been vindicated to the world

[38] pp. 42 f.
[39] Quoted by Robinson, at p. 43.

by the quality of life to which it led. As Robinson splendidly puts it, there is a vast difference between

> the son (as the parable puts it) who *says* 'I go' and ... the son who goes. There is no doubt that it is the going rather than the saying which is decisive, but no doubt also that in New Testament usage Christians are distinguished by acknowledging Christ, by naming him. They are those who 'believe in their heart, and confess with their lips that Jesus is Lord.' *Just* to say 'Lord, Lord', is fruitless. But to say, 'Lord', is an essential mark of being a Christian.

But when he adds that "the function of 'God' and 'Christ' language is precisely to identify the otherwise nameless, ineffable experience" (and bases this assertion on Paul's declaration at Athens that "What you worship but do not know—this is what I ... proclaim"),[40] he is, I think, stretching the basic concept of the essential lordship of Christ beyond biblical bounds. To attempt to worship some Person or Power beyond oneself is, no doubt, a step in the right direction; but it certainly falls very far short of Christian commitment.

Again, Robinson seems to me to show the same ambivalence when he says, on the one hand, that "Christians are those who name God—by pointing to the man.[41] They certainly don't claim to define God, to know what he connotes, what he is in himself; only what he denotes, what he's like if you meet him"; and then asserts, on the other hand, that "we must be open to the fact—whether we like it or not—that commitment to Christ and the 'idea of God' in *any* form are for many of our contemporaries antithetical."[42] It may, indeed, be possible, or even common, for men to commit themselves "to that which came to expression in Jesus Christ" without any belief in a "supernatural being" if, by such commitment, they mean no more than an

[40] p. 43.
[41] i.e., Christ.
[42] p. 46.

attempt to follow the ethical teaching and example of Jesus. But to go on to speak of the "real offence of the gospel, Jesus Christ and him crucified", without any reference whatever to what may be termed the God-ward side of the crucifixion, strikes me as quite inadequate;[43] to describe the traditional idea of God as a supernatural being as "crude" seems to me almost ludicrous (for wherein does the crudity lie; in the concept of "supernatural" or that of "being"?); and to assert that there is "more danger in a static doctrinal fundamentalism than in most heresy"[44] represents the age-old game of caricaturing those with whom one disagrees and then attacking the caricature rather than the real portrait. Robinson must know that the term "fundamentalist" (like "Puritan", "Methodist" and many other such terms down the centuries) is habitually used today of a wide variety of theologians and a large number of ordinary, but indubitably committed, Christians—even using the term "committed" in a strictly Robinsonian sense! And one wonders what, exactly, he means by "static" in this context. Is it static to regard the "fundamentals" of the faith as "given" and unchanging, or only so if one's mind is closed to any new understanding of those fundamentals?

IV

The fourth chapter is entitled "The Life—Now". It begins with a shortened form of the Johannine affirmation of the purpose behind the composition of the Fourth Gospel: "These things are written that you may believe, and that believing you may have *life*." Robinson emphasises, more-over, that the eternal life which is the burden of this Gospel "does not simply mean life after death, but real life, at a depth and of a quality that nothing merely biological can either give or take away. Of course it includes life after death—it simply would not be what it is if it could be finished by a bacillus or a bus. But it is life beyond self in

[43] Cf. pp. 158–195 above.
[44] pp. 47 f.

213

every sense of the word." Equally helpfully, we are reminded that "The life is the inside of the way. The way is a style of relationship to the world, and is primarily marked by doing. The life is the inner secret of the style, and is primarily marked by being." And this inevitably leads to the question "What then is the distinctively Christian life —now, individually and corporately?"[45]

Much more questionably, Robinson then summarises the concept of the Christian life which, he asserts, has hitherto prevailed as

> a pretty simple, uncomplicated version of the centre-periphery model. In this model, Christ is at the centre of a circle of light. The innermost ring comprises churchmen who are faithfully trying to live "the Christian life' (saying their prayers, going to church, receiving the sacraments, and so on). Thence there is a shading off to nominal, 'four-wheeler' Christians (who come to church in their pram to be christened, in the taxi to be married, and in the hearse to be buried), to those on the fringe, and finally to outsiders (who live in the darkness of 'the world'). On this view there is a simple equation: to join the Church is to come into the life, and to come into the life is to join the Church.[46]

But this must depend, of course, on the semantic question of what it really means to "join the Church", for this can scarcely be defined so simply as in terms of those graduated degrees of attendance, or non-attendance, at some place of worship to which such vivid and humorous reference has just been made.

The reality, we are told, is that the Christian life is not "a world of its own within the world";[47] it is "not distinctive by being distinct"; it does not mean "separate development"— whether this be "in the enclosed garden of the soul or the gathered fellowship of the congregation".[48] Instead,

[45] p. 49.
[46] Ibid.
[47] p. 50.
[48] p. 51.

214

Robinson somewhat questionably insists, the life is "the secret of what it means to be human". What distinguishes a Christian "is that he says with St. Paul, 'To me to live is *Christ*': for here—not only in the historical Jesus but in all that is meant by the new being 'in Christ'—he sees life defined and vindicated with a richness and a power that he does not see in Zen, or the Tao, or the Torah, or Marxism, however much all these and others may have to offer." This is, of course, splendid so far as it goes: but is the difference of life in Christ, on the one hand, and life in Zen or Marxism, on the other, merely a matter of degree? Is it not, in fact, a radically different and distinct form of life, however true it may be that this life is to be lived not only in the cloister or the church, but emphatically in the world? There is a very real sense, no doubt, in which the Christian life may be described, from the point of view of our everyday existence, as "common life uncommonly good, ordinary life transformed into something extraordinary".[49] But it is at least equally true that in the Bible, and especially in the Johannine writings, "life" is contrasted with "death", and that one of the most distinctive marks of a Christian is that he "has passed out of death into life". Of course this does not involve cutting himself off from other men, but an ever-increasing desire to share with them the eternal life which God has "given" him, through no achievement of his own, in his Son. But it stands written that "He who has the Son, has the life; he who has not the Son of God has not the life"; and the next verse specifies what this essentially means, when we read: "I write this to you who believe in the name of the Son of God, that you may know that you have eternal life"—and, indeed, when we read later in the chapter that "the whole world is in the evil one."[50]

This, surely, is the way in which the New Testament would express what Robinson caricatures as the "motive and goal" of Christian mission in the past,

to convert all men before they died. Otherwise they

[49] Ibid.
[50] I John 5:12, 13 and 19.

215

might be damned everlastingly. Certainly there was no assurance that they would be saved. Even in the early decades of this century 'the evangelisation of the world in this generation' was seen as a measured target. It was never really doubted that the object of evangelism was to make all men Christians, which for Roman Catholics meant quite simply make all men Roman Catholics—and the same for others *mutatis mutandis*, with varying discounts according to the hardness of your theology or the breadth of your charity.[51]

But it would be a major tragedy if the New Testament emphasis on evangelism, of which this is such a distorted picture, has in fact "got gradually—but rather rapidly—eroded", although I would take leave to take this statement with a large pinch of salt. For the evangel is still what it has always been: repent (i.e. turn both from sin and self-righteousness, from personal merit and demerit) and believe on the Son of God (who died for our sins and rose again for our justification). When we proclaim the evangel we are acting as ambassadors who plead with men, on behalf of Christ, to be reconciled to God—and that reconciliation is possible only because an ever-loving God "made him to be sin for us, who knew no sin: that we might be made the righteousness of God in him".

But Robinson obscures all this. He first asserts that "*koinonia* is where the Kingdom is, and the Kingdom is where *koinonia* is, in the world—whether in mercy or judgment" (whatever the last remark may mean). Next he tells us that *ecclesia* is

whatever formation is called for in a particular situation to meet the claims of *koinonia*, to embody life, love, justice, freedom—in other words to make life human. . . . And 'the clusters called for' (which is the root meaning of *ecclesia*) to make life human will be composed of many who cannot 'name' him[52] but who are just as concerned

[51] p. 53.
[52] i.e., Christ.

for *koinonia* in such basic human issues as the supply and distribution of bread, civil liberties, race, peace, pollution, population control, literacy, law reform, minority rights, etc., etc.[53]

Now again there can, of course, be no doubt whatever that Christians (who are, Robinson affirms, in the "special relationship" with God in Christ which *ecclesia* or being called out implies)[54] should be deeply concerned in all these issues. But that is a very different thing from implying that all who are concerned with such things—whether or not they feel any personal need for God's forgiveness, reconciling love and inward quickening—are all part of what the New Testament means by *ecclesia*. It is not enough to say that "the life made articulate, consciously and corporately appropriated, can be richer and deeper, freer and more joyful, than when it is lived with some levels of personality not engaged." Nor is it true to the New Testament to say that "Those *not* called to this special relationship of being in the Church ... are not *for that reason* condemned—though they may be for other reasons, which have to do with lovelessness"[55] (unless, of course, one uses the word "Church" with a narrowness of meaning for which I do not think the Bible gives any warrant, and the term "lovelessness" with a width of meaning for which I can find no warrant inside or outside the Bible). It is, I believe, perfectly true that in John 6 (which Robinson describes as the longest treatment of the Eucharist in the New Testament, but which in fact, as William Temple emphasised, refers not only to the Eucharist but to any "feeding" on Christ) the promise is to *whoever* comes to him; and that the bread he gives is "for the life of the *world*".[56] But the very same verse tells us unequivocally that it is those who actually eat of this bread who will "live for ever". So the burden of evangelism must

[53] pp. 54 f.
[54] But is not this statement itself somewhat inconsistent with what he has said, just before, on this subject?
[55] pp. 55 f.
[56] p. 58.

217

still be to plead with men both to "come" and to "eat"—with a meaning far wider than the Eucharist, but specifically centred on Christ himself.

V

With the way in which Robinson develops his thesis in the last two chapters, entitled "Tomorrow's Layman" and "Tomorrow's Priest", I am myself in very substantial agreement. He is here primarily concerned to get away from the stereotype of the past: the clear-cut distinction between the layman and the cleric. "To be a Christian," he justly remarks, is to be "at the disposal of all, yet at the mercy of none—save one." In the New Testament, he reminds us, the two words from which our terms "clergy" and "layman" are derived are both used to designate the whole people of God—whereas today they have all too often come to distinguish "two sorts of Christians, not good and bad Christians, but (in army parlance) officers and men".[57] Yet it remains true that "within the single vocation to be a Christian, there remain . . . diversities of functions and ministry. And these differences, unlike the status-marking clergy line, are native to the Church."[58]

It is particularly true of the layman, for example, that he should be what the New Testament describes as "in" the world but not "of" it; that he should be characterised by what Alec Vidler has termed "holy worldliness". This is not intended to denote

something particularly pious but a being in the world, up to the hilt, yet with a difference. . . . It means being wholly involved in the world, yet not deriving one's accreditation from it; being bound to it, yet not by it. It is . . . like walking on the knife-edge of a mountain ridge, with the ever present danger of slithering down into holy other-worldliness on the one side or into unholy worldliness on

[57] pp. 61 f.
[58] p. 63.

the other. And the layman is the man who walks that ridge with all the delicacy of balance and maturity of judgment which that requires.[59]

To say that "the Church has always recognised the vocation of some to a relative disengagement, to a standing back *from* the world in order to be free *for* it in special ways—to be set apart, for instance, to be ministers, missionaries or monks" is perfectly true, but carries with it, as Robinson justly remarks, two dangers: first, the "disastrous association" of the idea of "vocation" with this alone—"with the corollary that the majority who feel no call to this relative distancing have no vocation"; and, secondly, the "other distorting factor" of imagining that *all* ministers have the call "to forsake and set aside ... all worldly cares and studies".[60] But the fact remains that it is the *particular* function of the layman to be, to the society in which he lives, both salt and light. "Salt kept by itself in a salt-cellar is an agglomeration of useless white crystals: it does its stuff—it preserves, heals and savours—only as it is 'in solution', dissolved and assimilated in something else." Similarly, he pertinently remarks, "light too cannot be seen for itself alone: it can only be detected by the matter it falls on and the specks it illumines."[61]

Again, "a layman, as the derivation of the word implies, is a member of the *laos*, or 'holy people'. . . . And this is something you can only be in the plural, as a member of a group. In other words, to be a layman ... is necessarily to be in *ecclesia*, in that special relationship of corporate and conscious dedication to the kingdom of God which the Bible indicates by the people of God." But while this means that he will necessarily be a "Church-man", in the sense of being associated with his fellow Christians in some church, he may well fulfil his vocation, more and more, "through secular rather than religious groups".[62] I am sure this is true. But

[59] p. 64.
[60] pp. 64 f.
[61] p. 65.
[62] pp. 66 and 68.

again Robinson, to my mind, confuses what is a perfectly clear conception (however difficult it is to live it out in practice) by using the New Testament terms *koinonia* and *ecclesia* in this not "peculiarly Christian category", and by including in these terms those who would not call themselves Christians, and would have no desire whatever to be "baptised" as such. And he seems to imagine that the Lord's statement that "He who is not against us is for us" provides an adequate basis for this argument.

Now, of course there are, to our shame, many "sons of hope" who try, much more effectively than many church members, to "promote better understanding among men and work toward building a new world" (in Archbishop Helder Camara's words), yet who "could not call themselves Christians even in the loosest and most unpackaged sense".[63] But I very much doubt if we can conclude, with Camara, that they are thereby co-operating with "the Father's plan for redeeming the world". To say this, it seems to me, is to confuse two aspects of the Godhead which it is exceedingly important to distinguish: God as Creator and God as Redeemer. As our Creator, God is certainly most intimately involved in all that concerns his creatures: that they have enough to eat and decent houses to live in; that they enjoy social, economic and racial justice; that they should maintain moral standards, develop their artistic gifts, and engage in politics in a responsible way. But none of these things constitute what the New Testament means by redemption. It was specifically because of human sin and estrangement from himself that God the Creator became God the Redeemer, and came in Christ to "seek and to save that which was lost". We can indeed co-operate in God's plan to transform or reform the world in the way Camara describes; but we can co-operate in the Father's "plan of redemption" only in so far as we try to lead other men and women to the Redeemer.

When we turn to "Tomorrow's Priest" we are told that the "crisis of identity in which the contemporary Christian finds himself" is nowhere "focused and intensified more

[63] pp. 69 f.

than in the person of the ordained minister or priest" (which latter term is used throughout the chapter, Robinson emphasises, "for shorthand purposes without any ecclesiastical overtones").[64] The role of the professional ministry is under both sociological and theological pressure today: sociological, because the familiar role of the "priest" is threatened by the ever-increasing secularisation of society; and theological, because, "with the rediscovery of the priesthood of the whole laity his prerogative appears to be usurped."[65] In the past there have been certain functions "Which have been the preserve of the ordained ministry. . . . The more Catholic its ethos, the more the magic circle is centred in the Sacraments; the more Protestant, the more it is focused on the Word." This last remark is, perhaps, somewhat exaggerated, since there are in fact a number of laymen who preach, speak and teach as often and as widely as many of the clergy. But it is substantially true that "in the practice of all our traditions, priesthood or ministry has been defined and marked off as a clerisy *opposed* to a laity." Yet this, we are told, "is theologically a nonsense, as has always in theory been recognised. For clearly the priest is a part of the *laos*."[66]

"In Judaism, to be sure", he continues, "there was a priestly tribe set apart from the rest to do what the others could not do". But Christianity abolished all that.

> The veil of the Temple was rent from top to bottom. For nearly two hundred years the words 'priest' and 'priestly' were applied solely to the Body as a whole (*presbyteros*, elder, not *hiereus*, a priest, being the term for the particular order of ministry), and 'ministry', *diaconia*, was of course a description of the activity of the whole church prior to its technical use for the diaconate. In other words . . . priesthood and ministry are there not to do what the others cannot do but to carry out *on their behalf* what all

[64] p. 73.
[65] p. 74.
[66] p. 75.

must do. The relation of those specially ordained is representative rather than vicarious.[67]

In the New Testament, in point of fact, we find a variety of commissionings for particular ministries. But in the intervening centuries "this profusion has been disastrously restricted" and the "priesthood" now "includes the lot: all are swallowed up into one omnivorous order of ministry. One man is expected to do everything, the rest nothing."[68] And this has not only impoverished the laity but also deterred from ordination many who realise that they have not "got everything": "Indeed, it is too often those who are most discerning that are most deterred."[69]

Sociologically, moreover, the distinctiveness of the "Ministry" "has hitherto been assured by its being *a* profession amongst others, with its own carefully controlled entry, standards of training, professional code and career-structure".[70] But today much of this is breaking down. What, then, is to be the distinctive role of the "priesthood"? Robinson finds the answer to this question in the basic meaning of what it is to be a professional, a "man for others —speaking for them, acting for them, suffering for them. For that at their best is what the professions in society exist to do—like the doctor or the social worker or the advocate."[71]

In this the task of the minister is not, of course, *contrasted* with that of other Christians. "All laity are called to follow the man for others. But there is a true sense in which the priest is called to be that to them, to be ... 'the servant of the servants of God'. This again is a focussing and intensification of the role of the laity, not a difference from it." And an essential element in ordination (often obscured in our practice) is, he insists, that "the candidate is proposed and put forward by the congregation from which he comes

[67] Ibid.
[68] pp. 75 f.
[69] p. 76.
[70] p. 78.
[71] p. 79.

222

and commissioned to be there." The call to ordination is

> increasingly going to come this way, not from on high
> . . . but out of the midst, thrown up by the local group
> (with such wider acknowledgement, training and author-
> ization as is needed). It will not require the kind of
> person who 'has everything' in order, as at present, to be
> licensed for everything. It need not be for life in the
> sense of duration, though it will unreservedly be for
> life in the sense of direction. Nor will it necessarily be
> full-time in economic terms, though being a priest, like
> being a layman or being a man, is essentially a full-time
> vocation. . . . But there is room for every sort of ministry,
> and the more variety and equality and cross-fertilization
> between them the healthier.[72]

Much of this seems to me to make excellent sense, from
every point of view. It is no surprise, moreover, to find that
this little book ends on a note of confidence. For the
supreme vocation for the Christian (whatever his specific
function in Church or world) is that

> like his master, the complete layman as well as 'the high
> priest of our profession', who yet occupied no niche
> secular or ecclesiastical, he is there, ultimately, to *be* the
> place of at-one-ment. To serve as this for alienated human-
> ity he may be forced outside the camp—any camp—on
> to the cross. And this after all is the only *distinctive* place
> which the New Testament holds out for the Christian.
> The anxiety to find another, some less vulnerable *locus
> standi*, is a false anxiety. And this and no other is also the
> place of resurrection and of life.[73]

Like so much in this book, this is both true and deeply
moving so far as it goes. It sets an enormously high standard
for the Christian: a standard from which I must frankly
confess that I myself fall lamentably short. It is certainly

[72] p. 82.
[73] pp. 83 f.

true that the Christian is called to fulfil a ministry of reconciliation towards "alienated humanity", and that those who genuinely try to exercise this most costly ministry all too often are themselves rejected. It is also true that the only distinctive role which the New Testament holds out for the Christian is to follow in the footsteps of his crucified Lord. Only as we "share his sufferings, in growing conformity to his death" can we really "experience the power of his resurrection";[74] and only as we, like Paul, are "crucified with him" can we know what it is to cease to live our own self-centred lives and to have Christ live his life in us.[75]

Yet the way in which Robinson puts this leaves me with an uneasy feeling that, for all its truth and spiritual challenge, there is still something missing, something which is even misleading. For the cross of Calvary, and the atonement which the crucified Saviour there sealed with his blood, is not *only* our supreme example and the archetypal demonstration of the basic principle of life through death. It is much more than that. It is the unique act of God-in-Christ by which he reconciled mankind to himself, by taking the sinner's place and bearing the sinner's guilt; for it was there that "God caused Christ, who himself knew nothing of sin, actually to *be* sin for our sakes, so that in Christ we might be made good with the goodness of God."[76] It is only because he went to such incredible lengths to win us back to himself, and because he no longer counts our sins against us, that we can become "Christ's ambassadors" and, in his name, "implore" others to be "reconciled to God."[77] It is in that sense, and in that sense alone, that we can be what Robinson terms a "place of at-one-ment" between God and man; and only in that sense, too, that we can hope to do anything decisive and lasting to break down the enmity which stands like a dividing wall between man and his brother.[78]

[74] Phil. 3:10 and 11 (NEB).
[75] Gal. 2:20.
[76] II Cor. 5:21 (Phillips).
[77] II Cor. 5:19 and 20.
[78] Cf. Eph. 2:14.

VI

It is precisely at this point that this book, which is so good in parts, seems to me not to go nearly far enough. Robinson makes many references to the New Testament and its teaching, yet he completely ignores this elsewhere—and his basis of selection appears to be purely subjective. It is true, of course, that no one can be expected to cover the whole range of New Testament teaching in one slim volume; indeed, it would be absurd to make any such attempt. But the points which are omitted are, in this case, not peripheral to the subject in hand but absolutely basic. For surely it is only in the light of the fundamental doctrines of the Christian faith—the fact of sin, and the barrier it has inevitably erected between fallen man and a holy God; the redeeming love of God, displayed in all its fulness when Christ "in his own person carried our sins to the gallows";[79] and the miracle of regeneration by the Holy Spirit, whereby God has "delivered us from the dominion of darkness and transferred us to the Kingdom of his beloved Son"[80]—that we can really begin to answer the questions Robinson so pertinently poses.

When so viewed, the "difference in being a *Christian* today" seems to be just as radical and distinctive as it has always been—far more radical than the general tenor of this little book would lead one to suppose. "The difference in being a Christian *today*", on the other hand, appears to be much less radical than Robinson would suggest. It is no doubt true that the "preaching of the cross", in the way which Paul preached it, constitutes a "stumbling block" to many contemporary theologians, and "sheer nonsense" to philosophers and others; but so it was to the Jews and Greeks of the first century. Of course fashions of thought have changed, science has revolutionised many of our concepts, and we are always face to face with the challenge of how best to communicate the Gospel to our generation. But the facts of the Gospel do not change. It would be a grave mistake

[79] I Pet. 2:24.
[80] Col. 1:13 (RSV).

to limit the objective truth of the Gospel to the existential concept of our apprehension of it: the truth about God is first revealed and then, and only then, dimly apprehended.

Nor are we concerned only with this world. There are, indeed, a few passing references in this book to "eternal" life, and the fact that the new life in Christ cannot be ended "by a bacillus or a bus". But the almost exclusive emphasis throughout its pages is on this present human existence. It is true, of course, that Christians have sometimes been so occupied with the world to come that they have neglected their duties and responsibilities in the world in which God has placed them. Now, on the other hand, the pendulum seems to have swung almost to the opposite extreme. It may well be that this is characteristic, to a considerable degree, of contemporary society; but it is certainly not true of the New Testament. Robinson, moreover, did not set out merely to describe the way in which many people think today, but rather the difference it *should* make to be a Christian, as distinct from a humanist, in our contemporary society. And one of the distinguishing marks of a Christian, in any age or generation, should surely be that, while he in no sense ignores the importance of the "life he now lives in the flesh", he is able to view this life, in some measure, in the context of eternity.

It is that viewpoint, indeed, which gives all that concerns our lives here on earth their ultimate meaning and importance. For the Christian, moreover, it must always be true that "If in this life only we have hope in Christ, we are of all men most to be pitied." This is not to depict the Christian life in the terms of the Lenten hymn:

If I find him, if I follow, what his guerdon here?
Many a sorrow, many a labour, many a tear –

for that is a very one-sided picture of Christian experience. Why we should be "most to be pitied" if everything were to end with this life is not that we should have lived miserable lives here on earth to no purpose, but that our lives would have been illumined by a false hope and lived on a false foundation—that we should have invested our "treasure" in an unseen world which was no more than a shimmering mirage. But this is not the case. Instead, Jesus has told us, with sublime simplicity, that there are "many rooms in my Father's house. If there were not, should I have told you that I am going away to prepare a place for you?" And since that statement was made, God has confirmed it by giving us a "new birth into a living hope by the resurrection of Jesus Christ from the dead. The inheritance to which we are born is one that nothing can destroy or spoil or wither." Indeed, it is "kept" in heaven for us, who ourselves are "under the protection of his power until salvation comes—the salvation which is even now in readiness and will be revealed at the end of time".[81] This is the basic difference in being a Christ —whether yesterday, today or tomorrow. So why not say so?

A recent address by Peter Beyerhaus on "The Crisis of Faith in Western Europe"[82] seems to me to give the background against which this book must be viewed. After tracing the history of the Confessing Church in Germany from the dialectical theology of Karl Barth, through the "heilsgeschichtliche" approach to the Bible led by Oscar Cullman and Gerhard von Rad and then the "demythologising" approach of Rudolf Bultmann, he discussed the influence of philosophers and sociologists such as Herbert Marcuse and Ernst Bloch and the "theology of secularisation" as conceived by F. Gogarten and taken up by Harvey Cox and many others. This, he maintained, had now become "the accredited ideology of the W.C.C. which reached a new climax of its influence at its Geneva Conference on Church and Society in 1966 and its Uppsala Assembly in 1968". This theology could be summed up in the fact that God is not so much concerned with the Church as with "the whole world which he has created and which he, through the process of historical changes, leads to his appointed goal, the realisation of a new mankind united in Christ and governed by justice and peace." The Church is that part of the world "which knows already about the appointed goal of history and acknowledges the rule of Christ. The meaning of the church ... is to share with the

[81] 1 Cor. 15:19; John 14:2; 1 Pet. 1:3 ff. (NEB).
[82] Published in *The Churchman*, Autumn 1972, pp. 174 ff.

227

world its knowledge of and concern for a future more humanised state of society. This function is often described as sharing in the *Missio Dei*." The emphasis is always that

> the church only exists for its mission. But this mission does not consist so much in proclaiming the Gospel to unbelieving mankind or in saving souls; it rather consists in discovering the presence and saving activity of God within the events and turmoils of the world. But since God also and even mainly acts through non-Christian forces like Che Guevara in Latin America and Mao Tse Tung in China, mission is no one-way traffic. Rather the church is to engage in humble dialogue [with non-Christians] in order to find out what God wants to communicate to us through them. The Church-in-Mission must listen more than talk, receive more than give. [And he concludes:] If this concept is carried through to its logical conclusion, it must, according to my judgment, necessarily lead to the dissolution of the church into the world. Or, what is more likely, the church might be transformed into a syncretistic movement for innerworldly reforms, a movement which would not hesitate to use the power structures of this world.

Now I would not express myself in exactly the same terms as those used by Peter Beyerhaus, and I do believe (as he probably does, too) that there is a very real need for dialogue with those of other faiths, and that true dialogue always involves listening as well as speaking.[83] Nor do I for a moment believe that John Robinson thinks that God acts "mainly" through non-Christian revolutionary movements. But I can see several points of similarity between the theological position in Germany, as described by Peter Beyerhaus, and the spirit of Robinson's book. There is the same basic emphasis on a more humanitarian state of society and on social justice rather than on individual conversion; the same underlying picture of the Church being distinguishable from

[83] Cf. my book *Christianity and Comparative Religion* (Tyndale Press, 1970,) pp. 26 ff.

the world only by its greater apprehension of the goals towards which God is leading all men; and the same secularisation of the Gospel of redeeming grace. Robinson is far too steeped in New Testament studies to drive steadily along this road without, as I have put it, often "changing gear". But there can be little doubt about the general direction in which he is travelling.

Looking back at this book as a whole I do hope it will not appear too negative. The fact that I have been concerned with theologians and New Testament scholars has made it necessary to include numerous quotations from their writings; but I have done my best to balance the positive against the negative. I must confess, however, that as an academic from another discipline—together, I believe, with a lot of other people who are neither theologians nor ministers of religion—I am becoming increasingly tired of the attitude of mind betrayed by many members of theological faculties and occupants of pulpits. It seems to me of very questionable propriety (I nearly said honesty) for them to cite New Testament texts freely when these texts accord with their own views, but ignore (or even evade) them when they do not; to quote passages from the Bible freely, but give them a meaning and application which I very much doubt if any court of law would regard as what their authors meant or intended; and to make dogmatic assertions about what can, and what cannot, be accepted as authentic or historical without any adequate evidence for these statements. As I said at the beginning of this book, members of theological faculties seem to me to indulge in more mutual contradictions, and more categorical statements about matters which are still wide open to debate, than any other academics. They are, of course, fully entitled to their opinions; but I do wish they would distinguish between theory and fact, and treat their evidence in a fair and responsible way.

I am well aware that some of the scholars I have criticised earnestly desire to make the Christian message credible to those who live in a technological age. But I am convinced that they are going about it in the wrong way, and that their attempt to rid the Faith of all that might offend has left them with a milk-and-water substitute for the New Testament message which will satisfy no-one. Indeed, I believe that this is part of the reason for our empty churches, and for the pathetic search, in some quarters, for a spiritual or mystical experience of some sort, from wherever, and in whatever form, it may come. The New Testament is emphatic, moreover, that "A man who is unspiritual (or 'natural') refuses what belongs to the Spirit of God; it is folly to him; he cannot grasp it because it needs to be judged in the light of the Spirit."[84] So our paramount need is not for a change of message or even its presentation (although we should, obviously, do our utmost to communicate the message in an intelligible way) but rather for a change of heart in those who hear it. And for this we must always remain dependent on God alone.

[84] 1 Cor. 2:14.

Addendum

Since these pages went to the printer, John Robinson has written another book, *The Human Face of God* (SCM Press, 1973). Had this been available earlier I should certainly have included quotations from it at relevant points in this book, and I might even have devoted an additional chapter to the crucial – and bafflingly complex – subject of Christology.

I think that it is fair to say, however, that Robinson's latest book represents little that is basically new in his thought, although he certainly tackles the problem of Christology in much more detail than in any other of his books which I have read. We find the same curious mixture of careful, and even conservative, New Testament scholarship with recurrent examples of what seem to me wild speculations and unwarranted conclusions; the same amalgam of a very real reverence with a singular lack of sensitivity, taste or judgment; and the same combination of clarity of mind and expression with what I can only describe as a woolliness of both. When I read his books with a pencil in my hand I find myself writing, in the margin, a whole series of question marks, together with comments ranging all the way from "Excellent" to an emphatic "No".

Of John Robinson's devotion to the person of Jesus as the unique manifestation in history of the 'human face of God' there can be no question. It is noteworthy, moreover, that he usually seems to do his best, within his frame of reference, to preserve what he regards as the essentials of the biblical revelation; and that he seldom, if ever, passes over from the questioning, and suggested re-interpretation, of these essentials to any downright denial of them. But even on his own premises many of his conclusions seem to me neither

231

necessary nor convincing, while some of them appear to be directly contrary to the natural interpretation of the relevant passages in the New Testament. In particular, I can find no adequate evidence to support the way in which he merges the Jesus of history in the cosmic Christ (even to the point of asserting that "the mystery of the Christ is primarily a matter of recognition – not, Can you believe this individual to be the Son of God?, but, Can you see the truth of your humanity given its definition and vindication in him?");[1] caricatures (by his repeated use of loaded phrases like "a divine being arriving to look like a man", or "the myth of a supernatural, heavenly Redeemer visiting this earth in the form of a human being")[2] belief in *any* pre-existence of the Christ other than the concept that "one who was totally and utterly a man—and had never been anything other than a man or more than a man – so completely embodied what was from the beginning the meaning and purpose of God's self-expression (whether conceived in terms of his Spirit, his Wisdom, his Word or the intimately personal relation of Sonship) that it could be said, and had to be said, of that man, 'He was God's man', or 'God was in Christ', or even that he *was* 'God for us' ";[3] and insists on the logical impossibility that a Jesus conceived in any other terms could be really a man at all (as against those Docetic views which he rightly rejects). But in regard to the basic mystery of the Incarnation human logic seems to me an essentially inadequate tool. Robinson's Christology would, as I see it, rob both the Atonement and the Parousia (and I deliberately retain both the definite articles and capital letters!)[4] of their essential meaning—as discussed, in part, in chapters 5 and 6 of this book. Indeed, Robinson seems to regard any post-existence of the risen Lord as meaning no more than that "the representation of God continues. The incognito by which he must be represented by man is not abrogated. God has emptied himself into Christ, and Christ into his fellow men."[5] The "eternal

---

[1] p. 16
[2] pp. 161 f.
[3] p. 179
[4] *Pace* Robinson, p. 230
[5] p. 215

humanity of Christ, the mediator, who ever lives to make intercession for us" is, he suggests, a myth which means no more than that "the Christ lives on – in the lives of those who represent now the human face of God. The *prosōpon*, the face or person, of the Son is henceforth the faces of men and women"[6] – or, as he puts it elsewhere, "a new humanity composed of *all men* brought to life' ".[7]

Again, he seems to me far too dogmatic in his assertions that this or that concept is now 'dead'. He confidently affirms, for example, that "The realisation is fitfully dawning that 'God' now means, for us, not an invisible being with whom we can have direct communication as it were on the end of a telephone, but *that by which he is represented*, his surrogate – the power of a love that lives and suffers for others"; and he asserts that "If men are to believe in God, it can only be 'a-theistically', that is, as he is represented – above all in the irreplacibility of man."[8] But was it really nothing more than an abstraction of that sort which inspired Jesus himself to live and to suffer, or which he habitually addressed as 'Abba, Father'? When, moreover, Robinson says that "People rightly ask how one man's death two thousand years ago can alter their lives today", the only answer is that men and women not only ask that question but also, in many cases, find an answer which satisfies them both intellectually and experimentally – as I can confirm from practical experience. To assert with Sydney Carter that

> The Jesus who
> keeps saying 'I am Jesus,
> look at me,
> there is no substitute'
> is an imposter . . .

> So forget
> my name was ever Jesus.
> From now on
> I am anonymous

[6] *Ibid*
[7] p. 235
[8] pp. 218 f.

is to be guilty of perpetrating a caricature of both Christianity and its Founder. The marvel to me is that Robinson can mix quotations of this calibre with others which are superb – and, indeed with passages of his own of a totally different quality—without, it would seem, any sense of incongruity.

Index of Bible References and Quotations

Index of Authors Mentioned

A LAWYER AMONG THE THEOLOGIANS

Norman Anderson is a lawyer. For one trained to evaluate evidence according to rules worked out through the years, he says, it is astonishing to see how some theologians operate—the presuppositions and convictions with which they approach the ancient documents and the "positively staggering assurance" of their pronouncements on issues that are, on any showing, open to question.

In *A Lawyer Among the Theologians*, Anderson takes to task a significant number of those theologians, pointing out the evidential discrepancies and contradictions he discovers in their works. Closely examining the Jesus of history and the Christ of faith, the basic historicity of the resurrection and the detailed evidence for it, and the meaning of such New Testament concepts as sin, forgiveness, and judgment, Anderson concludes that an objective reading of the available evidence argues strongly in favor of accepting the scriptural account as accurate and reliable.

In a final chapter, Anderson provides an extended critical review of John A.T. Robinson's recent book, *The Difference in Being a Christian Today*, finding there a "combination of clarity of mind and expression with what I can only describe as a wooliness of both." Citing numerous examples from the book, Anderson takes issue with what he regards as Robinson's attempt to reinterpret the message of the New Testament.

"A very valuable piece of work which provides a much needed corrective to what for too long has been an almost unchallenged fashion among theologians, to forget theology and to indulge instead in a rather sterile 'did Bacon write Shakespeare' type of controversy."

—E. Garth Moore, Chancellor
Corpus Christi College, Cambridge

Norman Anderson, a prominent Anglican layman, is Director of the Institute of Advanced Legal Studies at the University of London, and editor of *The World's Religions*, also published by Eerdmans.

$3.95
ISBN 0-8028-1565-0

WM. B. EERDMANS
PUBLISHING CO
255 JEFFERSON AVE. S.E., GRAND RAPIDS, MICH. 49502